THE LITTLE BOOK OF

GOLF LAW

SECOND EDITION

JOHN H. MINAN

Cover design by Andrew O. Alcala/ABA Publishing.

The materials contained herein represent the opinions and views of the authors and/or the editors, and should not be construed to be the views or opinions of the law firms or companies with whom such persons are in partnership with, associated with, or employed by, nor of the American Bar Association, unless adopted pursuant to the bylaws of the Association.

Nothing contained in this book is to be considered as the rendering of legal advice, either generally or in connection with any specific issue or case. Readers are responsible for obtaining advice from their own lawyers or other professionals. This book and any forms and agreements herein are intended for educational and informational purposes only.

©2013 American Bar Association. All rights reserved.

No part of this publication may be reproduced, stored in a retrieval system, or transmitted in any form or by any means, electronic, mechanical, photocopying, recording, or otherwise, without the prior written permission of the publisher. For permission, contact the ABA Copyrights and Contracts Department at copyright@americanbar.org or via fax at 312-988-6030, or complete the online form at http://www.americanbar.org/utility/reprint.html.

Printed in the United States of America.

17 16 15 14 13   5 4 3 2 1

Library of Congress Cataloging-in-Publication Data

Cataloguing-in-Publication data is on file with the Library of Congress.

ISBN: 978-1-62722-419-2

Discounts are available for books ordered in bulk. Special consideration is given to state bars, CLE programs, and other bar-related organizations. Inquire at Book Publishing, ABA Publishing, American Bar Association, 321 North Clark Street, Chicago, Illinois 60654-7598.

www.ShopABA.org

*This book is dedicated to
my grandchildren and
future golfing partners:
Andrew, Darby, Maddy, Jack,
Tatum, Charlie, and Jackson.*

Table of Contents

xiii   **Preface**

1   **Part I: Torts**

    3   **Hole One:**
        Golfer Liability to a Playing Partner:
        Slow play and "ready golf"
        California: *Shin v. Ahn*,
        42 Cal. 4th 482 (2007)

    13   **Hole Two:**
        Golf Course Liability:
        Golf ball bounces off the cart path
        Hawaii: *Yoneda v. Tom and Sports Shinko (Mililani) Co., Ltd.*, 133 P.3d 796 (2006)

    23   **Hole Three:**
        Golf Course Liability:
        Warning golfers of lightning
        Kansas: *Sall v. TS, Inc.,d/b/a Smiley's Golf Complex*, 136 P.3d 471 (2009)

    33   **Hole Four:**
        Golfer Liability to a Spectator:
        "Duty or breach of duty?"
        Indiana: *Pfenning v. Lineman*,
        947 N.E.2d 392 (2011)

    41   **Hole Five:**
        Golfer Liability to a Playing Partner:
        "Shanks a lot"
        New York: *Anand v. Kapoor*,
        942 N.E.2d 295 (2011)

51 Hole Six:
Product Liability:
Golf cart maker in "hot seat"
California: *Mendoza, et al. v. Club Car, Inc.*,
81 Cal. App. 4th 287 (2000), reh'g denied
(June 27, 2000), review denied (Aug. 23, 2000)

61 Hole Seven:
Product Liability:
"Golfing Gizmo" training aid
California: *Hauter v. Zogarts*,
14 Cal. 3d 104 (1975)

73 Hole Eight:
Product Liability:
Defectively manufactured golf clubs
Federal: *Price v. Wilson Sporting Goods Co.*,
2005 WL 1677512 (D. Colo. July 18, 2005), modified
on reh'g (damages), 2006 WL 1409519 (2006)

79 Hole Nine:
Golf and the Loss of Consortium:
You can lose more than your golf balls during a round of golf
California: *Kurash v. J.C. Resorts, Inc.*,
00703109 Super. Ct., San Diego, Cal. (1996)

87 Part II: Contracts

89 Hole Ten:
Covenants, Conditions, and Restrictions:
Errant golf balls
California: *Masters, et al. v. Burton, et al.*,
2013 WL 3866516 (Cal. Ct. App. July 25, 2013)

99 Hole Eleven:
Hole-in-One Contest: Mistake
Pennsylvania: *Cobaugh v. Klick-Lewis, Inc.*,
561 A.2d 1248 (1989)

107 Hole Twelve:
Hole-in-One Rules:
The ladies' red tees
South Dakota: *Harms v. Northland Ford Dealers, et al.*, 602 N.W.2d 58 (1999)

117 Hole Thirteen:
Hole-in-One Fraud:
Off to the hoosegow
Federal: *United States v. Krilich*,
159 F.3d 1020 (7th Cir. 1998)

127 Hole Fourteen:
Insurance:
19th Hole drunken assault
Iowa: *Dolan v. State Farm Fire & Casualty*,
573 N.W.2d 254 (1998)

133 Hole Fifteen:
Insurance: Golf cart accidents
and policy exclusions
Mississippi: *Dowdle v. Mississippi Farm Bureau Mutual Insurance Co.*,
697 So. 2d 788 (1997)

141 Hole Sixteen:
Insurance:
Hole-in-one insurance scam
Washington: *State of Washington v. Kevin Kolenda d/b/a Hole-in-Won*,
case no. 12-1-04505-1 (2012)

147 Part III: Property

149 Hole Seventeen:
Misappropriation:
The USGA handicap index formula
California: *U.S. Golf Association v. Arroyo Software Corp.*, 60 Cal. App. 4th 607 (1999)

157 Hole Eighteen:
Right of Publicity: Commercial use of videotaped hole-in-one
Federal: *Pooley v. National Hole-In-One Association*, 89 F. Supp. 2d 1108 (D. Ariz. 2000)

167 Hole Nineteen:
Right of Publicity:
"The Masters of Augusta" painting
Federal: *ETW Corporation v. Jireh Publishing, Inc.*, 332 F.3d 915 (6th Cir. 2003), reh'g denied (Sept. 8, 2003)

173 Hole Twenty:
Trespass and Nuisance:
Golfer liability
Texas: *Malouf v. Dallas Athletic Country Club*, 837 S.W.2d 674 (Tex. Ct. App. 1992)

179 Hole Twenty-One:
Trespass and Nuisance:
Golf course liability
Georgia: *DeSarno v. Jam Golf Management, LLC*, 670 S.E.2d 889 (2008), cert. denied (2009)

187 Hole Twenty-Two:
Trespass and Nuisance:
Assault and battery
Rhode Island: *Hennessey v. Pyne*,
694 A.2d 691 (1997)

193 Hole Twenty-Three:
Golf Course Private Easement:
Abandonment
California: *Bernardo Heights Country Club v. Community Association of Bernardo Heights* (D024460), Fourth Appellate District (April 6, 1998)

201 Part IV: Intellectual Property

203 Hole Twenty-Four:
Patent Infringement:
Doctrine of equivalents
Federal: *Wilson Sporting Goods v. David Geoffrey & Associates d/b/a/ Slazenger*, and *Dunlop Slazenger Corp. aka Dunlop Sports Corp.*, 904 F.2d 677 (Fed. Cir. 1990), cert. denied, 498 U.S. 992 (1990)

213 Hole Twenty-Five:
Patent Infringement:
Novelty and obviousness
Federal: *Callaway Golf Co. v. Acushnet Co.*, 576 F.3d 1331 (Fed. Cir. 2009), reh'g and reh'g en banc denied (2009), cert. denied, 130 S. Ct 1525 (2010)

227 Hole Twenty-Six:
Golf Equipment and the *Rules of Golf*:
The battle over grooves
Federal: *Gilder, et al. v. PGA Tour, Inc.*, 936 F.2d 417 (9th Cir. 1991)

239 Hole Twenty-Seven:
The Right of Publicity:
"Grip it and rip it"
Federal: *John Daly Enterprises, LLC v. Hippo Golf Co.*, 646 F. Supp. 2d 1347 (S.D. Fla. 2009)

249 Hole Twenty-Eight:
Copying Famous Golf Holes:
Legal "gimmies"
Federal: *Pebble Beach Co. v. Tour 18 I, Ltd.*, 155 F.3d 526 (5th Cir. 1998)

265 Hole Twenty-Nine:
Resale of Trademarked Golf Balls:
Finders keepers, losers weepers
Federal: *Nitro Leisure Products, LLC v. Acushnet*, 341 F.3d 1356 (Fed. Cir. 2003)

275 Part V: Environmental Law

277 Hole Thirty:
The Federal Endangered Species Act (ESA):
"Can't we all just get along?"
Federal: *Wild Equity Institute, et al. v. City and County of San Francisco*, 2012 WL 14581178 (N.D. Cal. April 26, 2012)

289 Hole Thirty-One:
Forfeiture:
Clubbing wildlife is a no-no
Hawaii: *State v. Terry Pupus*, LNR T1, LNR T2 (1997)

297 Hole Thirty-Two:
Water Quality: Golf course use of reclaimed water
California: City of Santa Barbara Against the Use of Potable Water by the Tsukamoto Sogyo Company, Department of Water Resources Control Board, Decision 1625, Feb. 15, 1990

305 Part VI: Equal Protection

307 Hole Thirty-Three:
Gender Discrimination: Men's only golf tournaments at a public golf course
Federal: *Joyce v. Town of Dennis*, 705 F. Supp. 2d 74 (D. Mass. 2010)

321 Hole Thirty-Four:
Country Club Membership Rules: Sexual-orientation discrimination
California: *Koebke, et al. v. Bernardo Heights Country Club*, 36 Cal. 4th 824 (2005)

331 Part VII: Sovereign Immunity

333 Hole Thirty-Five:
Federal Sovereign Immunity: Military golf course liability
Federal: *Ventimiglia v. United States of America*, 2009 WL 2982001 (N.D. Cal.)

341 Hole Thirty-Six:
Local Government Immunity: Municipal golf course liability
Iowa: *Summy v. City of Des Moines*, 708 N.W.2d 333 (2006)

351 **Part VIII: Antitrust**

353 Hole Thirty-Seven:
The USGA and Handicap Competition: GHIN (without the tonic)
Federal: *Handicomp v. United States Golf Association* (USGA), 2000 WL 426245 (3d Cir. 2000), cert. denied, 531 U.S. 928 (2000)

363 **Part IX: Tax**

365 Hole Thirty-Eight:
Internal Revenue Service: Wannabe tour player teed off at IRS
Federal: *Courville v. Comm'r*, 71 T.C.M. (CCH) 2496 (U.S. Tax Court) (1996)

373 **Part X: Americans with Disabilities Act**

375 Hole Thirty-Nine:
Americans with Disabilities Act of 1990 (ADA): The nature of the game of golf
Federal: *PGA Tour, Inc. v. Martin*, 532 U.S. 661 (2001)

385 **Index**

392 **About the Author**

Preface

This revised and greatly expanded second edition of *The Little Book of Golf Law* is written to appeal to readers with an interest in golf and the law. It explores a wide array of legal issues affecting golfers, golf courses, and the golf industry generally.

Golf is a multibillion dollar industry. It encompasses recreational golf activities, amateur and professional tournaments, golf course operations, equipment manufacturers, patents and other forms of intellectual property, insurance, golf course design, sales and leasing of golf equipment, and so on. With so many facets and complexity, litigation is inevitable. In fact, one sports authority ranked golf as the second most litigated sport.[1]

The Little Book of Golf Law examines thirty-nine reported federal and state court cases that involve golf in one way or another. The cases were selected because they present interesting facts and consider core legal principles.

The cases are grouped by general subject matter, such as torts, contract, property, and so on. The cases deal with such subjects as golfer and golf course liability, manufacturer liability for defective golf clubs and training devices, disputes over hole-in-one contests, golf cart injuries and insurance claims, sex discrimination disputes, intellectual property issues, environmental claims, legal immunity, and much more.

Each case is presented as a story involving real people. The facts are identified, the applicable law discussed, and a conclusion offered. The discussion often includes interesting references to the Rules of Golf. These rules govern how the game is played, and are written and interpreted by the United States Golf Association (USGA) and the Royal and Ancient Golf Club of Saint Andrews Scotland (R&A).

The game of golf is not normally considered a dangerous or contact sport. But injury and damage frequently happens

---

1. Litigation involving baseball ranked first.

because the trajectory of a golf ball is never guaranteed. There probably isn't a golfer alive who hasn't wondered about liability after hitting an errant shot that unexpectedly veers toward another player or leaves the golf course headed for a neighboring house or car. In some cases, the end result is a blood-curdling scream, the sound of breaking glass, or worse.

One does not have to be a lawyer or have legal training to enjoy the cases. The reader is taken on a journey canvassing a wide variety of legal issues. The book is suitable as a reference work for those grappling with golf-related legal issues, as well as for use in conferences and continuing legal education programs.

The Little Book of Golf Law is not a substitute for legal advice. Readers are cautioned that the law of one state is not a reliable guide to the law of another state. Statutes vary between states, and courts are not always consistent in the treatment of similar factual and legal issues. In addition, the law is dynamic and may be changed at any time by the legislature or subsequent judicial decision. Thus, each case should be considered simply a snapshot of the law applied to the facts at a point in time.

For the love of the game

The game of golf is loved by many. Others may not be so enthusiastic or embracing. William Wordsworth saw golf as "a day spent in a round of strenuous idleness." H. L. Mencken, America's beloved curmudgeon and full-time satirist, argued that if he had his way "no man guilty of golf would be eligible to any office of trust or profit in the United States." Mark Twain's quip that "golf is a good walk spoiled" suggests skepticism.

Other popular commentators appear to have a more tolerant attitude toward golf. The humorist P. J. O'Rourke remarked that golf "combines two favorite pastimes: taking long walks and hitting things with a stick." O'Rourke was obviously speaking metaphorically. The game is actually played with a "club," which must meet certain specifications promulgated by the Rules of Golf, and not with a "stick."

But there are many who unconditionally love the game, no matter how fleeting or episodic their success at getting the golf ball to behave properly. Golf can be an amazing teacher about joy and contentment. It can also teach one to set aside and accept one's shortcomings. There are worse things in life, after all, than a triple bogey or missing a short putt. Finally, golf can teach you about fair play and the importance of playing by the rules.

In the 1996 film classic *Tin Cup*, Roy "Tin Cup" McAvoy (played by Kevin Costner) developed a romantic interest in Dr. Molly Griswold (played by Rene Russo). During a practice session at the driving range, Molly undergoes a transformation in her attitude toward the golf. She initially tells "Tin Cup" that golf is "without a doubt, the stupidest, silliest, most idiotic grotesquery masquerading as a game that has ever been invented." But after experiencing the satisfaction of hitting a solid shot, she beams at her success. She now gets it. Golf can be fun. And as Roy quipped, "sex and golf are two things you can enjoy even if you're not good at them."

I have been teaching law for more than forty years. I am also an avid golfer with a love for the law and golf. My hope is that you enjoy the following stories of legal intrigue as much as I have enjoyed writing about them. I also wish to thank those who have invited me to share and speak about my affection for golf and the law.

John H. Minan
Professor of Law
University of San Diego
San Diego, CA 92110
November 2013

THE LITTLE BOOK OF

GOLF LAW

SECOND EDITION

Part I
Torts

Hole 1

Golfer Liability to a Playing Partner:
Slow play and "ready golf"

California: *Shin v. Ahn*, 42 Cal. 4th 482 (2007)

The *Rules of Golf* state: "The player shall play without undue delay."[1] But slow play is a problem on many golf courses. Wiggles, waggles, agonizing over club selection, stalking putts like a homicidal maniac, and generally being unconscious of one's effect on the pace of play all contribute to slow play.

"Being on the clock" and the potential imposition of penalties help to speed up slow play at the professional level.[2] At many golf courses, the problem of slow play is acerbated by those golfers who feel entitled to take as much time as they want because they've paid their greens fees. Slow play also happens because the course is tough, or a player can't find the ball,

---

1. Rule 6-7.
2. Players are expected to keep up with the group playing in front of them. The PGA Tour slow play rules call for a rules official or Tour official to put the group "on the clock." Although failure to speed up play can result in up to a two-stroke penalty, fines, or disqualification, such consequences are as rare as a double eagle.

or love is in the air.[3] Course marshals can be effective in monitoring and moving players along, but there are no easy answers.

"Ready golf" is an informal way of dealing with slow play by encouraging golfers to speed up. Simply put, playing "ready golf" encourages players to hit when they are ready. But playing "ready golf" may expose a player to legal liability.

Ben Hogan remarked that "golf is a game of misses." A lawyer might add that missing another player with a golf shot is a good way to avoid being sued for negligence. In simple terms, the law of negligence is conduct that falls below the legal standard to protect others from the risk of harm and causes injury.

In most cases, successfully suing another player for negligence is difficult. Courts frequently reason that golfers assume the risks inherent in the game, including being hit by an errant shot. But all is not lost for the injured player. Other legal theories, such as recklessness or intentional conduct by the defendant, may be available under the right circumstances.

In the popular movie *Sideways,* Miles Raymond (played by Paul Giamatti) and Jack Cole (played by Thomas Haden Church) decide to play a round of golf during a California wine-tasting road trip. The banter between Jack and Miles slows down the pace of play. This prompts a frustrated golfer playing behind them to "hit into them" to encourage them to pick up the pace. It doesn't. Miles hits the offending ball back at the group. The return volley rattles off the offender's golf cart, and things

---

3. The following story was reported by a golfer who wanted to play through because of slow play: "Played behind a couple that was going slow due to them continually making out. They were grabbing each other's butts on the tee, stopping their cart to kiss, etc. On a couple of greens the guy would be lining up his putt and the woman would sit down spread-eagled in front of the cup. They showed no signs of letting us play through, even when our cart was by the tee box while they were teeing off (or groping each other). To be honest we enjoyed the show for a few holes, but over an hour to play three holes was just too long." http://golf.about.com/u/ua/golfetiquette/badgolfetiquette.htm (last visited March 13, 2013).

Hole 1: Golfer Liability to a Playing Partner

escalate from there. Ultimately, Jack charges the group, wildly swinging a club and yelling, "This is going to be fun." On the one hand, the offending salvo, the return volley, and the wild charge are certainly not risks inherent in the game of golf. On the other hand, being "hit into" is common and often causes heated exchanges.[4]

Another illustration of slow play and where it can lead is depicted in the movie *Happy Gilmore* (played by Adam Sandler). After Happy takes seven putts, the "guy on the green" says, "It's about time!" Happy responds, "Yeah, it's about time. I mean, I just couldn't get the ball in the hole. I wanted to but I just couldn't do it." Happy, in a not-so-happy frame of mind, then rips off the guy's shirt and punches him in the stomach. Once again, you don't have to be a lawyer or have a crystal ball to know that being battered is not an inherent risk of the game.

The Facts

The setting was the par-4, 13th hole at the Rancho Park Golf Course in Los Angeles. This popular public course, which was built in the late 1940s, is owned and operated by the city of Los Angeles. The fairways are lined with mature trees, and the terrain is generally hilly. By all accounts, it is a pleasant place to play golf.

On the ill-fated day, Johnny Shin, Jeffrey Frost, and Jack Ahn were playing together as a threesome. After putting out on the 12th hole, Ahn headed for the 13th tee box, presumably to play ready golf. Shin and Frost finished putting and followed

---

4. In real life, violence on the golf course occasionally occurs. In April 2007, for example, an argument escalated over who owned a golf ball retrieved from a water hazard on the sixth hole of the Oceanside Municipal Golf Course in Southern California. Tempers flared so much that one golfer landed in the hospital. The other two (Bishop Michael Babin, a minister, and his playing partner) were charged with felony assault.

Ahn. Shin took a shortcut up the hill toward the tee box, which placed him in front of Ahn and to his left.

Unwilling to be electronically disconnected from the outside world, Shin stopped to check his cell phone for messages and to get a bottle of water from his golf bag. He was then about 25 to 35 feet in front of Ahn, who was getting ready to tee off. Shin was at approximately at a 40- to 45-degree angle from the intended path of Ahn's ball. Ahn said he was focused on hitting the shot, and therefore did not shout "fore" or any other warning.[5]

With Shin in front of Ahn, the stage was set for disaster. But some facts were disputed. Shin claimed that Ahn saw him standing in front of him, which Ahn denied. Ahn claimed that he did not see Shin either when he took a practice swing or when he actually teed off.

His tee ball didn't go as planned. Ahn, who is right-handed, pulled his tee shot to the left, whacking Shin in the head. It is not certain how much distance he lost by Shin getting in the way. In any event, Shin sued Ahn in negligence for his "disabling, serious, and permanent" injuries.

The Law

As a general matter, two types of implied assumption of the risk exist: primary and secondary. Primary assumption exists when a golfer is considered to have impliedly accepted the risks inherent in the game. In such a case, the courts will reason that

---

5. As golfers know, "fore" is shouted to warn others on a golf course when there is a danger of hitting them with a golf ball. While the exact etymology of the term is uncertain, one popular view traces the term "fore" to military operations. During the 17th and 18th centuries, the infantry advanced in formation while artillery batteries fired over their heads. When an artilleryman was about to fire, he would yell "beware before." This forewarning allowed the infantrymen to drop and cover to avoid being hit. Golfers have shortened the warning to "fore."

Hole 1: Golfer Liability to a Playing Partner

the defendant owes the plaintiff *no duty* to protect the plaintiff from conduct that is a foreseeable and customary part of the game. Without the existence of a duty, a plaintiff's claim of negligence fails. Some jurisdictions have adopted statutes that provide that a person who takes part in a sport accepts, as a matter of law, the inherent risks that are obvious and a necessary part of the game. You might think of it in the following terms: If you are a boxer, you should not complain if you get hit while boxing.

In the secondary form of implied assumption of the risk, the plaintiff knows about a particular risk and acts unreasonably in voluntarily encountering that risk. It may or may not bar recovery. In some jurisdictions, for example, this form of assumption of risk doctrine does not bar recovery, but results in the application of principles of comparative negligence, in which liability is apportioned between the plaintiff and the defendant.

In *Shin*, the trial court initially granted the defendant's motion for summary judgment. The court then changed its mind and ordered a new trial to determine if Ahn's actions increased the risk beyond those assumed by Shin. The defendant disagreed with the court's change of heart and appealed, arguing that he should prevail as a matter of law.

The court of appeal affirmed. It found that Ahn had breached the duty to ascertain Shin's whereabouts before hitting, and ordered a new trial to apportion the fault between the parties. It saw the matter as fitting with the category of secondary assumption of the risk. The appellate court reasoned that the no-duty rule of primary assumption applied only when the injured golfer was playing with a different group of golfers. Therefore, because Shin and Ahn were playing in the same threesome, the primary assumption of the risk (no-duty rule) was inapplicable.

The California Supreme Court stepped into the fray, framing the decision as the "next generation" of jurisprudence following the landmark case of *Knight v. Jewett*, which was based on avoiding legal rules that impose liability in "contact sports" for "ordinary careless conduct."[6]

The court applied the *Knight* primary assumption of the risk doctrine to golf even though it is not considered a contact sport. It also rejected the appellate court's reasoning that assumption of the risk was limited to situations where the plaintiff and defendant are playing together in the same group. Assumption of the risk applies to playing partners as well as to other golfers on the course. The duty of a golfer turns on the nature of the game, and not on whether the defendant is playing with the plaintiff in the same group.

The court cautioned that being hit by a poorly struck golf ball is an inherent risk of the game. Under the assumption of the risk doctrine, a golfer has a "limited duty" to other golfers. It is breached only if the defendant intentionally injures the plaintiff or acts recklessly. In short, a mishit ball that strikes another is simply a risk that any golfer assumes. As a matter of policy, holding a golfer liable for a mishit shot would have the undesirable effect of encouraging lawsuits and preventing golfers from playing the game.

The court agreed with the trial court that summary judgment was inappropriate, and therefore remanded the matter. In order to prevail on remand, Shin would have to prove to the jury that Ahn acted either intentionally or recklessly. The record was too sparse to support such a finding as a matter of law.

---

6. Knight v. Jewett, 834 P.2d 696 (1992) (holding that participants in contact sports breach the duty of care only if they act recklessly or intentionally). The court addressed the application of this principle to non-contact sports, such as golf, in Shin v. Ahn.

Under the court's reasoning, Ahn had the limited duty to check to see where Shin was before hitting. Once he addressed the ball, Ahn was not required to break his concentration before hitting.

Conclusion

The *Shin* decision reflects the general reluctance to apply principles of simple negligence to mishit shots that cause injury. It was based on the concern of turning a pleasant day on the golf course into a visit to the courthouse. As a result, a golfer who hits another golfer in California is not likely to be found negligent due to the application of assumption of the risk. Consequently, injured golfers bear the full risk of harm. The exception is that liability is possible for conduct that is considered reckless or intentional. In such cases, assumption of the risk will not bar recovery.

When a risk associated with the injury-causing conduct is not considered "inherent," the negligence standard continues to apply. The difficulty is determining what situations other than mishit shots are included within the concept of "inherent risk." This determination ultimately demands fact-specific inquiries.

States approach golfer negligence differently. In *Zurla v. Hydel*, the plaintiff was struck by a ball hit by another member of his threesome.[7] He argued that the proper standard of care was ordinary negligence, which was rejected in *Shin*. The Illinois Court of Appeal reasoned that inherent risk may be useful when applied to contact sports, but golf is not a contact sport:

> In our view, golf is simply not the type of game in which participants are inherently, inevitably or customarily struck by the ball. Unlike the contact sports recognized

---

7. Zurla v. Hydel, 681 N.E.2d 148 (Ill. 1997).

by the cases, the only defense of the target in golf is made by the principles of Sir Isaac Newton, the natural obstacles of Mother Nature, and the cunning of those who have designed the course. There is never a need for players to touch one another. Rather, golf is a sport which is contemplative and careful, with emphasis placed on control and finesse, rather than speed or raw strength. Although the game of golf certainly presents significant dangers, these dangers are more psychological than physical. Moreover, the physical dangers that exist are diminished by long-standing traditions in which courtesy between the players prevails. In such an environment, players have the time to consider the consequences of their actions and to guard against injury to those who may be in harm's way.

The Rules of Golf and Safety

The etiquette section to the *Rules of Golf* addresses safety.[8] The USGA has explained that the rules of etiquette are simply guidelines as to how golf "should" be played so that all players will gain maximum enjoyment from the game. The word "should" was deliberately chosen to convey the idea that safety guidelines are simply recommended.

In light of the USGA's admonition, the court in *Shin* understandably found that the appellate court relied too heavily on

---

8. Rules of Golf, Etiquette

    1. Players should ensure that no one is standing close by or in a position to be hit by the club, the ball, or any stones, pebbles, twigs or the like when they make a *stroke* or practice swing.

    2. Players should not play until the players in front are out of range.

    3. Players should always alert greenstaff nearby or ahead when they are about to make a stroke that might endanger them.

    4. If a player plays a ball in a direction where there is a danger of hitting someone, he should immediately shout a warning. The traditional word of warning in such situations is "fore."

Hole 1: Golfer Liability to a Playing Partner

the rules of etiquette involving safety, which are only intended to govern socially acceptable behavior. It reasoned that the sanction for violating a rule of etiquette is social disapproval, not legal liability.

Violating the *Rules of Golf* generally subjects the violator to the internal sanctions prescribed by the rules. Imposing legal liability for a violation has the potential to alter the fundamental nature of the game by deterring golfers from vigorously engaging in activity that falls close to violating, but on the permissible side of, a prescribed rule. In other words, if a golfer violates the *Rules of Golf*, the complaining party should take the complaint to the Rules Committee at the golf course, not to the judiciary.

Hole 2

Golf Course Liability:
Golf ball bounces off the cart path[1]

Hawaii: *Yoneda v. Tom and Sports Shinko (Mililani) Co., Ltd.*, 133 P.3d 796 (2006)

Hawaii is known for its tropical breezes, surfing, great beaches, and wonderful golf courses. The Mililani Golf Course is a par-72, 6,455-yard public course owned and operated by Sports Shinko. The golf course is located near the U.S. Army's Schofield Barracks on a plateau or "central valley" between two volcanic mountains somewhat near the center of the island of Oahu.

The Hawaiian word *"mililani"* means "beloved heaven." Arguably, the Hawaiian words *"kolepa pilikia"* ("golf trouble") more correctly describes the following dispute.

The Facts

On August 20, 1999, Ryan Yoneda was playing golf with his buddies at the Mililani Golf Club. They finished playing the fifth

---

1. Not all cart path ricochets result in tragedy. During the 2013 WGC-Cadillac Championship at the TPC Blue Monster at Doral, Phil Mickelson hit the long drive of the tournament on the par 4, 17th hole. His ball bounced and bounced on the cart path, rolling some 450 yards. Phil then chipped 30 yards off the cart path to within about 10 feet of the hole, and sank the putt for a birdie.

hole, got in their golf carts, and headed toward the sixth hole. Yoneda was on the passenger side of the cart.

The golf course had a "cart-path-only" rule. It required them to stay on the cart path as they headed to the sixth hole, which they did. The cart path between the fifth green and sixth tee looped in a "U-turn" behind a restroom building. Once clear of the restroom, the cart path headed in a straight line to the sixth tee box.

Andrew Tom and his playing partners were in the foursome behind the Yoneda group. They waited on the fifth fairway for the Yoneda group to clear the green before hitting their next shots. Tom was about 175 yards from the green when he hit. His ball soared off in an unintended direction. After some intermediate detours, the ball bounced off the cart path just as Yoneda and his cart partner came around the restroom on the cart path heading to the sixth tee box. Tragedy struck when the ball bounced off the cart path and hit Yoneda in the eye.

The cart Yoneda was riding in did not have a protective Plexiglas™ windshield.[2] No expert testimony was offered on the value of one in preventing injury. Consequently, it is not clear whether a Plexiglas windshield would have actually protected him. The Plexiglas windshields on many carts are hinged, so they can be flipped up or down by those riding in the cart. If the windshield is up and properly sceured, it "may" provide some

---

2. The *Rules of Golf* would apply had the errant shot hit Yoneda's cart and bounced elsewhere. Rule 19-1 deals with the situation when a ball in motion is accidentally deflected or stopped by an "outside agency," which is defined as something that is not part of the match or, in stroke play, not part of the competitor's side. It typically includes such things as yardage markers, signs, sprinkler heads, and so on.

The golfer generally is required to play the ball where it comes to rest without any penalty. Special rules apply under Rule 19-3 when the accidental deflection occurs by the player, partner, or equipment, as well as when the deflection occurs by an opponent or the opponent's equipment. Undoubtedly, when a golfer hits another person, that golfer is less likely to be concerned with correctly tallying penalty strokes under the rules and more concerned with the penalty of being sued.

Hole 2: Golf Course Liability

additional protection.[3] Not surprisingly, Yoneda argued that the presence of a Plexiglas windshield on his cart would have prevented his injury.

Tom didn't yell "fore" or provide any other warning. The reason he argued was straightforward: no one was in sight as the ball veered off after hitting the cart path. The design of the cart path, which looped around the restroom, prevented him from seeing Yoneda until it was too late.

After being hit in the eye, Yoneda was rushed to Saint Francis Medical Center West for treatment. The injury to his left eye included loss of peripheral vision, permanent pupil dilation, blurred vision, angel recision glaucoma, traumatic ecchymosis, and retinal edema.

Yoneda sued both Sports Shinko and Tom to compensate him for his physical injuries.[4] He alleged that Sports Shinko:

(1) is strictly liable for the defective design of its golf course, which (a) required golfers, following the laid-out cart path, to face oncoming shots without adequate or reasonable protection and (b) prevented Tom from seeing anyone near or approaching the vicinity of his errant shot; (2) negligently failed to provide safe rental carts for use on the premises by failing to equip them

---

3. In Donnelly v. Club Car, Inc., the defendants (Glen Lakes Country Club and the golf cart manufacturer) offered expert testimony that Plexiglas was an appropriate material for the golf cart windshield and that the injury-causing accident would not have happened had the windshield been properly secured. Therefore, the appellate court sustained the grant of summary judgment by the trial court in favor of the defendants because the plaintiff failed to present contrary expert evidence raising a genuine issue of material fact about whether the construction and composition of the windshield on the cart were defective. Donnelly v. Club Car, Inc., 274 So. 2d 25, 27 (Ala. Civ. App. 1998).

4. The focus here is on the golf course's liability. For the interested reader, the lower court applied the implied primary assumption of risk doctrine to bar Yoneda's claim of negligence against Tom. The supreme court affirmed, finding no evidence that Tom had acted in a reckless or intentional manner.

with windshields; and (3) had a special relationship with Yoneda as an invitee, and, thus, was required to take greater care by placing warning signs or safety netting to minimize the risk that golfers will be hit by golf balls.

The trial court granted Sports Shinko's motion of summary judgment based on implied assumption of the risk. Not surprisingly, this didn't sit well with Yoneda.

On appeal, the Hawaii Supreme Court reasoned that the dispositive issue was whether the "implied assumption of the risk" doctrine applied, and if so, whether the plaintiff's claims against the defendant were barred as a matter of law. The three separate counts contained in Yoneda's complaint, the court reasoned, "essentially fall under the category of creating or increasing the risks beyond those inherent in the sport."

The Law

"Express assumption of the risk" exists when the parties expressly agree to allocate risk by contract or written agreement. As such, it furthers their expectations. This type of express agreement between the parties was not before the court.

"Implied assumption of the risk" doctrine is more controversial than express assumption. It commonly comes in two recognizable forms. The first implied form is often called "primary assumption of the risk," and it typically is argued in sport and recreation cases. It completely bars any recovery by the plaintiff based on the rationale that the defendant either had no duty to the plaintiff or did not breach any duty. In short, the plaintiff is impliedly considered to have assumed the risk by participating in the activity that caused the injury.

Hole 2: Golf Course Liability

The second implied form is called "secondary assumption of the risk." It analyzes the activity under principles of comparative negligence. Secondary assumption doesn't bar recovery, but rather is used to apportion the liability between the plaintiff and the defendant based on principles of comparative fault. Any financial recovery by the plaintiff is reduced by the comparative fault of the plaintiff.

The Hawaii Supreme Court explained the difference between the two forms of implied assumption:

Implied assumption of risk has been used in the context of negligence cases to describe two distinct theories under which a defendant may avoid liability. The "primary" sense of implied assumption of risk emerged, along with the global doctrine itself, out of the common law action of a servant against his master. Used in its primary sense, assumption of risk describes the act of a plaintiff, who has entered voluntarily and reasonably into some relation with a defendant, which plaintiff knows to involve the risk. It is an alternative expression of the proposition that a defendant owes no duty to a plaintiff. . . . In its "secondary" sense, implied assumption of risk focuses on a plaintiff's conduct, and describes a situation where plaintiff knows of the danger presented by a defendant's negligence and proceeds voluntarily and unreasonably to encounter it. A plaintiff's assumption of risk is unreasonable, and a form of contributory negligence, where the known risk of harm is great relative to the utility of plaintiff's conduct. It is implied assumption of risk in this secondary sense, *i.e.*[,] unreasonable assumption of risk, that has been merged with comparative negligence by the decisions of this court in products liability cases.[5]

The Hawaiian Supreme Court had previously limited the use of primary assumption. For example, the court had rejected its application in implied warranty and strict liability tort actions. A defective product, the court had reasoned, is one that causes injury when the product is used in a reasonable manner, and therefore it is not available to bar recovery. Primary assumption unnecessarily duplicates the "defect" analysis on which liability is based and has the clear potential to generate confusion.

Although the "primary assumption" doctrine is not available in cases of implied warranty and strict liability, Hawaii has not abandoned the doctrine in other contexts. It continues to be recognized as a discrete and complete defense in sport injury cases. Thus, absent intentional or reckless conduct by a defendant, the implied primary assumption of the risk doctrine insulates the defendant from liability when the plaintiff's injury is considered an "inherent risk" of the activity. When the risks are fully apparent, the plaintiff is considered to have consented to the risks by electing to participate in the activity.

Increasing the Inherent Risk

The court found that a golf course owes a duty to golfers to exercise ordinary care for the golfer's safety and protection.[6] This includes the duty to warn golfers of latent or concealed defects known to owners and operators of the golf course. But this duty does not include the responsibility to eliminate or protect golfers from risks considered inherent in the game.

---

5. Yoneda v. Tom, 133 P.3d 796, 800 (2006).
6. *See* RESTATEMENT (SECOND) TORTS 314A (1965).

Hole 2: Golf Course Liability

A defendant golf course may be held liable for creating or permitting risks that are considered beyond those inherent to the game.[7] As the owner and operator, Sports Shinko has the duty to design the golf course in a way that minimizes the risk that golfers will be hit.

Determining what risks are "inherent" calls for the consideration of the "nature of the activity," whether the conduct is "totally outside the range of ordinary conduct," and "the relationship of the defendant to the plaintiff." A risk is likely to be considered "inherent" if its elimination would chill the vigorous participation in the game or would fundamentally change its

---

7. PGA Tour, Inc. v. Martin, 532 U.S. 661, 699–702 (2001) (holding that the federal Americans with Disabilities Act (ADA) public accommodation rules applied to Tour events). In his dissent, Justice Scalia criticized the Court's reasoning:

> [W]e Justices must confront what is indeed an awesome responsibility. It has been rendered the solemn duty of the Supreme Court . . . to decide What Is Golf. I am sure that the Framers of the Constitution, aware of the 1457 edict of King James II of Scotland prohibiting golf because it interfered with the practice of archery, fully expected that sooner or later the paths of golf and government, the law and the links, would once again cross, and that the judges of this august Court would some day have to wrestle with that age-old jurisprudential question, for which their years of study in the law have so well prepared them: Is someone riding around a golf course from shot to shot *really* a golfer? The answer, we learn, is yes. The Court ultimately concludes, and it will henceforth be the Law of the Land, that walking is not a "fundamental" aspect of golf. Either out of humility or out of self-respect (one or the other) the Court should decline to answer this incredibly difficult and incredibly silly question. To say that something is "essential" is ordinarily to say that it is necessary to the achievement of a certain object. But since it is the very nature of a game to have no object except amusement (that is what distinguishes games from productive activity), it is quite impossible to say that any of a game's arbitrary rules is "essential." Eighteen-hole golf courses, 10-foot-high basketball hoops, 90-foot baselines, 100-yard football fields—all are arbitrary and none is essential. The only support for any of them is tradition and (in more modern times) insistence by what has come to be regarded as the ruling body of the sport. . . . I suppose there is some point at which the rules of a well-known game are changed to such a degree that no reasonable person would call it the same game. If . . . competitors were required to dribble a large, inflated ball and put it through a round hoop, the game could no longer reasonably be called golf. But this criterion—destroying recognizability as the same generic game—is surely not the test of "essentialness" or "fundamentalness" that the Court applies, since it apparently thinks that merely changing the diameter of the *cup* might "fundamentally alter" the game of golf.

Bay Course at Kapalua, Maui: Looking for good bounces.

nature. In the end, these are elastic considerations best left to a jury.

Sports Shinko failed to meet its burden of showing that no material facts were in dispute. Although it argued that the grant of summary judgment was proper based on implied primary assumption of the risk, the court found that at least one genuine issue of fact existed—namely, whether the golf course actually increased the risk of a golfer being hit by routing the cart path behind the restroom building. Thus, summary judgment was inappropriate. A jury should resolve this factual dispute.

Conclusion

Golf course owners and operators have a duty to design and maintain their facility in a way that does not increase the risk of injury beyond that "inherent" in the game. Whether Sports Shinko met this duty in routing the cart path behind the restroom was a question for the jury to decide on remand.

In a "beloved heaven," or perfect world, the implied assumption of risk doctrine would be sent to the dustbin of legal theory. The existing rules of negligence make its separate existence unnecessary and often confusing. No compelling reason exists for not deciding tort cases using the traditional concepts of duty, breach of duty, or principles of comparative fault. Alas, the world is far from perfect. Thus, the implied assumption of risk doctrine continues to be the law in many states, including Hawaii.

Hole 3

Golf Course Liability:
Warning golfers of lightning

Kansas: *Sall v. TS, Inc., d/b/a Smiley's Golf Complex*, 136 P.3d 471 (2009)

Lightning is a dreaded natural phenomenon that poses a significant hazard to golfers and golf course property. In the United States alone, lightning kills up to 300 people per year and injures as many as 1,500. The National Climatic Data Center statistics show that about one in every 20 lightning deaths occurs on golf courses.[1]

Because it is largely unpredictable, a lightning strike that causes injury or death may be considered an "act of God," which is another way of saying "don't blame me, blame God." The "act of God" legal theory effectively acts as a bar to recovery when the plaintiff's injury would have occurred regardless of the defendant's actions.

Too many golfers ignore the dangers of lightning because they are having "the game of their life." The film classic *Caddy-*

---

1. Sunny days can also be a problem for golfers. In 1934, the U.S. Supreme Court rejected a life insurance claim brought by the widow of a golfer who suffered sunstroke while playing golf and died. The insurance policy provided that the insurance would be paid if death should result "directly and independently from external, violent and accidental means." Notwithstanding that an autopsy revealed that there was no bodily infirmity or disease that contributed to the golfer's death, the sun's rays were not considered an external accidental means. *Landress v. Phoenix Mut. Life Ins. Co. et al.*, 291 U.S. 491 (1934).

shack I humorously made this point. Movie fans will recall the scene in which Bishop Pickering, played by Henry Wilcoxon, and Carl Spackler, played by Bill Murray, are hoping to finish the round of golf under threatening weather conditions at Bushwood Country Club.

After sinking an unbelievable putt in the middle of a torrential thunder and lightning storm, the bishop asks his caddy for advice about continuing: "Well, what do you think?" Carl says, "I'd keep playing, I don't think the heavy stuff is going to come down for quite a while." The bishop agrees: "You're right. Anyway, the good Lord would never disrupt the best game of my life. I'm infallible, young fella." The bishop is then struck by lightning, which is a reminder that the "good Lord" does not play favorites on the golf course.

Although golf fatalities from lightning are rare, you don't have to be an electrical engineer to know that lightning and golf don't mix. Perhaps the most widely publicized case involving professional golfers occurred in 1975 during the Western Open golf tournament. Tony Jacklin and Bobby Nichols were both hit by lightning. Jacklin's eight-iron, which acted like a lightning rod, was sent flying about 20 feet through the air. Jerry Heard and Lee Trevino, affectionately known as the "Merry Mex," were also hit during the event. During a subsequent interview, Trevino famously quipped, "I should have held up a one-iron. Not even God can hit a one-iron."

There are other notable cases involving lightning and golfers.[2] Retief Goosen was a teenage amateur when he was struck by Thor's hammer while playing golf at Pietersburg Golf Club in

---

2. Professional golfer John Daly is known for his big stick on the golf course. He also has a big heart. During the 1991 PGA Championship, which he won, he learned that a lightning strike had claimed the life of gallery patron. "Big John" donated $30,000 of his winnings, his first significant check as a professional, to the victim's family.

Hole 3: Golf Course Liability

South Africa. He still has a scar on his wrist from the incident. News reports said his mom kept what was left of his clothes, which had been burned off his body, as a reminder of the close call.

In the 1930s, Bobby Jones recalled his close run-in with lightning after quitting the East Lake Golf Course due to a severe thunderstorm. As he was walking in front of the clubhouse, lightning hit the main chimney. Falling parts of the chimney ripped through his shirt and cut his shoulder. Just as in putting, an inch or two can make the difference between disaster and success.

The Facts

Smiley's Golf Course (SGC) is an 18-hole, par-60 executive course in Lenexa, Kansas. The course layout is as follows:

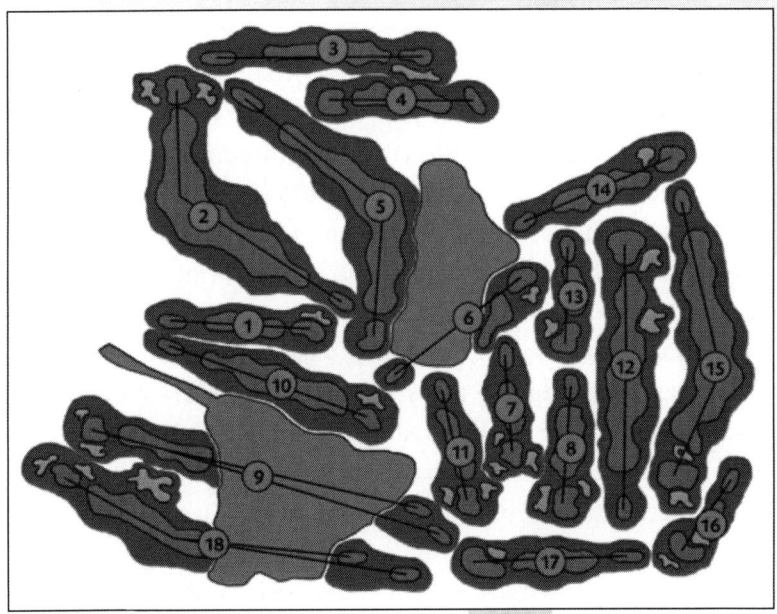

Smiley Golf Course

SGC has a policy and procedure for dealing with inclement weather. It calls for the manager to monitor the local television stations and weather radio, check weather radar images on the Internet, and visually inspect the weather by stepping outside. No written policy exists concerning the frequency of checking these weather resources, but they are consulted more frequently when storms are in the area.

Patrick Sall and his buddy, Chris Gannan, decided late in the afternoon to play golf at Smiley's. Thunderstorms had been moving in and out of the area, so Patrick called the course to see if it was open. Patrick's mom was concerned about the weather. Patrick reassured his mother: "Mom, don't worry; they wouldn't be open if it wasn't safe." So off they went.

They paid their greens fees and arrived at the first tee shortly before 5:00 p.m. They teed off sometime between 4:45 and 4:50 p.m. As they were walking to the second tee, it started to sprinkle, and they wondered whether storms might be moving back into the area. They discussed the fact that SGC would blow an air horn as a danger signal to golfers to return to the clubhouse.

At approximately 4:50 p.m., the manager checked the weather on the Internet. While he waited for the radar image to appear, an employee informed him that a television news teaser had just reported that storms were moving back into the area. The computer screen showed storms to the southwest of the golf course. The manager then went outside and saw dark clouds and lightning to the southwest. He immediately went inside, grabbed the air horn, stepped outside, and sounded the horn for two 7- or 8-second periods. He estimated that he sounded the air horn at approximately 4:57 or 4:58 p.m. At the time, three golfers were on the course: Patrick, Chris, and Toby Mills, who was playing golf by himself and several holes ahead of the twosome.

Hole 3: Golf Course Liability

It was raining harder when Patrick and Chris started putting on the second green. Chris saw a lightning bolt off to the west, but it was far enough away that they were not concerned. Nevertheless, according to Chris, they agreed to walk back to the clubhouse after putting out. As they were walking on the green, Chris saw a flash, heard a loud boom, and was knocked unconscious. When he came to, Patrick was facedown and unresponsive. A meteorologist calculated that Patrick was struck by lightning approximately two to three minutes after the horn sounded.

Eyewitness accounts are not always reliable. At the trial, Toby Mills testified that he heard the horn when he was playing the sixth hole and returned immediately to the clubhouse. On the way there, he said he passed Chris and Patrick as they were walking toward the second green. He claimed to have looked at them and wondered why they were still golfing. But he recalled the facts differently in his deposition.

During his deposition, Toby said that he saw Patrick and Chris getting ready to tee off on the second hole as he was playing the fifth. He also testified that he had just teed off on the seventh hole, not the sixth hole, when he heard the horn. In his deposition, he said that he did not immediately return to the clubhouse, whereas at trial he said he did. At his deposition, he also said that he never saw Patrick and Chris on his way back to the clubhouse.

After Patrick was hit by the lightning, Chris said he headed to the clubhouse to get help, which he estimated took him between five and 10 minutes. A person at the clubhouse called 911, and the call was logged in between 5:16 and 5:17 p.m.

Patrick never fully recovered from being hit, and he now requires total care. Patrick and his parents sued SGC for negligence.

The Law

The plaintiffs argued that SGC had a duty to warn Patrick of the danger it knew or should have known about. The plaintiffs also argued that SGC was negligent in monitoring the weather, in failing to sound a timely warning, and in failing to utilize lightning detection equipment. The defendant moved for summary judgment.

The trial court ruled that SGC was entitled to summary judgment because it owed no duty to Patrick to protect him from lightning-related injuries. Without the existence of a duty, the negligence claim faltered. It also reasoned that even if it owed Patrick a duty, it was not breached.

On appeal, the court of appeals affirmed the trial court. It reasoned that lightning is not a foreseeable risk and that SGC did not breach any standard of care by failing to have a lightning detection system. In addition, if a duty to foresee the lightning existed, no breach occurred because SGC provided approximately 10 minutes of notice, and no evidence existed that this warning was insufficient. It also found that Patrick and Chris saw the lightning and yet chose to remain on the golf course.

The Kansas Supreme Court reversed and remanded the case. It found that a legal duty to Patrick existed under Section 323 of the Restatement (Second) of Torts:

> One who undertakes, gratuitously or for consideration, to render services to another which he [or she] should recognize as necessary for the protection of the other's person or things, is subject to liability to the other for physical harm resulting from his [or her] failure to exercise reasonable care to perform his [or her] undertaking, if, (a) his [or her] failure to exercise such care increases the risk of such harm, or (b) the harm

is suffered because of the other's reliance upon the undertaking.

The court reasoned that SGC undertook the task of warning golfers of the impeding storm for the purpose of protecting them. As a result, it owed the golfers the duty of reasonable care in implementing those warnings and safety precautions. This determination did not mean that the plaintiffs should prevail, but only that a legal duty was owed to Patrick.

The court also found that the appellate court erred in reasoning that if a duty existed, SGC was not negligent based on its own findings of fact. The appellate court sits not as an independent finder of fact, which was the basis of its finding that no breach of the duty occurred. The court scolded the appellate court for misconceiving its function in reviewing summary judgment, which is to resolve all facts and reasonable inferences in favor of the party against whom the ruling is sought.

The United States Golf Association (USGA) and the Royal and Ancient Golf Club of Saint Andrews (R&A) write, interpret, and revise the *Rules of Golf* every four years. The 2012 rule book is more than 200 pages long. The accompanying Decisions on the Rules of Golf (Decisions) is another authoritative source governing the game. It is more than 500 pages long.

Most avid golfers are familiar with events beyond human control. The expression "rub of the green" is one way the *Rules of Golf* effectively say "accidents happen, play the ball where it lies." Lawyers are familiar with an analogous concept. Unforeseeable natural forces, such as lightning, may be called acts of God. It is a roundabout way of saying that accidents happen and the defendant should not be held liable. The *Sall* case avoided the acts of God doctrine by focusing on whether SGC's monitoring practices and warning increased the risk of harm to Patrick. SGC's actions triggered the finding of the existence of a duty and not the existence of the lightning strike.

The *Rules of Golf* deal with lightning. Rule 6-8 allows a player to unilaterally decide to discontinue play when the player "believes there is a danger from lightning." A note to Rule 6-8 confirms the dangers from lightning: "There have been many deaths and injuries from lightning on golf courses; all clubs and sponsors are urged to take precautions for the protection of persons against lightning."

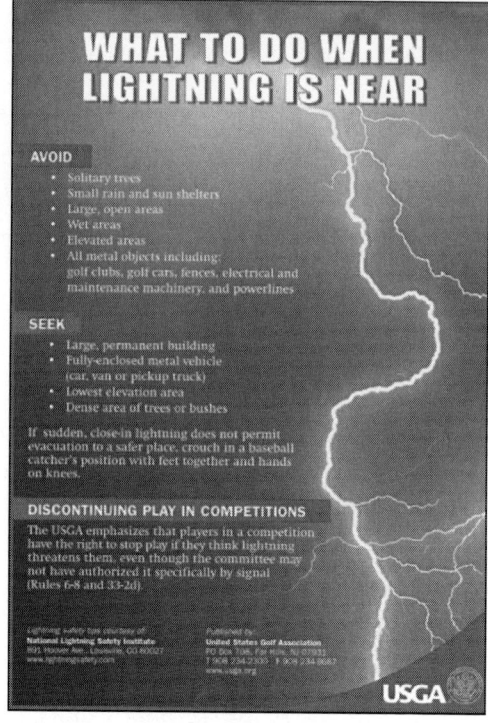

USGS Safety Warning

The committee[3] may provide, in the conditions of a competition under Rule 33-1, that in potentially dangerous situations, play must be discontinued immediately following a suspension of play by the committee. If a player fails to discontinue play immediately, he or she is disqualified, unless circumstances warrant waiving the penalty as provided in Rule 33-7.

---

3. The "committee" is defined as the committee in charge of the competition or, if the matter does not arise in a competition, the committee in charge of the course. RULES OF GOLF, *Definitions*.

Conclusion

Lightning is unpredictable and difficult to protect against. Golf course owners or operators may argue that they have no duty to prevent injuries caused by lightning because lightning is an "act of God."

Although generally available as a theory to avoid liability, there are limits to its effectiveness. The owners and operators of golf courses that use a weather warning system to warn players of lightning must operate the system with reasonable care to avoid increasing the risk of harm to golfers who rely on it.

In *Sall*, SGC had assumed a duty to Patrick to operate its warning system in a non-negligent manner. Material issues of fact remained to be determined on whether SGC breached the duty it assumed in operating the warning system on remand to the trial court. If SGC were found to be negligent on remand, a jury would have to determine whether Patrick was comparatively negligent for not heeding the obvious storm conditions. SGC's liability would be reduced to the extent of Patrick's own negligence based on the Kansas comparative fault statute.

The Supreme Court did not address what, if any, type of technical warning system a golf course should or must employ. Those important questions were left to future litigation and debate.

Hole 4

Golfer Liability to a Spectator:
"Duty or breach of duty?"

Indiana: *Pfenning v. Lineman*, 947 N.E.2d 392 (2011)

All too often a spectator may be on the receiving end of an errant golf shot. Anyone who has watched professional golf on television can't help but be amazed when spectators crowd together, creating a small window for the intended flight of the ball. There seems to be no fear that the ball will fly off-line.

Even the pros hit wild shots. During a practice round at the 2012 Ryder Cup at Medinah Country Club in Illinois, Tiger Woods's tee shot on the 18th hole didn't go as intended. He nailed an unsuspecting spectator on the head. The next day, Woods's tee shot veered off-line on the 7th hole. The ball, which dropped the unfortunate spectator like a heavy golf bag, careened some 50 yards off the spectator's head. Some commentators wondered whether the spectator was a hardheaded Chicagoan or a steelworker. A third spectator during the tournament got whacked by another of Woods's wayward drives. To make amends, Woods gave the spectator a signed golf glove.[1]

---

1. Perhaps during a post-round interview, an intrepid sport's writer will ask the following fantasy question: "Tiger, how many gloves do you carry in your golf bag during a tournament?"

Other nonparticipants are at risk of getting hit. For many golfers, the beverage cart that often circles the golf course may be considered a traveling oasis on wheels. Most beverage carts serve snacks and beverages, including what some call necessary "swing lubricants." Depending on the attractiveness of the driver, some golfers are drawn to the cart for other reasons. Sometimes it is to check on the health and well-being of the cart girl or to practice their lame comedy routine.

Although a welcome sight for many golfers, beverage carts carry certain risks, especially for the overly thirsty golfer. In 2006, for example, Adam Thompson was charged with felony criminal vehicular operation for driving a golf cart at the Mississippi Dunes Golf Links while under the "influence."[2] As bad luck would have it, he flipped the golf cart and pinned his playing partner underneath. The police were called, and Adam was summoned to appear in court. He argued, among other things, that the golf club bore some responsibility for the accident by putting an attractive woman in charge of dispensing a full load of booze within his thirsty reach.

The Facts

The Marion Elks Country Club 18-hole private golf course is located in Marion, Indiana. It is a par-72 course that stretches more than 6,300 yards from the back tees. It has a course rating of 70.3 and a slope rating of 125 from the back tees. The golf course is popular and has been featured in *Golf Digest*. It also has been featured in a judicial opinion of the Indiana Supreme Court.

In 2006, Cassie Pfenning was driving the beverage cart on the cart path of the 18th hole when she was hit in the mouth by

---

2. United Press Int'l, *Man faces DWI for golf cart crash*," June 10, 2006.

Hole 4: Golfer Liability to a Spectator

a golf ball served up by Joseph Lineman, one of several defendants in the case. The cart had a large cooler on the back, which was loaded with swing lubricant beverages being dispensed by her cart companion, Christie Edwards. Pfenning, who was age 16, was a volunteer, whereas Edwards was an employee of the tournament sponsor, Whitey's 31 Club Tavern. The cart had no windshield, and the record is not clear whether it had a protective roof.

The ball that hit Pfenning was a low drive from the 16th tee, which was approximately 80 yards away from her. The ball traveled straight for approximately 60 to 70 yards before deciding to change course and severely hook to the left. Lineman said he shouted "fore," but neither the plaintiff nor her beverage-serving partner heard the warning. After hearing what he described as a "faint yelp," Lineman ran in the direction of the errant ball to investigate. He discovered the injured and soon-to-be plaintiff, Pfenning.

The Law

Pfenning sued Lineman in negligence for the injuries she suffered to her mouth, jaw, and teeth.[3] Because her legal theory against Lineman was negligence, the plaintiff was required to prove the following: First, the defendant owed her a duty of care; second, the defendant breached the duty; and finally, the breach was the factual and legal cause of her injury.

The defendant argued at trial that, under established Indiana precedent, he had no duty to a "co-participant" with respect to the risks inherent to the game. Thus, he should prevail as a matter of law.

The trial court granted the defendant's motion for summa-

---

3. The lawsuit also named the country club, Whitey's Tavern, and the estate of Jerry Jones.

ry judgment on the theory that no duty was owed to a "co-participant" for risks inherent to the game. The court of appeals affirmed. The Supreme Court of Indiana affirmed the result, but said the reasoning was wrong. In doing so, it clarified the appropriate analysis for future cases.

The court held that if a golfer acts within the "range of ordinary behavior," the conduct is reasonable as a matter of law and does not constitute a breach of duty. Looking at "inherent risk" to define the duty was out. The status of the injured party as a participant or co-participant also was out. The principal question was whether the defendant acted within the range of ordinary behavior. A golfer hitting an errant drive "is clearly within the range of ordinary behavior." Therefore, the conduct is reasonable as a matter of law and does not establish the element of breach necessary to support a claim of negligence.

Comparative Fault Law

Most American systems using a comparative fault system reduce the plaintiff's recovery of damages when the plaintiff is partially at fault. This approach rejects the harshness of barring the plaintiff from recovery when the plaintiff is considered to be "slightly," or to some degree, negligent. This situation may arise when the injured golfer carelessly or intentionally walks in front of a playing partner.

Under Indiana statutory law, a plaintiff may be barred from recovery when the plaintiff's level of fault reaches a specified breakpoint. Section 6 bars recovery when the plaintiff's contributory faulty to the injury "is greater than" that of the defendant or defendants.[4] This will occur when the plaintiff is found to be more than 50 percent negligent.

---

4. IND. CODE ANN. § 34-51-2-6 (West).

Hole 4: Golfer Liability to a Spectator

Section 6 provides:

(a) In an action based on fault that is brought against: (1) one defendant; or (2) two or more defendants who may be treated as a single party; the claimant is barred from recovery if the claimant's contributory fault is greater than the fault of all persons whose fault proximately contributed to the claimant's damages.

(b) In an action based on fault that is brought against two (2) or more defendants, the claimant is barred from recovery if the claimant's contributory fault is greater than the fault of all persons whose fault proximately contributed to the claimant's damages.[5]

Absent being barred from recovery, the degree of plaintiff's fault results in the reduction of any recovery under Section 5.

Section 5 provides: In an action based on fault, any contributory fault chargeable to the claimant diminishes proportionately the amount awarded as compensatory damages for an injury attributable to the claimant's contributory fault, but does not bar recovery except as provided in section 6 of this chapter.[6]

"Fault" is considered any act or omission by the plaintiff that is negligent, willful, wanton, reckless, or intentional toward the defendant. It includes, for example, an unreasonable assumption of risk by the plaintiff. A plaintiff's unreasonable failure to avoid an injury or to mitigate damages also triggers a finding of fault.

The court concluded that using an "inherent risk" analysis to find no duty of care was inconsistent with the Indiana Com-

---

5. IND. CODE ANN. § 34-51-2-6 (West).
6. IND. CODE ANN. § 34-51-2-5 (West).

parative Fault Act. In doing so, it joined a handful of states that insist upon applying an ordinary concept of negligence.

The policies of encouraging participation in the sport and discouraging excessive litigation by those suffering injury from a participant's conduct were also important. These policies, the court found, could be achieved within the framework of the comparative fault statute by basing the analysis on the element of breach of duty. The court also noted that focusing on breach, rather than duty, was consistent with the approach taken by New Hampshire and Arizona.

The court left unanswered the methodology to be used in determining the "range of ordinary behavior." It did clearly recognize, however, that hitting the errant drive, which injured a plaintiff, is within the range of ordinary action of golfers.

Conclusion

In Indiana, the analysis of a golfer's liability does not depend on whether the injured party is a cart girl, a spectator, or another golfer. It also does not depend on whether the injured person has assumed the risk of injury. Rather, the legal analysis focuses on whether the conduct of the defendant golfer was within the ordinary range of conduct for playing the game. If it is, then the conduct is reasonable as a matter of law and does not constitute a breach of duty for a claim based on negligence. Indiana's Comparative Fault statute was instrumental in shifting the analysis from duty to breach of duty.

In *Pfenning*, the parties agreed that conventional golf etiquette includes shouting "fore" when a shot presents a danger to others. The court was not prepared, however, to let either the presence or absence of this warning control. It offered two principal reasons. First, the court found that the effectiveness of such a warning depends on numerous other factors, such as the

Hole 4: Golfer Liability to a Spectator

distance between the plaintiff and defendant, wind velocity and ball flight, the timing and the volume of the warning, and so on. These variables "inevitably call for speculation and surmise." Second, the court reasoned that yelling "fore" or not yelling it is within the range of ordinary behavior of golfers, "and that, as a matter of law, neither the manner of doing so nor the failure to do so constitutes a breach sufficient to support a claim for negligence."

The shift in analysis to breach of duty is significant and seemingly at odds with the approach taken by New York and California, which rely on assumption of those risks inherent to the game. Whether Indiana is the wave of the future is yet to be seen.

Hole 5

Golfer Liability to a Playing Partner:

"Shanks a lot"

New York: *Anand v. Kapoor*,
942 N.E.2d 295 (2011)

A shanked shot can provide comic relief. In the golf movie *Caddyshack*, for example, golf ace Ty Webb (played by Chevy Chase) hilariously shanks a shot through the window of assistant greenskeeper Carl Spackler (played by Bill Murray). The ball, which comes to rest on a slice of pie on Spackler's coffee table, is then played out a window by Ty after taking what appears to be a free drop.

Pro golfers are not immune from the dreaded "shank." During the 2010 Ryder Cup, one of the world's most recognized professional golfers, Tiger Woods, shanked a shot that was captured on film in mid-flight. A picture of the ball was taken by a photographer just before it smashed into the lens of his camera. Dramatic, yes; funny, not so much.[1]

---

1. An alligator attack is rarer than a shanked shot. The Georgia Supreme Court recently held that the golfer either assumed the risks of walking in areas inhabited by alligators or failed to exercise ordinary care. The fatal attack occurred at The Landings, a planned residential development with a golf course located on Skidaway Island off the Georgia coast. The day after the attack, the golfer's body was found floating in an adjacent lagoon. The decedent's right foot and both forearms had been bitten off. An eight-foot alligator later was caught in the same lagoon, and, after the alligator was killed, parts of the decedent's body were found in its stomach. Landings Ass'n, Inc. v. Williams, 728 S.E.2d 577 (2012).

Golfers have a general duty to warn anyone in the foreseeable zone of danger from a shot. The customary warning "fore" is used by the golfer either before hitting or once the misbehaving ball threatens another. The *Anand* case looks at the duty to warn a playing partner of a "shanked" golf shot, which unfortunately ended the plaintiff's medical career as a neuroradiologist.

The Facts

The events unfolded at the Dix Hills Park Golf Course on Long Island, New York. Owned by the town of Huntington, Dix Hills is a 9-hole golf course that plays to a par 31 for men and a par 32 for women. It has a driving range and chipping area to work one's game prior to playing. Although the first hole is a 280-foot par 4 that plays slightly uphill, the course has mostly par 3's. Its "slope rating" of 97 generally places the course in the category of relatively easy. But being relatively easy is no protection against a shanked shot.[2]

Dr. Azad Anand and Dr. Anoop Kapoor were close friends for many years and often golfed together. By his own admission, Kapoor said he was not an "expert" and only "played" at the game. The record does not reveal whether he had a predisposition to shank.

Their 25-year friendship took a turn for the worse on the morning of October 19, 2002. The doctors had expected to play a friendly round of golf with their mutual friend, Balram Verman. The record also does not mention whether the threesome warmed up on the driving range, or whether it would have made a difference. After teeing off on the first hole, a 283-yard par

---

2. A golf course slope rating is a way of measuring the degree of difficulty for bogey golfers, who are those players with an 18 handicap.

Hole 5: Golfer Liability to a Playing Partner

4, they each hit a mulligan.[3] After hitting their mulligans, they headed toward their respective balls.

Without waiting for Kapoor to find or hit his ball, Anand went to look for his ball, which was off to the right on the fairway. Meanwhile, Kapoor found his ball in the rough and hit. At about the same time Kapoor hit, Anand turned around to see where his playing partners were. The timing couldn't have been worse. The ball was mishit off the heel and hosel area of Kapoor's club, which cause it to dart in an unexpected direction, striking Anand in the left eye.[4] As a result, Anand suffered a retinal detachment and permanent loss of vision in his left eye.

Hosel Shank

---

3. Several theories and considerable debate exists as to the origin of the term "mulligan." One commonly accepted view traces it to David Mulligan, who played at the St. Lambert Country Club in Montreal, Canada, during the 1920s. But several versions of the story exist. One version says that the first "mulligan" was simply an impulsive act to correct a poor shot. After hitting his drive off the first tee, Mulligan simply re-teed and hit again. His playing partners found this amusing, and decided that the shot that Mulligan called a "correction shot" deserved a better name, so they called it a "mulligan." Another version is that the extra shot was given to Mulligan on the first tee because he was jumpy and shaking from his automobile drive to the golf course. A third version has Mulligan showing up late to the course. As a result of being harried from his last-minute arrival on the first tee, Mulligan hit a poor shot and simply re-teed. One discredited theory is that the term is really a contraction of the phrase "maul it again."

4. During the 2012 BMW Championship, Webb Simpson, the reigning U.S. Open winner, shanked his tee shot so badly on the sixth tee that the ball couldn't be found. Although rare for a professional golfer, most recreational golfers have shanked a golf shot more than a few times.

Anand sued Kapoor in tort seeking damages for the personal injuries he sustained.

During the trial, there was disagreement as to some of the facts. The plaintiff admitted that it is customary for players in the same group to stand behind the player hitting the ball. He estimated that he was approximately 15 to 20 feet ahead of the defendant when he was hit by the shanked shot. Their playing partner, Verma, agreed that the plaintiff was about 20 feet in front of the defendant. Their view of how far the plaintiff was in front of the defendant was generally consistent. Verma also testified that the plaintiff was at an angle of about 50 degrees from the defendant's intended target—the green—when he was struck.

The defendant, Kapoor recalled the distances and angles differently. He testified that the plaintiff was considerably further ahead of him and off his line of play by perhaps 60 to 80 degrees when he shanked his shot. But he also admitted that he "did not actually know" where either the plaintiff or Verma was prior to actually hitting. He did claim, however, that he did not see anyone standing between his ball and the green when he hit the ill-fated shot.

The defendant testified that he shouted a warning when he realized the ball was moving off-line, but both the plaintiff and Verma testified that they did not hear any such warning. There was sufficient evidence in the record to support the conclusion that the plaintiff was not in the intended line of flight of the defendant's shot.

The Law

Every lawsuit requires a legal theory to support a finding of liability. Three theories of liability exist when a golfer is injured by another player on the golf course: negligence, willful and reck-

Hole 5: Golfer Liability to a Playing Partner

less misconduct, and intentional tort. In simple terms, negligence is conduct that falls below the standard of care that the law imposes to protect others from the unreasonable risk of harm. In order to support a claim of negligence, the defendant must breach some duty that is owed to the injured party. Establishing that the defendant breached a duty is not enough to prevail, however, because the defendant has the chance to assert certain defenses, such as assumption of the risk.

Under New York law, a golfer has the duty to give a timely warning to other players who happen to be within the "foreseeable ambit of danger" from a shot, and failure to do so may constitute negligence. Before hitting a shot, a golfer has the duty to warn those players in the same group of the impending shot and also those potentially at risk of being hit.

Custom dictates that a golfer warns those players by yelling the warning "fore" before hitting or once it becomes clear that another player is in danger of being hit. Although this is the customary practice, many golfers find it interesting, as well as surprising, that yelling "fore" is not mandated by the *Rules of Golf*.

As might be expected, a factual question often arises as to whether the defendant actually yelled the warning "fore." An injured plaintiff often will deny having heard the warning, while the defendant will argue that such a warning was given. In most cases, the jury will be tasked with deciding whether the warning was given based on the testimony of the parties and any witnesses. In *Anand*, this factual question never reached the jury because the case was decided as a matter of law on a motion for summary judgment. In other words, the presence or absence of the warning was not relevant to the outcome of the case.

Determining whether the plaintiff was within the zone of danger is critical to finding that the defendant owes the plaintiff a duty. Unlike the "out of bounds" signs that mark the boundary to the playing area, no fixed rule or formula exists for determining the legal boundaries to the zone of danger. The zone of danger often depends on the facts and circumstances of the case. The intended line of flight of the ball is a starting point to fixing the legal zone, but it is not determinative because the duty to warn extends beyond the boundaries of the intended path of the ball. If golf balls always followed the "intended path," there would be no lawsuit.

Depending on the jurisdiction, assumption of the risk is treated either as a defense to the claim of negligence, which is the traditional approach, or as a way of examining the duty component of negligence. It works to bar liability in the following way. As a matter of law, golfers are considered to accept the risks that are inherent to the game. They are generally considered by the law to have consented to the known risk of being injured by wayward golf balls, because mishit and errant shots are simply part of the game.

Only those risks that are foreseeable and inherent to the game are within the assumed risk. A player who walks ahead of a playing partner who has yet to hit may be considered to voluntarily accept the risk of a mishit shot, and therefore be precluded from recovering on the theory of negligence by assumption of the risk.

To the extent that the defendant is considered to have acted recklessly or intentionally, which are alternate theories of liability, assumption of the risk does not bar recovery. An injured player, for example, does not assume the risk that he or she will be hit by the reckless or intentional actions of another player.

In *Anand*, the plaintiff's legal theory was that the defendant's failure to warn of his shot amounted to negligence and was the proximate cause of his injury. The trial court was not convinced that this alleged failure should control the outcome.

Hole 5: Golfer Liability to a Playing Partner

As a result, it granted the defendant's motion for summary judgment, reasoning that the plaintiff was not physically in the "foreseeable zone of danger."

The plaintiff appealed but had no better luck before the appellate division. It offered three reasons for ruling against the plaintiff: first, the defendant had no duty to warn of his intent to hit; second, the plaintiff assumed the risk of being hit by a poorly executed shot by advancing in front of the defendant; and finally, the plaintiff's failure to yell the warning "fore" before hitting the ball did not unreasonably increase the risk to the plaintiff beyond those inherent in the game.

Even when a plaintiff is considered to be within the zone of danger, assumption of the risk may preclude liability. Rather than focusing on whether the defendant has a duty to the plaintiff, assumption of the risk may shift the focus to the actions of the plaintiff. The plaintiff may be considered to have consented to the known risk of being injured by the shanked shot hit by the defendant because it is simply part of the risk of playing the game. Moreover, a player who walks ahead of a playing partner who has yet to hit may be considered to voluntarily accept the risk of being hit by a mishit shot.

The existence and scope of duty are questions of law that require the court to consider and weigh competing public policies. One important policy is facilitating the free and vigorous participation in the game without being exposed to legal liability. To conclude that the defendant could be held liable in tort for a shanked golf shot because he may have negligently failed to shout "fore" was, in the court's view, inimical to this policy.

Anand had one last shot or legal mulligan. He asked the highest court in New York, the Court of Appeals of New York, to decide in his favor. In a brief opinion, the court of appeals rejected the argument that the defendant's failure to warn of his shanked shot amounted to negligence. It found that the failure to yell "fore" or otherwise warn Anand did not unreasonably increase the risk to which the plaintiff consented. In short, being hit without warning by a shanked shot by a playing partner while searching for one's own ball is a commonly appreciated risk of golf.

The plaintiff submitted an affidavit of a golf expert. He opined that the defendant violated the "universally recognized" rules and procedures by hitting before determining the whereabouts of the other players and in failing to give a warning before hitting. The affidavit did not affect the outcome.

The court of appeals reasoned that the plaintiff assumed the risk of injury. As a result, the failure to yell "fore" before hitting a golf ball did not unreasonably increase risk to the plaintiff beyond those inherent in the game. Thus, the factual disagreement on whether the defendant yelled "fore" never reached the jury.

A warning makes sense only if it would make a difference. Yelling "fore" applies when another person is within the foreseeable zone of danger. Assuming that a golfer fails to ascertain where the other members of his party are before hitting, such a lapse does not rise to the level of creating a dangerous condition over and above the usual danger inherent in playing golf.

The court of appeals did not expressly endorse the idea of defining the foreseeable zone of danger by reference to the intended line of flight of the ball. The intended line of flight is, however, a relevant starting point for determining the zone of danger.

Conclusion

Plaintiff's injury was the result of a terrible accident, but not all accidents result in a finding of liability. One must advance

Hole 5: Golfer Liability to a Playing Partner

an adequate legal theory to support liability. In most golf injury cases, the plaintiff will argue that the defendant acted negligently, but he or she generally faces an uphill legal battle.

Several lessons can be taken from *Anand*. In New York, a golfer who shanks a shot by more than 60 degrees can breathe a bit easier about being held liable for not yelling "fore." For playing partners, the parody to the lyrics of the song "Sixteen Tons" offers the following advice: "When you see me tee up, you'd better step aside. A lot of men didn't, a lotta men died"—or were severely injured.[5]

You might recall that the players hit mulligans. Would the outcome have been different had the plaintiff had been hit by the defendant's mulligan? A golfer who hits a mulligan without warning and injures another player in the same group is apt to be found liable. As an aside, the *Rules of Golf* prohibit a golfer from having more than one ball in play at the same time, with one exception. Under Rule 27-2, a "provisional ball" is one that is played as a conditional substitute for a ball that may be lost outside a water hazard or may be out of bounds. Mulligans don't fit this exception.

---

5. In 1992, the singer and songwriter John Denver offered the following parody of the song "Sixteen Tons" that was first recorded by country singer Merle Travis in 1947:

When you see me tee up, you'd better step aside
A lot of men didn't, a lotta men died
I hook it to the left, I shank it to the right
I'll be looking for my ball until the dark of the night
You play eighteen holes, what do you get
Another day older and deeper in debt
Saint Andrew don't you call me, 'cause I can't go
I owe my soul to the country club pro . . . I owe my soul to the country club pro
Yeah

Hole 6

Product Liability:
Golf cart maker in "hot seat"

California: *Mendoza, et al. v. Club Car, Inc.*, 81 Cal. App. 4th 287 (2000), reh'g denied (June 27, 2000), review denied (Aug. 23, 2000)

Motorized golf carts are common in the United States. About a million are in use today, of which approximately 75 percent are used to ferry golfers, golf clubs, and miscellaneous items during a round of golf.

Some golf courses require golfers to use motorized golf carts, while other courses simply make them available as a courtesy. Any golfer who has paid a separate fee to rent a motorized golf cart may not be surprised to learn that the golf cart industry is big business. The industry is estimated to generate more than $1 billion a year in revenue for the manufacturers and golf cart owners, which is often the golf course.

Motorized carts are not inherently dangerous. Nevertheless, a statistically significant number of personal injuries and deaths result from golf cart accidents each year. Except for "governors," which mechanically control speed, golf carts have few safety features.

Many accidents involving carts are attributable to operator error, often quick turning or general inattentiveness. Riding golfers may be injured when they fall out of a cart or it tips over on them. Collisions between two or more carts also occur. In cases of operator error, the driver of the cart may be sued for negligence. Because golf carts are used on sloped and hilly terrains, a golf course may be swept into the litigation on the theory of premises liability for unsafe design, maintenance, or construction of the golf course or cart paths.[1]

When injury or death is caused by a cart defect, the golf cart manufacturer will be sued on the theories of strict product liability, negligence, and breach of warranty. The golf course and others in the chain of distribution are also likely to be named as defendants

The Facts

Steele Canyon is a 27-hole, public/private golf course designed by Gary Player. It offers three 9-hole tracts: the Meadow, the Ranch, and the Canyon. The popular course is located about a 25-minute drive east of San Diego, California.

The Canyon 9-hole is descriptive. It offers dramatic elevation changes, breathtaking views, and numerous canyons that are seemingly magnetized to attract wayward golf balls. As part of their 18-hole loop, David Mendoza and three of his buddies were playing the Canyon the day of the accident. They had rented two carts from the golf course.

David had parked his cart on the dirt cart path on a hillside. The slope runs toward a lateral hazard, which was a dry creek bed filled with rocks and vegetation. David pushed the parking brake to lock the cart against moving. Setting the brake was necessary to prevent the cart from rolling into the lateral hazard.

---

1. Premises liability is a body of law that subjects the owner or possessor of land to liability suffered by persons injured on the land. Generally, the owner or possessor must be negligent or commit some other wrongful act before being found liable.

The cart was stationary when David got out to help O'Hara, his playing partner, find his ball. The two other players in the foursome, John and Bill Watkins, testified that the cart was stationary. A few minutes after leaving the cart, John and Bill both heard the distinctive sound of the brake releasing. As a result, the cart started down the hillside on its own.

David was about 10 yards behind the now driverless cart, which began to pick up speed. In hot pursuit and halfway down the hillside, David grabbed the roof strut of the cart with his left hand, thinking he could stop it. At the last minute, he rethought his plan and let go. As he did, the runaway cart hit a bump or depression on the hillside and turned on him.

The cart threw David into the air and launched him onto the large rocks in the creek bed. As a result, he suffered numerous injuries, including multiple spinal vertebrae fractures and a spinal cord injury in the neck area.

The parking brake design and condition

The parking brake on the golf cart is designed to engage by applying pressure on the upper left side of the brake pedal. The brake is released by either depressing the pedal or stepping on the accelerator. The design engineer for the golf cart manufacturer testified that the parking brake is operated by engagement of a pawl with a latch. He described the braking assembly mechanism as follows:

> When the parking brake pedal is depressed, the narrow tip of the pawl fits into one of six teeth in the latch, depending on how hard the parking brake pedal is depressed. The pawl is connected to the parking brake pedal by linkages. The latch is also connected to the accelerator pedal by linkages. The linkage to the accel-

erator is mounted on two plastic bearing blocks on the undercarriage of the cart. When the parking brake is set, the depth of the engagement of the pawl is approximately one-tenth of an inch. The pawl and latch are designed to be movable. To prevent the latch and pawl from unintentionally disengaging, the direction of the force exerted by the pawl upon the latch goes directly through the center of rotation of the accelerator pivot shaft, to which the latch is attached by linkages. If the force is directed rearward of that point, a rotational force is created that moves the latch rearward (as if the pedal is depressed) and the parking brake can spontaneously release. The harder the brake pedal is pushed and the deeper the tooth is engaged, the more force is generated, the more load on parts and the greater the tendency of the pawl to push away and the parking brake to spontaneously disengage.

The expert for the plaintiffs, a registered mechanical and safety engineer, testified that a design defect in the cart's braking system caused the parking brake to fail on the date of the accident. He opined that the close tolerance of the latch and pawl made it easy for a number of different factors to cause the latch and pawl to not match up at the correct angle and redirect force rearward, causing the brake to spontaneously release. These factors included wear, adjustment, load on the linkages, alignment, and/or deflection of parts.

The same expert also testified that the parking brake assembly had been altered after the accident. Between the accident and the expert's inspection, the golf course's mechanic worked on the cart. The parking brake assembly had been washed with high-power water and air hoses, and the brake drums were

Hole 6: Product Liability

removed. The brake assembly had been sprayed with thick black graphite to provide, according to the golf course mechanic, lubrication and preservation.

The plaintiffs' expert analyzed the golf course "maintenance" differently. He testified that from the way it was applied, the graphite had no anti-corrosion benefits and served no lubrication purpose. Rather, the effect of the spraying was to simply cover up or mask the oxidation and tool marks on the parking brake parts. As a result, when the expert removed the latch, he was unable to tell if the latch had moved on its pad because graphite was between the latch and pad.

Consequently, David and his wife sued Club Car, Inc. for strict product liability as well as negligence and breach of warranty.[2]

The Law

Strict product liability is imposed by operation of law to further the public policy of protecting the public from defective products. The theory applies not only to the manufacturers of the golf cart, but also to distributors, retailers, and owners and lessors of the golf cart.

In California, the criteria for determining whether a product is defectively designed are generally set out in *Baker v. Lull*.[3] Under *Baker*, a product may be found defective in design through either of two alternative tests. One test analyzes consumer expectations—namely, whether the product failed to perform as safely as an ordinary consumer would expect when using the product as intended or in a reasonably foreseeable manner.

---

2. The golf course was also sued, but the focus of discussion is on the manufacturer of the golf cart, Club Car, Inc.

3. Baker v. Lull, 143 Cal. Rptr. 225 (1978).

The other test analyzes the design defect in terms of "risk utility" or "risk benefit." Essentially, the jury is asked to balance the likelihood of harm against the burden of taking additional precautions. This approach permits a jury to consider the feasibility of a safer alternate design.

The jury was given the following instruction based on consumer expectation: "A product is defective in design if it fails to perform safely as an ordinary consumer would expect when used in an intended or reasonably foreseeable manner."

The parties jointly drafted a special verdict form that asked the jury to answer a number of specific questions concerning liability.

Question 7 asked: "Was the harm to the plaintiff caused by a use of the product that was reasonably foreseeable?" The jury was asked to answer "yes or no." After deliberating, the jury answered "no."

The answer "no" was presumably based on its finding that the harm was caused by something other than the reasonably foreseeable use of the cart. Club Car, Inc. inferred that the jury reasoned the cart was not being used in "an intended or reasonably foreseeable manner." But it wasn't clear why the jury said "no." Perhaps the jury reasoned that the work on the cart after the accident necessitated the "no" response.

Question 10 asked the jury to attribute or apportion any conduct or negligence to the plaintiff, the golf course, and the golf cart manufacturer. The jury allocated responsibility as follows: The plaintiff (16 percent); the golf course (44 percent); and the golf cart manufacturer (40 percent).

There was a problem. The answers to questions 7 and 10 were inconsistent. The court explained the inconsistency to the jury before asking it to redeliberate:

Hole 6: Product Liability

Ladies and gentlemen, in the view of the court, your answers to question number seven and 10 present an inconsistency. . . . You will notice in question number seven your answer was no. That was reflected with 12 no votes. By answering no to question number seven, that eliminates liability for Club Car. So when you get to question number 10 then, Club Car should not be included in the breakdown of the percentages. So what I am going to ask you to do is reflect on seven and 10 and make any appropriate changes. . . .

At this time there is an inconsistency between the [response to the] two questions. I am not telling you how to rectify it. I am not necessarily saying leave seven as it is and change 10 or leave 10 as it is and change seven. That is your responsibility as jurors. I am just saying in my interpretation of the situation the answers are inconsistent.

The court asked the jury to resume deliberations to resolve the inconsistency. Eleven minutes after redeliberating, the jury returned and informed the court that it had changed the answer to question 7 from "no" to "yes." The revised verdict established the liability of Club Car.

The question of liability and damages was bifurcated at the outset of the trial. In 1998, a new jury presided over the damages phase of the trial. It awarded the plaintiff $610,823 in economic damages and $1 million in noneconomic damages, jointly and severally, against the cart manufacturer and the golf course.

Club Car, Inc. appealed solely that portion of the judgment finding it liable. It argued that the trial court committed reversible error. The appellate court rejected each of its arguments. It found that the special verdict was in fact inconsistent with respect to the answers on causation (question 7) and apportionment of fault (question 10), and the trial court's subsequent instruction to correct the inconsistency did not constitute a prejudicial error.

California law provides: "Proceedings When Verdict Is Informal. When the verdict is announced, if it is informal or insufficient, in not covering the issue submitted, it may be corrected by the jury under the advice of the Court, or the jury may be again sent out."[4] The terms "informal" and "insufficient" have been broadly construed, and the appellate court used this provision to uphold the trial court.

Conclusion

David Mendoza suffered multiple injuries after the parking brake on the golf cart spontaneously released after being properly set. David and his spouse sued the Club Car, Inc. alleging strict product liability as well as negligence and breach of warranty.

Product liability law protects the public from defective products that cause injury. In *Mendoza*, the golf cart braking system failed to perform safely when being used in a reasonably foreseeable manner. Expert testimony supported the claim that a properly designed braking system does not spontaneously release after being properly set. Eyewitness testimony by the other players in the foursome supported the plaintiffs' factual claim.

The jury was asked to make special findings. When the jury returned its verdict on liability, the court found that the answers to two of the questions that were part of the special findings were inconsistent. After explaining the inconsistency to the jury,

---

4. C.C.P § 619.

Hole 6: Product Liability

the court directed the jury to redeliberate. It then found Club Car liable.

Club Car appealed, arguing that the trial court had abused its discretion in dealing with the inconsistency. The appellate court rejected the claim, finding that there was no prejudicial error in the trial court's instruction regarding the jury's correction of the inconsistency.

Many cart rental agreements contain a "no liability" or exculpation clause. No mention of such a clause was made in this case. Even if such a clause were included in the rental agreement, its presence would not preclude a finding of strict product liability. To hold otherwise would defeat the essence of strict liability, which is imposed as a matter of law to protect the public from defective products.[5]

---

5. See Villa Olivia Country Club v. Club Car, Inc. 380 N.E.2d 819 (Ill. App. Ct. 1978).

Hole 7

Product Liability:
"Golfing Gizmo" training aid

California: *Hauter v. Zogarts*,
14 Cal. 3d 104 (1975)

At one time or another, most golfers have either tried or thought about using a golf training aid. For those with an unquenchable thirst for new training aids and equipment, the annual PGA Merchandise Show is a golf oasis.

But finding "just the right one" is like finding the "just the right life partner"—it can be challenging and doesn't always work out. YouTube, the Golf Channel, and *Golf* magazine offer endless "tips" that are "sure to improve your game" or add "10 to 15 yards" to your drive, or fix your chipping around the green, or turn you into a better putter once on the green.

Is hitting the ball squarely your problem? Use the right aid and you'll be hitting the ball like PGA Tour player Jack Nicklaus in no time at all. *Hauter v. Zogarts* is a classic case dealing with a "home driving range" designed to help the golfer hit the ball like a pro. It explores the realities through the legal theories of strict liability, warranty, and misrepresentation.

The Facts

In 1966, Louise Hauter bought the Golfing Gizmo for her 13½-year-old son, Fred, as a Christmas gift. About six months later, Fred was seriously injured while using the aid. He suffered brain damage and, in one doctor's opinion, is currently an epileptic. Not surprisingly, the Hauters sued both the manufacturer and the seller.

The Golfing Gizmo instructions said: "The Golfing Gizmo enables you to improve your golf at home, without the costly expense of a driving range, or the waste of time chasing practice shots at your golf club. Many golfers prefer to practice their shots without any onlookers; the Golfing Gizmo lets you practice your shots in the privacy of your own home, at your own convenience."

The sales pitch convinced Louise that this would be a great Christmas gift for her son, an aspiring golfer. It would be a low-cost training aid that could be used without the prying eyes of onlookers and other "experts" who are usually more than happy to share their unsolicited and often contradictory advice. You know the type: "keep your head down, tuck your elbow in on the back swing, use the swing plain, rotate your hips, follow through," and so on.

The Golfing Gizmo was a simple, albeit potentially dangerous device. It consisted of two metal pegs, two cords—one elastic, one cotton—and a regulation golf ball. After the stakes were driven into the ground approximately 25 inches apart, the elastic cord was looped over them not unlike a sling shot. The cotton cord, measuring 21 feet in length, was tied to the middle of the elastic cord. The practice golf ball was then attached to the end of the cotton cord. When the cords were extended, the Gizmo resembles the shape of a large letter "T," with the ball resting at the base or bottom of the tee.

When the ball was hit, the elastic cord stopped the golf ball from going the distance it would ordinarily go, perhaps into a neighbor's window. If hit properly, the laws of physics stepped

Hole 7: Product Liability

in and caused the ball to spring back to a point near its original spot. A Kevlar® vest and visored helmet were not provided with the device.

There were three simple instructions and accompanying illustrations to aid the golfer on the journey to better golf by using the Golfing Gizmo:

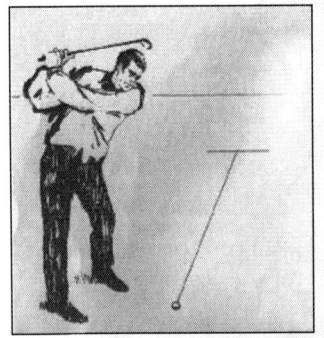

1. Use your yard, parkway, or any area that allows 40 feet of space. Insert stakes at each end of the elastic, stretch 25 inches. Place in turf flush with ground. Place ball at right angles to elastic, full length of cord. Tee the golf ball in your usual manner.

2. Drive golf ball with full power, with iron or wood clubs. You are hitting a real golf ball, not a toy or plaything. Concentrate on your own improvement in coordination, rhythm, and power. Golfing Gizmo gives you more practice, in less time, at less cost.

3. When hit correctly, ball returns near tee, indicating 175-yard drive. If ball returns to your left, it shows a slice; if ball returns to your right, it shows hook. If ball is topped, it will not return, must be retrieved. Regular practice will improve your game.

The Little Book of Golf Law

The label on the shipping carton and the cover of the instruction booklet assured the golfer: "COMPLETELY SAFE BALL WILL NOT HIT PLAYER."

At the time of his injury, Fred was a beginner golfer, or, as golfers would say, a "duffer." He had practiced at driving ranges and had played only a few rounds of golf. His dad instructed him in the correct use of the Golfing Gizmo, and Fred had read the printed instructions that accompanied the device. He had practiced with it about a dozen times before being injured.

On the day of the mishap, Fred set up the training aid in his front yard according to the printed instructions. The area was free of objects that might cause the ball to inadvertently ricochet, and no nosy onlookers were nearby. Fred took his normal swing with a 7-iron. After hitting the ball, the last thing Fred remembered was extreme pain and dizziness. After a period of unconsciousness, he staggered into the house and told his mother that he had been hit on the head by the ball.

So how was Fred injured?

A safety engineer and expert on the analysis and reconstruction of accidents testified that Fred had hit underneath the ball and had caught the cord with his golf club on his follow-through. The ball looped over the ascending club, producing a "bolo" effect, and struck him on the left temple. The expert concluded that the Golfing Gizmo was a "major hazard."

A professional golfer also was called as an expert witness. He personally tested the Golfing Gizmo by intentionally hitting low shots, and found that his club became entangled in the cord, looping the ball back toward him as he completed his swing. He added that a beginner's golf swing usually is very erratic, and thus rarely hits the ball squarely. In his view, the looping problem was not unusual.

The defendants (the manufacturer and the seller) did not

dispute the plaintiffs' version of the facts or how the injury occurred. They argued the law.

The Law

The plaintiffs' suit against the defendants was based on the theories of defective design, false representation, and breach of express and implied warranties. Following a jury verdict in favor of the defendants on each of these theories, the trial court said the evidence did not support the verdict in favor of the defendants and entered a verdict in favor of the plaintiffs.

The defendants appealed, and the case found its way to the Supreme Court of California. The court affirmed the trial court and sent the case back to determine of the amount of damages.

Strict Liability

Many books and legal treatises have been written about strict liability, which is also known as liability without fault. As a general matter, in order to prevail on the theory of strict liability, a plaintiff must show that a defendant is in the business of selling the product, that the product was not substantially changed before being used by the plaintiff, and that the product is the cause in fact as well as the legal cause of the plaintiff's injury.

In a design defect case, the plaintiff must prove that the product is defective. A consumer expectation test was the earliest legal test used in evaluating design defects. It remains a common, albeit controversial, test used in such cases today. It is most frequently used when the defect can be assessed using common knowledge or experience as to safety of the product.

In contrast to a consumer expectation test, the *Restatement Third, Torts: Product Liability*[1] uses a more nuanced "risk-

---

1. Restatement (Third) of Torts: Prods. Liab. (1998).

utility" balancing test for determining design defectiveness. Section 2(b) of the Restatement classifies a design as defective if the plaintiff suffered a foreseeable injury that could have been prevented by a reasonable alternative design. Numerous factors are relevant to "whether an alternative design is reasonable and whether its omission renders a product not reasonably safe" under 2(b), including the likelihood and seriousness of foreseeable harm from the chosen design, warnings accompanying the product, and the costs and benefits of the alternative design relative to the chosen design.

The Restatement rejects consumer expectation as a freestanding or independent basis for ascertaining the defectiveness of product designs. Rather, it includes consumer expectation as simply one of the factors to be considered in the risk-utility balancing. The Restatement drops all references to strict product liability based on the view that courts typically use a negligence standard to determine design defects notwithstanding the fact that they continue to use the language of strict liability.

In *Hauter*, the California Supreme Court found that the existence of the design defect was supported by the record. The court reasoned that a person using the Golfing Gizmo under normal conditions was likely to be injured by the club becoming entangled in the cord attached to the ball. Although this reasoning is tied to consumer expectation, the court also found that the evidence showed that the risk of harm built into the Golfing Gizmo was greatest when it was being used by a player of limited ability, such as the injured Fred.

Based on these considerations, the court affirmed the trial court's decision that the Golfing Gizmo was defectively designed as a matter of law, and that the defective design was the proximate cause of Fred's injuries.

Express and Implied Warranty

Plaintiffs also alleged breach of express and implied warranty under the Uniform Commercial Code (UCC), which has been adopted by California. The UCC governs contracts for the sale of goods, such as the Golfing Gizmo.

The essence of the law of warranty is the determination of what the seller has agreed to sell to the buyer. A seller creates an express warranty by any affirmation of fact or promise that relates to the goods and that becomes part of the basis of the bargain with the buyer.[2] It typically is created by something the seller says or does. The warranty assures the buyer that the goods conform to the promise or affirmation regardless of whether the seller uses technical words of art, such as "warrant" or "guarantee." If they don't conform to the promise or affirmation, the buyer has an actionable claim for breach of the express warranty.

Defendants argued that their "representations" were not a warranty, but were simply statements of opinion and "puffing." In support of this, they cited the sales catalogue language: "You may be a duffer and divot digger, but just give yourself a few hours with this and you'll be challenging Jack Nicklaus!" They claimed this hyperbole was hardly a believable basis for an express warranty.

The court wasn't buying it. The law traditionally has allowed a seller considerable latitude in describing the virtues of a product, so-called "puffing," without being considered to have warranted the product. But the court reasoned the modern tendency is to liberally construe language used by the seller in making affirmative statements of fact regarding quality to be a warranty. The representation of the Golfing Gizmo as "completely safe"

---

2. Uniform Commercial Code § 2-313.

and that it would "not a hit player" were statements of fact and important characteristics of the training device. As a matter of policy, treating such statements as express warranties is necessary to counteract the shrewd technique of sellers seeking to slip around and avoid their responsibility by cloaking the representations as mere puffing and opinion.

The UCC also imposes an implied warranty of merchantability on the sale of goods, unless the implied warranty is properly excluded or modified. The implied promise arises automatically by operation of law regardless of the seller's statements, conduct, or intentions, unless specifically excluded.[3]

Under the implied warranty of merchantability, the focus is on the performance of the product when it is used in the customary, usual, and reasonably foreseeable manner. To the extent the product is not minimally safe for its expected purposes, the seller will be deemed to breach this implied warranty. The implied warranty of merchantability also may be predicated on the failure of the product to conform to the promises appearing on the label or container.

Under section (UCC) 2-316, an implied warranty of merchantability may be excluded or modified by the seller.[4] The defendants argued that the instructions for using the Golfing Gizmo indicated that it was completely safe only when the user hit the ball properly; hit the ball improperly, and safety is not assured. In essence, they argued that Fred didn't hit the ball properly, and thus there was no breach of the implied warranty.

Section 2-316 is designed to protect buyers from the nasty surprises that accompany unexpected and inconspicuous disclaimers of liability by a seller. The court found that the illus-

---

3. Uniform Commercial Code 2-213.
4. Uniform Commercial Code 2-316.

tration showing the golfer properly hitting the ball did not clearly communicate any disclaimer. To the extent that the seller is not clear, the disclaimer of liability is strictly construed against the seller. The fact that golf may be dangerous under certain circumstances wasn't persuasive for the simple fact that Fred wasn't playing golf. Rather, he was learning to play golf using the Golfing Gizmo in his front yard.

The fact that Fred did not himself purchase the Golfing Gizmo but received the training device as a Christmas gift raised the question of privity of a contract because a breach of warranty claim is contractual in nature. The court quickly dealt with the fact that Fred wasn't the purchaser. The court reasoned that Fred, as a minor, came "within the well-recognized exception" of being a member of the purchaser's family.[5]

Misrepresentation

Under section 402(B) of the *Restatement of Torts*, a commercial seller is potentially liable to anyone who relies upon the misrepresentation of a material fact.[6] The principle contained in this section, which has now been superseded by section 9 of the *Restatement of the Law Third*, Torts: Products Liability, is that one engaged in the business of selling products who, by advertising, labels, or otherwise, makes a misrepresentation of a material fact concerning the character or quality of the purchased product is subject to liability for the physical harm caused by justifiable reliance upon the misrepresentation.

The defendants argued that it was unreasonable for the plaintiffs to rely on the Golfing Gizmo as completely safe under all circumstances, particularly when a player hits beneath the

---

5. Uniform Commercial Code 2-318 provides three alternative approaches who may bring a breach of warranty cause of action.
6. Restatement (Second) of Torts § 402(B) (1965).

ball. They argued that any improperly hit golf shot exposes any golfer, as well as others who happen to be nearby, to the serious risk of harm. In other words, golf injuries happen.

The court had previously rejected this argument and was not persuaded to accept it as it applied to misrepresentation. The defendants' illustrations and instructions clearly indicated that the company anticipated that users would hook, slice, or top the ball. They expected their customers to commit the errors that normally plague duffers. Thus, when they declared their product "completely safe," the only reasonable inference was that the Golfing Gizmo was in fact a safe training device for all golfers regardless of their ability and regardless of how squarely they hit the ball. Moreover, the representation would be illusory if it were limited to only those infrequent cases when the ball was hit solidly.

More generally, the court reasoned that Fred was not "playing golf." Rather, he was home on his front lawn learning to play the game with the aid of the defendants' supposedly danger-free training device. By practicing with the Golfing Gizmo in an open, isolated area apart from other golfers and free of objects off which a poorly hit shot could ricochet, he eliminated most of the dangers present during a normal round of golf. Furthermore, even though certain dangers are inherent in playing golf, the risk that the golfer's own ball will wrap itself around the club and strike the golfer on the follow-through is nonexistent when actually playing the game.

Conclusion

Some products may be considered reasonably safe if they are accompanied by a warning and a safety instruction. If the instructions had identified the dangers associated with the looping problem and also a warning had been included in place of

Hole 7: Product Liability

the statement "COMPLETELY SAFE BALL WILL NOT HIT PLAYER," it might have been a closer case. But that wasn't the case.

Some contemporary lessons from *Hauter* exist. To the extent that the golf professional at a country club sells training aids or equipment, the pro may be in for a surprise. He or she may be treated as a "seller" for the purposes of strict liability in tort, or as a "merchant" for the purposes of an implied warranty of merchantability under the UCC. The pro would be treated no differently from other sellers when bodily injury or property damage results from defective equipment.

The doctrine of strict liability may also apply. In *Sipari v. Villa Olivia Country Club*, for example, the plaintiff was seriously injured when the cart he was riding in overturned and fell on top of him.[7] He sued the cart manufacturer and the golf course that leased the cart. The court held that suit could proceed against the golf course even though there was an exculpation clause in the rental lease that the plaintiff signed. The court stated that strict liability imposed applies not only to manufacturers but also to distributors, retailers, and lessors.

---

7. Sipari v. Villa Olivia Country Club, 63 Ill.App.3d 98520 (1978).

Hole 8

Product Liability:
Defectively manufactured golf clubs

Federal: *Price v. Wilson Sporting Goods Co.*,
2005 WL 1677512 (D. Colo. July 18, 2005), modified
on reh'g (damages), 2006 WL 1409519 (2006)

In the 2000 movie *Cast Away*, Chuck Nolan, a harried Federal Express executive played by actor Tom Hanks, winds up on a deserted island after a plane crash. His silent companion, Wilson, helps Nolan cope with his struggle to make it back to civilization. Wilson, you may recall, is the image of a face (complete with spiked hair) that Nolan paints on a Wilson beach volleyball. The volleyball arrives on the island courtesy of the same downed plane.

Name recognition is important in advertising. Undoubtedly, Chuck's companion provided a memorable boost to the Wilson brand. But this boost to the company's brand image suffered somewhat of a setback when Wilson Sporting Goods Company was successfully sued for manufacturing a defective golf club in federal district court in Colorado.

The Facts

David Price purchased a set of Wilson Ultra golf clubs from Target.[1] Sometime thereafter, David and his son were playing a

---

1. Since 1938, a player cannot exceed carrying fourteen clubs during a "stipulated round" of golf. If a player has more than the maximum allowed, the player is

round of golf when disaster struck. His son was teeing off on the 9th hole when the head of the Wilson Ultra pitching wedge separated from the shaft.[2] David, who was standing approximately 20 yards to the side and 10 to 20 yards in front of the teeing ground, was hit by the airborne club head. As a result of the impact, he suffered severe head lacerations, a skull fracture, and momentary unconsciousness.

David sued Wilson Sporting Goods, Target (the seller), and True Temper Sports.[3] He moved for summary judgment against

---

penalized under Rule 4-4. In stroke play, there is two-stroke penalty for each hole at which any breach occurred up to a maximum of four strokes. In match play, the match is adjusted by deducting one-hole for each hole at which the breach occurred up to a maximum of two holes.

In 2001, Ian Woosnam was leading the final round of the British Open when this Rule came into play. His caddie, Miles Byrne gave him the bad news after he nearly made a hole-in-one on the first hole:

Byrne: You're going to go ballistic.

Woosnam: Why?

Byrne: We've got two drivers in the bag (Woosnam had fifteen clubs in his bag, and thus had to call a two-stroke penalty on himself).

His caddie was right. Suffering a temporary meltdown, Woosnam bogeyed two of the next three holes. He finished the Open tied for third.

The reason for the rule limiting the maximum number of clubs a player can carry seems straightforward. Without some limit, golfers would insist on carrying any number of specialty clubs to fit every imaginable situation, and golf bag manufacturers could not build large enough golf bags to carry the assembled arsenal of weapons. Fourteen was selected by the USGA because it was considered a "standard set" of two woods, two wedges, a putter, and nine irons.

2. The Rules of Golf have a special rule for situations when a club is substantially damaged during "normal" play, which would have applied had David been able to continue his round of golf with his son instead of being rushed off to receive medical attention. The Rules allow the damaged club to be replaced so long as replacing the club does not "unduly" delay play. Rule 4-3.a.(iii). But the replaced club cannot be borrowed from another player playing the course. If a club is broken or damaged outside normal play, such as in a burst of anger, the club may not be replaced.

3. The Restatement of Products Liability applies its liability rules to those in the business of either selling or distributing a defective product that causes harm to a person or property. Restatement (Third) of Torts: Products Liability 1 (1997).

4. The court ruled against David on his motion for summary judgment based on negligence. The court reasoned that there were important factual questions to be determined, such as whether Wilson Sporting Goods should have foreseen that David would be standing in front of his son when he was injured. These and other factual

74

Hole 8: Product Liability

Wilson Sporting Goods on his claim of strict product liability. The court granted David's motion.[4]

The Law

The Supreme Court of Colorado has expressly adopted the doctrine of strict product liability of Section 402A of the *Restatement (Second) of Torts*. It provides:

> (1) One who sells any product in a defective condition unreasonably dangerous to the user or consumer or to his property is subject to liability for physical harm thereby caused to the ultimate user or consumer, or to his property, if (a) the seller is engaged in the business of selling such a product, and (b) it is expected to and does reach the user or consumer without substantial change in the condition in which it is sold.

Under Section 402A a product is considered defective if, considering its reasonably foreseeable use, it leaves the seller's hands in an unreasonably dangerous condition not contemplated by the consumer.[5]

David presented two experts to support his claim of strict liability, whereas Wilson Sporting Goods Company failed to disclose its experts in a timely manner in accordance with the *Federal Rules of Civil Procedure*. Wilson also failed to file a timely response to David's motion for summary judgment. Thus, David made the case for why he should prevail on summary judgment, while Wilson's attorneys presumably were out looking for the beverage cart.

---

questions were for a jury to decide, and thus were not appropriate to resolve on the motion for summary judgment. The claim of negligence would have to be sorted out by a jury at trial.

5. Under the Restatement (Third) of Torts: Products Liability (1997), consumer expectation is one factor in deciding whether a product is defective.

David's two experts testified that the pitching wedge was defectively manufactured. They reported that the epoxy used to connect the golf shaft to the club head was not evenly distributed around the shaft. This failure weakened the bond between the two components and created the opportunity for abnormal stress on the club while it was being normally used. The problem was compounded by the misapplication of epoxy, which was not in accordance with "good adhesive bonding practice" in the industry.

The experts also reported that the end of the shaft where it fit into the club head was not properly prepared. While some grinding of the shaft is necessary to promote the proper bonding to the club head, the grinding on the shaft of the pitching wedge was deeper than required. During the manufacturing process, the chromium plating on the shaft was completely removed. This exuberant grinding at the end of the shaft compromised its structural integrity and made it prone to stress fracture during the golf swing. Finally, there was evidence of a potential welding defect, which also suggested defective manufacturing.

The set of clubs, including the pitching wedge, was relatively new at the time of the accident. The defective club did not show any sign of improper use or abuse, so that defense was not available to Wilson. Moreover, the defect was not readily observable because a fixed-plastic ferrule located immediately above the hosel prevented the discovery of the defects. As a result, the problem with the wedge was from a manufacturing defect and not from the use of the club.

The fact that David's son was using the club at the time of he was injured didn't matter. David was a regular golfer and thus was a person who could reasonably be expected to use the pitching wedge or be affected by its use. The court reasoned that David was someone who would reasonably be expected to either use the Wilson golf clubs or, as a result of sharing them with his son, be affected by their use.

Based on the evidence, the court held that reasonable people could draw only the following conclusions: the pitching wedge was defectively manufactured, the wedge was unreasonably dangerous to David, and the defect was the cause of his injuries. The Wilson Ultra wedge was a real Wilson "cast away."

Conclusion

David demonstrated that no genuine issues of material fact existed. He affirmatively presented specific facts probative of Wilson's strict liability. This evidence that the pitching wedge was defective was uncontradicted by Wilson due to its failure to timely file a response in accordance with the *Federal Rules of Civil Procedure*.

Based on the evidence, the court found that reasonable persons could draw only the following inferences: (1) that the pitching wedge was defectively manufactured; (2) that the defect created an unreasonable danger to the plaintiff; and (3) that the defect caused David's physical injuries. It granted him summary judgment on his strict product liability claim against Wilson. The lawyering by Wilson's attorneys appeared to match the quality of the defective wedge.

Hole 9

Golf and the Loss of Consortium:
You can lose more than your golf balls during a round of golf

California: *Kurash v. J.C. Resorts, Inc.*, 00703109 Super. Ct., San Diego, Cal. (1996)

A below-par performance is great during a round of golf. It's not so great in the bedroom. This case involves the latter type of performance.

The Facts

The Oaks North Country Club is a popular executive-type course managed by J.C. Resorts, Inc. There are three 9 hole, par 30 tracts: East, South and North. Its advertising says that golfers may start the day on the best driving range in north San Diego County: "Well organized, striped hitting area, bright targets, with good golf balls and even a great view."

August 29, 1995, was a great day for golf in Southern California. The weather was perfect for a day on the links. Stanley Kurash and three of his friends, Ed Brown, Bob Steele, and Alexander Sirpis, decided to take advantage of a clear, calm, and sunny day by playing golf on the North Course at Oaks North Country Club in Rancho Bernardo, California.

The Little Book of Golf Law

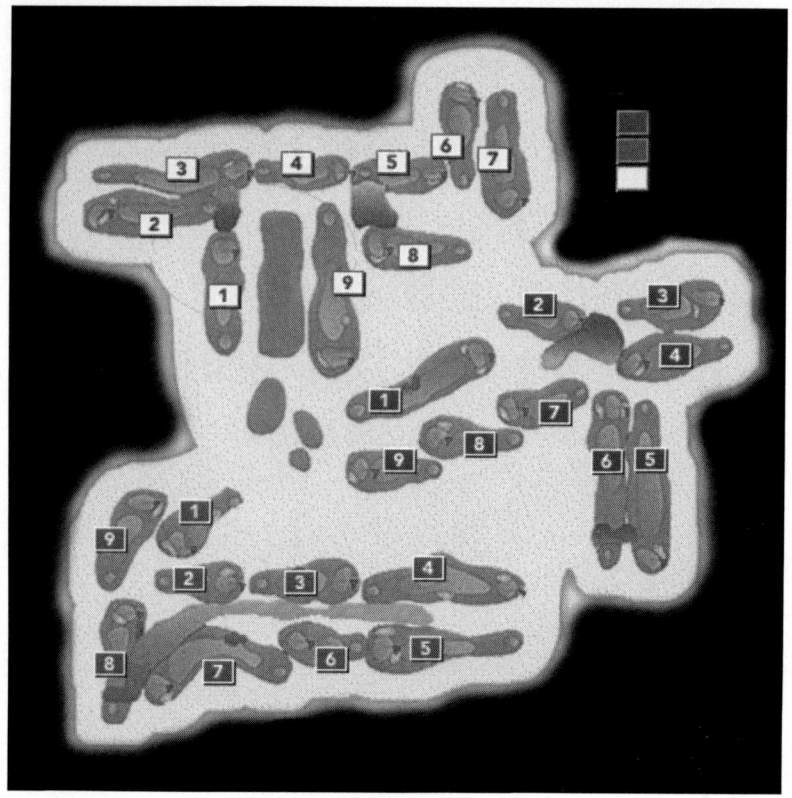

Oaks North Country Club Layout

The North Course winds its way through a well-manicured planned community. There are numerous trees on the course that beautify it and provide golfers, as well as adjacent property owners, with sanctuary from errant shots. The golf club's employees often trim the trees on the course with handsaws or pole saws. In addition, the club contracts with a tree-trimming service.

Stanley and his friends golfed without incident through the eighth hole. The ninth hole is an uphill par 4 that runs parallel and adjacent to the driving range, which appears as a shaded

Hole 9: Golf and the Loss of Consortium

area between hole one and hole nine in the top portion of the layout on page 80. It is separated by a line of mature trees, mostly pines, from the driving range teeing area located on the right, which is out-of-bounds to players coming up the ninth fairway to the green. Stanley and Ed drove their cart to the right side of the fairway to retrieve a golf ball that Bob had inadvertently sliced. After retrieving the ball, Stanley approached his ball, which was also in the tree line.

Stanley heard a loud crack. Thinking that a golf ball from the adjacent driving range had hit the tree above his head, Stanley looked for the responsible golfer. There was none. Moments later, he heard a second, louder crack, which was followed by a large tree limb falling on him. The limb was some 12 inches in diameter and was estimated to weigh 750 pounds. Stanley found himself in an unplayable lie not covered by the *Rules of Golf*.[1] He was unable to extricate himself from the physical embrace of the limb until Ed lifted it high enough so that he was able to crawl from under it.

---

1. Although the Rules of Golf don't deal with being pinned under a tree limb, Rule 28 does deal with golf balls deemed unplayable. In order to declare a ball unplayable, the player must first identify it as his or her own ball. During the U.S. Open at Pebble Beach in 1993, golfer Nick Faldo practiced his Tarzan-like skills by climbing up a tree to identify his ball in order to declare it unplayable. His feat is a useful aid in remembering the identification rule. Once identified, the ball may be declared unplayable by a golfer at any place on the course with one exception. That exception is when the ball is in a water hazard.

By declaring a ball unplayable the player incurs a one-stroke penalty. The player then has three options. First, the player may go back to the spot from which the last stroke was played and take a drop. Second, the player may drop within two-club lengths of the unplayable ball, but no nearer the hole. If the unplayable ball is in a tree or bush, the ball is dropped within two-club lengths of a point immediately below the unplayable ball. The final option is a little more complicated. A player may draw an imaginary line between the unplayable ball and the hole, and drop anywhere on that line so long as the drop is no nearer the hole than where the ball lay. It is possible to drop from one unplayable lie into a second unplayable lie triggering a second penalty, so care must be exercised before taking a drop under the unplayable-ball rule.

Stanley was taken by ambulance to a nearby hospital. He suffered various cuts, abrasions, and a broken nose. X-rays revealed that he had a broken left rib. He also suffered a bruised tailbone and other medical problems.

Stanley and his wife, Naomi, sued the golf course management. Among other injuries, Stanley claimed that he suffered sexual dysfunction from the fallen limb. He maintained that he was rendered permanently impotent, and claimed he was able to reach coitus with his wife of 53 years only after painful injections of Alprostil or suppositories. Both he and his wife were understandably unhappy.

The Law

Stanley said that J.C. Resorts was negligent in failing to properly trim the pine limb that fell on him. He argued that the golf club was in control of the property and that its maintenance crew had inadequately trimmed and pruned the tree. This failure resulted in the growth of foliage at the end of the tree limb, creating a strain on the limb, which snapped unexpectedly and hit Stanley. While Stanley may have assumed some risk by playing golf, he did not, in his view, assume the risk of being struck by a limb from a failing tree.

J.C. Resorts argued that the trees were intentionally maintained in a dense fashion to serve as a safety screen against balls hit from the driving range striking players on the ninth hole. They also claimed that they regularly inspected the trees, had no notice of any safety risk from falling tree limbs, and that the accident was caused by an act of God.

The case is a somewhat typical tort claim. The interesting part of the case is "why Naomi was able to make a legal claim against J.C. Resorts when it was her husband who was injured." The answer is the law of consortium.

Hole 9: Golf and the Loss of Consortium

The *Restatement (Second) of Torts* outlines the legal rights of Naomi for harm that was caused by a tort against her husband, Stanley. It provides:

(1) One who by reason of his tortious conduct is liable to one spouse for illness or other bodily harm is subject to liability to the other spouse for the resulting loss of the society and services of the first spouse, including impairment of capacity for sexual intercourse, and for reasonable expense incurred by the second spouse in providing medical treatment.

(2) Unless it is not possible to do so, the action for loss of society and services is required to be joined with the action for illness or bodily harm, and recovery for loss of society and services is allowed only if the two actions are so joined.[2]

Naomi's claim was legally joined with her husband's claim of negligence. She maintained that his inability to function sexually was her loss as well as her husband's.

She testified that while she knew that sex might not always be present in their marriage if they lived long enough, having it suddenly torn asunder from their marriage by J.C. Resorts' failure to act prudently was more difficult than accepting it as nature's way.

J.C. Resorts didn't take her claim lying down. It argued that Stanley had erectile dysfunction before the accident. It also claimed that Stanley's age, 74, was the other factor causing his increased sexual dysfunction and poor performance.

Historically, only a husband had a cause of action for loss of consortium when his wife suffered a non-fatal injury. A hus-

---

2. Restatement (Second) of Torts § 693 (1977).

band's claim was originally considered to be for loss of his wife's services. The theory was similar to a master's claim for loss of his servant's services in cases where the servant suffered physical injury. The claim was gradually expanded to include recovery for the "three Ss": society, services, and sexual intercourse.

In contrast to a husband's claim for loss of consortium, a wife historically had no reciprocal cause of action for her loss because she had no separate legal status. Without legal status, a wife had no analogous claim to her husband's. By the end of the nineteenth century, most states had enacted Married Women's Property Acts. These laws were enacted to remove a woman's legal disabilities that were based on her servile status as a wife and the absence of her independent legal status.

Beginning in the 1950s, most states expanded the claim on a gender-neutral basis to permit wives to recover for the losses they sustained when their husbands were injured. Today, the overwhelming majority of states, either by statute or judicial decision, allow wives to sue for loss of consortium. The cause of action generally is limited to those in a legally recognized marital relationship. Unmarried cohabitants generally are barred, at least in most states, from suing for loss of consortium based on various public policy arguments. Thus, the loss of consortium is strictly a "family affair."

Although legally independent, a claim of consortium is legally dependent on the principal victim's claim.[3] In order to prevail for loss of consortium, Stanley was required to prevail. To avoid duplicating any award of damages, the loss of consortium claim is frequently joined in the same lawsuit with the principal victim's claim. Thus, the claims are litigated together.

---

3. In Hennessey v. Pyne, *infra* Hole 22, William, Eileen Hennessey's husband, joined the litigation also alleging a loss of the three S's.

Conclusion

A claim for loss of consortium is compensable by a separate damage award either for the period of incapacity or for the spouse's life expectancy if the incapacity is shown to be permanent. After a five-day trial, the jury found for the plaintiffs. Stanley was awarded $55,000 to compensate him for his injuries. Naomi was awarded $5,000 for her loss of consortium.

The recovery by the plaintiffs in the *Kurash* case was modest in comparison to the plaintiff in *Stackhouse v. Royce Realty and Management*.[4] In this case, the plaintiff also was injured by a falling tree limb. It fell on her while she was walking near the 13th teeing ground at the Lakemoor Country Club in Illinois. The tree limb struck her on the back between her shoulders, throwing her forward, facedown on the ground. She was subsequently transported to the hospital by helicopter.

She sued the country club for negligence. Although the tree did not fall until almost two years after the golf course manager had notice that the tree was possibly diseased, this fact did not extinguish the duty to inspect and remove the tree if it was rotten. The jury awarded the plaintiff slightly more than $4.5 million in damages.

---

4. Stackhouse v. Royce Realty and Management Corp., 2012 Il App (2d) 11602 (2012).

Part II
Contracts

Hole 10

Covenants, Conditions, and Restrictions:
Errant golf balls

California: *Masters, et al. v. Burton, et al.*,
2013 WL 3866516 (Cal. Ct. App. July 25, 2013)[1]

A golf ball that curves to the right is called a "slice" for a right-handed golfer. A ball that follows the same general trajectory as a "slice" but to a lesser degree is called a "cut" or "fade." For a left-handed golfer, a golf ball that curves to the right is called a "hook" or a "draw." For most players, a ball that behaves exactly as expected is often called a miracle.

When miracles don't happen, a lawsuit is possible. A homeowner living next to a golf course who suffers a personal injury or property damage from errant golf balls may sue. Likely defendants include the golfer who hit the errant shot, the golf course, and perhaps even the architect who designed the course.

The homeowner also may sue the prior owner who sold the property. Possible claims against the seller include rescission of the purchase contract and restitution as well as damages for breach of the purchase contract or in tort.

---

1. The decision was not certified for publication in the official reports. Under the California Rules of Court, the decision may not be cited as judicial precedent. The decision is binding, however, upon the parties. In addition, the court's reasoning may be persuasive in other cases.

The Little Book of Golf Law

The Facts

Spanish Hills Country Club is a private country club located just north of Los Angeles in Camarillo, California. It features an 18-hole, par 71 golf course. From the longest tee setting, it plays to slightly more than 6,700 yards. From the men's tee, the seventh hole at Spanish Hills is a 350-yard-or-so straight-away par 4. The hole is about 25 yards shorter from the ladies tee.

Scott Burton and Linda Burton owned a home located on the seventh fairway. In early 2007, they listed their home for sale after Scott changed jobs and relocated to northern California. Scott's new employer hired a third-party relocation company, SIRVA, to assist the Burtons with the sale.

The relocation company intended to sell the property as soon as possible, and thus did not hold the property for investment purposes. Its job was to facilitate the sale to a third party. Laura Means, who worked for Troop Real Estate, Inc., was the Burtons' and SIRVA's real estate agent.

In May 2007, Carolyn Masters and Mark Moore (purchasers) entered into a contract to purchase the Burtons' property. Masters, a licensed real estate agent, acted on behalf of Moore and herself in completing the transaction. She was both an agent and buyer.

During the two-month escrow period prior to closing, the purchasers visited the property several times. On one occasion, Moore was with Linda Burton when a golf ball hit a palm tree near the house. Linda said, "That happens sometimes." Before leaving that day, Moore and his son picked up somewhere between 20 and 25 golf balls from the backyard and stacked them in a pile. Errant golf ball storm warnings ought to have been on the horizon.

The purchasers were given a copy of the Covenants, Conditions, and Restrictions (CC&R's) indicating that the owner

Hole 10: Covenants, Conditions, and Restrictions

assumes the risk of any property damage, personal injury, death, or any trespass or nuisance caused by errant golf balls. The CC&R's warned that "there is a possibility that golf balls may damage the Property or injure persons or pets on it."

Multiple disclosures about the errant golf balls were given to the purchasers. They included the "ERRANT GOLF BALLS" Statewide Buyer and Seller Advisory signed by the Burtons, a California Association of Realtors (CAR) Seller Property Questionnaire by the Burtons disclosing "some golf balls on the property," the Burtons' Transfer Disclosure Statement (TDS),[2] and the Real Estate Agent's Inspection Disclosure by Laura Means. Finally, the CAR Statewide Buyer and Seller Advisory warned, "There is a possibility that golf balls may damage the Property or injure persons or pets on it."

Before closing on the purchase, Masters executed a Real Estate Agent's Inspection Disclosure form certifying that she had made a reasonably competent and diligent inspection of the property and saw no conditions that required disclosure. Upon closing, she received a $53,000 real estate commission in connection with the purchase.

The transfer of title involved two steps. First, the Burtons deeded the property to SIRVA. Second, the relocation company then deeded the property to Masters and Moore. The Burtons/SIRVA deed was recorded the same day as the SIRVA/Masters-Moore deed was recorded. Although two deeds were used, SIRVA never took possession or occupancy of the property. The SIRVA/Masters-Moore purchase agreement indicated that the relocation company was selling the property in its present condition and "acting as a conduit in the sale." In their legal

---

2. A Seller's Real Estate Transfer Disclosure Statement is required by California Civil Code 1102.6.

complaint, the purchasers argued that the relocation company "acted as the agent" for the Burtons and was an intermediary in the sale.

After taking title to the house, the new owners became alarmed at the number of golf balls being sliced and hooked onto their property from the seventh fairway. They found themselves being bombarded by an average of three or four balls a day. Although most of the golf balls didn't hit the house, it was not immune. Some balls pelted the exterior stucco, a window, and the roof tiles. Others landed in their yard or swimming pool.

In 2008, less than a year after taking title, the unhappy purchasers sued the Burtons and SIRVA. They claimed they were defrauded by not being apprised of the number of errant golf balls landing on the property, which they maintained constituted a significant hazard that could not be guarded against. They also claimed that SIRVA breached its statutory duty of disclosure.

The purchasers asked for damages as well as rescission of their purchase contract. They maintained that the property had zero market value, and that they suffered "at least" $2.15 million in damages, which was the equivalent of playing litigation Lotto.

After a 30-day trial, the court granted SIRVA and the Burtons summary judgment.

The purchasers appealed.

The Law

Under the common law of California, as well as many other states, a seller has a duty to disclose those facts generally unknown or not discoverable by the buyer. If the facts materially affect the value or desirability of the property, the seller is

Hole 10: Covenants, Conditions, and Restrictions

required to disclose them. Materiality is judged by whether the facts "would have a significant and measurable effect on market value." Failure of the seller to disclose material facts may result in a court granting rescission and damages.

California imposes a statutory duty to disclose and utilizes a standardized disclosure form. Although automatic rescission is not contemplated for breach of the statutory requirements, damages are potentially available. Damages will not be granted, however, if the failure to accurately disclose "was not within the personal knowledge of the transferor . . . and ordinary care was exercised in obtaining and transmitting (the disclosure statement)."

The purchasers argued that SIRVA breached the statutory disclosure it owed to them. The fact that the Burton's had provided a TDS wasn't good enough. They claimed that the relocation company knew or should have known that a significant errant golf ball problem existed and this should have been revealed in the company's TDS to them.

The appellate court rejected the argument because the relocation company's duty to disclose is limited to information within its personal knowledge. The California Civil Code dealing with Transfer Disclosure Statements provides:

> Neither the transferor nor any listing or selling agent shall be liable for any error, inaccuracy, or omission of any information delivered pursuant to this article if the error, inaccuracy, or omission was not *within the personal knowledge* (emphasis added) of the transferor or that listing or selling agent, was based on information timely provided by public agencies or by other persons providing information as specified in subdivision (c) that is required to be disclosed pursuant to this article,

and ordinary care was exercised in obtaining and transmitting it.[3]

It was undisputed that SIRVA had no discussion or communication with the Burtons, Troop Real Estate, or the Burtons' real estate agent about the golf balls landing on the property or how they might impact the value of the property. The company had no personal knowledge. As a result, the appellate court rejected the plaintiff's argument.

The plaintiffs also argued that they should be entitled to rescind the contract based on mistake and fraud. The trial court found that the Burtons failed to disclose the errant golf ball problem. It reasoned:

> The Burtons knew at the time they put their home up for sale that approximately a thousand errant golf balls a year (3 to 4 balls per day on the average) were landing in various locations on their premises below the orchard, particularly on the side of the yard closest to the 7th fairway, [and] . . . from time to time, . . . impacting on the walls and roof of their residence (causing damage) as well as landing in the BBQ and pool area in the backyard. At the time the Burtons put their house up for sale and filled out various disclosure forms, the Burtons knew that because of numerous errant golf ball impacts, they had to repair resulting damage to their residence's roof tiles, plaster walls and windows, and outdoor lights . . . [T]he Burtons intentionally chose not to disclose to anyone connected with this transaction . . . this information . . . in order to enhance the saleability of their property.

---

3. Cal. Civ. Code 1102.4 (a).

Hole 10: Covenants, Conditions, and Restrictions

The Burtons had clearly failed in their duty to disclose. But the trial court also found that the purchasers failed to make reasonable inquiries based on the facts they had, and that Masters, who acted as their real estate agent, was negligent in failing to investigate the need for any repairs to the house from errant golf balls.

Rescission based on the theory of fraud or mistake requires justifiable reliance. When a buyer is on notice of a problem affecting the desirability and value of the property being purchased, the buyer is under an obligation to investigate the problem and determine its severity. The buyer cannot simply ignore the facts.

The evidence demonstrated that the purchasers visited and inspected the property several times, were provided written errant golf ball disclosures, and were told that stray golf balls were landing on the property. In fact, Moore picked up stray golf balls in the backyard with his son, and actually saw a golf ball hit a palm tree during an inspection of the property. Additionally, they had played golf in the past. As a real estate agent, Masters was sophisticated in real estate matters.

Moore testified at the trial that he would not have bought the property had he known golf balls were hitting the house and causing stucco damage. He said, with presumably a straight face, that "a single golf ball strike to the house was too great a risk." If it happened once, it "could happen again at any time. And it's uncertain as to where the ball would wind up . . . And that would potentially mean someone in the backyard could be hurt . . . I would say, no. I would not have bought the house."

Masters corroborated his testimony. She testified that Moore would not have purchased the property had he been told that a stray golf ball ever hit the house or swimming pool. Masters also believed that Moore would not have bought the property had he known or been told that errant golf balls landed in the area between the house and the pool.

Justifiable reliance is a question of fact. The claim about not buying the house was difficult to believe. Based on the information the plaintiffs had and their experience as golfers, they ought to have known the property was the unintentional landing zone for errant slices and hooks.

On appeal, the unhappy purchasers failed to show that the evidence was so uncontradicted and unimpeached as to compel reversal of the trial court. The factual determinations would stand on appeal.

Conclusion

When the seller of real property knows of facts materially affecting its value or desirability and also knows that such facts are not known to, or within the reach of, the diligent attention and observation of the purchaser, the seller is under a duty to disclose them to the purchasers. Breach of the seller's duty to disclose may give rise to a cause of action for both rescission and damages as well as other legal claims.

In California, residential property owners have a common law and statutory obligation to make the full disclosure of facts materially affecting the value or desirability of their property. But a relocation management company that sells residential property to purchasers as an "agent" or intermediary may have no independent duty to investigate a prior owner's transfer disclosure statement. The Transfer Disclosure Statute requires personal knowledge.

Prior residential property owners are not necessarily immune from liability to a purchaser from the relocation company acting as an intermediary. The prior owner may be liable under statute and common law to a subsequent purchaser,

Hole 10: Covenants, Conditions, and Restrictions

despite the absence of privity of contract, on the theory of fraud or misrepresentation.

But in order for liability to attach, the subsequent purchaser from the relocation company must prove justifiable reliance, which is a subjective standard measured by the subsequent buyer's conduct and experience. Justifiable reliance by the purchaser is also required when the sale occurs without the assistance of a relocation company.

Hole 11

Hole-in-One Contest:
Mistake

Pennsylvania: *Cobaugh v. Klick-Lewis, Inc.*,
561 A.2d 1248 (1989)

The ultimate thrill for most golfers is hitting a hole in one. Most involve some degree of luck. Andrew Magee's good fortune fits in this category. He is the only player to hit a hole in one on a par 4 during a PGA Tour event. While the foursome ahead of his group was on the green, he teed off with his driver on the 17th hole at the Phoenix Open. To his surprise, the ball reached the green of the 322-yard hole, bounced off Tom Byrum's putter, and incredibly went in the hole. On style points, his feat is unlikely ever to be repeated.[1]

Many amateurs dream of hitting the "perfect shot," one where the ball finds the bottom of the hole, which is only 4¼ inches in diameter, after only one stroke.[2] Yet hitting a hole in one is a rarity for most amateurs. Some years ago, the magazine *Golf Digest* estimated that an average golfer had only a 1

---

1. The spectacular shot can be seen on YouTube. *See also*, Davis, "Magee Gets an Ace on Par-4," Ariz. Republic, Jan. 26, 2001.

2. The exact reason for the hole being 4-1/4 inches in diameter is lost to history. Legend has it that the hole cutting tool to make the golf hole was a piece of excess pipe that was laying around the Royal Musselburgh Golf Club in Scotland. In 1891, the R&A standardized the size, and the rest of the golf world followed.

in 20,000 chance of acing a par 3 hole of standard difficulty. The U.S. Golf Register estimated the chance of hitting any hole in one at 1 in 33,000.

Hitting an ace and winning a court case to claim a new car as the prize for a hole-in-one contest that officially ended several days earlier is a Ripley's "Believe It or Not" story.

The Facts

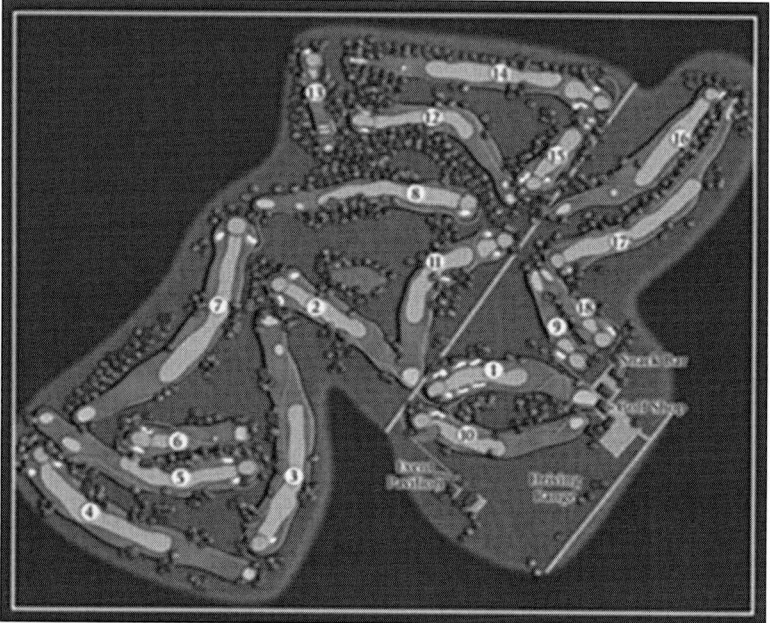

Fairview Golf Course, Cornwall, Pennsylvania

In late spring, Amos Cobaugh was playing in the East End Open Golf Tournament on the Fairview Golf Course in Cornwall, Pennsylvania. When he arrived at the ninth tee, he saw a new Chevrolet Beretta tantalizingly positioned, together with signs that said:

Hole 11: Hole-in-One Contest

"HOLE IN ONE Wins this 1998 Chevrolet Beretta GT Courtesy of KLICK-LEWIS Buick Chevy Pontiac."

The offer seemed clear: a free car to anyone who made a hole in one. Game on.

Amos hit the perfect shot, a hole in one. The court records do not reveal the details of the shot, but who cares? A hole in one is an impressive feat regardless of how the ball finds its way to the bottom of the cup. In any event, when Amos attempted to claim his prize, the matter became more complicated.

The sponsoring automobile dealer, Klick-Lewis, refused to award him the prize. It claimed that the car was for a charity golf tournament sponsored by the Hershey-Palmyra Sertoma Club. That tournament had finished two days earlier, so his hole in one was two days late. The dealer apologized for inadvertently neglecting to remove the car and the signs. The dealer said "sorry," but it had no obligation to honor the expired promotional.

Amos was not satisfied with the explanation. It was time to call in the lawyers. He sued the dealer to compel delivery of the Chevrolet Beretta.

The Law

The facts weren't disputed. Thus, the parties entered a stipulation regarding them. The trial court granted Amos's motion for summary judgment, and the dealer appealed.

The appellate court found that the dealer made an offer that was accepted by Amos. A unilateral contract came into existence when Amos performed in accordance with the terms of the offer by hitting the hole in one.

The appellate court relied on the established legal principle that the promoter of a prize-winning contest makes an offer by making public the conditions and rules of the contest. If, before the offer is withdrawn, a person acts on the offer, the promoter is bound to perform the promise by paying up. The dealer's advertising signs offered to award the car as a prize to anyone who made a hole in one. When Amos hit his ace he accepted the offer, thus forming a binding unilateral contract.

In order to be enforceable, a contract requires consideration, which confers a benefit on the promisor or causes a detriment to the promisee. The appellate court rejected the dealer's argument that the contract failed for lack of consideration. By making the offer to award a car as a prize, the dealer benefited from the continued publicity generated by the promotional advertising. This benefit, the court found, was the required consideration.

The defense of mistake

Having determined that a contract existed, the dealer argued that the doctrine of mistake should excuse its performance of the contract. This argument is an extremely difficult one to win, as the automobile dealer learned.[3]

---

3. The Rules of Golf also deal with mistake. When a golfer mistakenly plays the wrong ball, the consequences are generally straightforward under Rule 15. In match play, the golfer loses the hole. In stroke play, the player incurs a two-stroke penalty, and must rectify the mistake by "playing the correct ball or by proceeding under the Rules."

In the most common case, which involves a player mistakenly hitting the ball of another golfer in the same group before finishing the hole, the player must replace the ball hit in error, and find and hit the correct ball. Some golfers go to extraordinary effort in marking their balls in order to avoid the identification problem. Professional golfer Duffy Waldorf, for example, comes to mind. Duffy's wife and children mark his ball with messages and reminders. As a result, his golf ball is next to impossible to mistake.

The governing rule is that a player must play the same ball from the teeing ground until the player finishes the hole, unless a specific exception allows otherwise. The term "wrong ball" includes a ball belonging to another player, an abandoned ball, and the original ball when it is no longer in play.

Some recreational golfers, especially when they have to hit over a hazard or risk losing a "favorite" ball, change balls during a hole. Other golfers may tee off with one ball and replace it with a different "putting ball" once they are safely on the putting green. These changes are no-nos. Even when the change is inadvertent, the Rules provide no exception to such wrong-ball substitutions.

Hole 11: Hole-in-One Contest

Several factors led the court to reject the defense. First, there was no basis for Amos to think that the offer applied only to the earlier Hershey-Palmyra Sertoma tournament. The signs announcing the availability of the prize did not include dates or other such limitations. Thus, the court found that Amos had formed a reasonable expectation based on the apparent terms of the bargain proposed by the dealer. There was no mistake on his part.

Second, the court found that any mistake was due to the dealer's failure to remove the signs after its tournament. When the mistake is unilateral and is due to the negligence of the party seeking to rescind, performance will not be excused.

The hard lesson learned by the dealer: clean up after yourself by taking down your signs after a tournament. It's also prudent to specify who is eligible to participate in a contest.

One judge, who presumably was not a golfer, dissented. He argued that under Pennsylvania law, a hole-in-one contest had all the elements of illegal gambling. There was payment of money (the entry fee paid to enter the tournament), a reward (the car), and the element of chance.[4] This being the case, he reasoned that because all wagering contracts are illegitimate transactions, which the law declares void, the illegal contract should not be enforced. He would leave the parties where it found them: Amos with the satisfaction of hitting the hole in one, and the dealer with the car. How would you like to have this fun-loving judge direct your next golf tournament?

---

4. The author of the majority opinion, Judge Wieand, had this to say about the element chance.

Even if this Court could legitimately consider the "acts" which the dissent introduces from a popular magazine, those statistics demonstrate that a professional golfer is generally twice as likely to shoot a hole-in-one as an amateur golfer. Under these circumstances, it cannot be said that skill is "almost an irrelevant factor."

Conclusion

Cobaugh v. Klick-Lewis is admittedly a factually strange case. Who "wins" a hole-in-one prize after the event is over? Notwithstanding the unusual facts, the legal principles applied to the facts are straightforward.

To be enforceable, a contract requires an offer, acceptance, and consideration. The car dealer made an offer to award the prize of a car to a person hitting a hole in one. Amos accepted the offer by hitting it. The dealer benefited from the publicity generated by the promotional advertising, which furnished the consideration. Thus, all the elements for an enforceable unilateral contract were present.

The dealer was left arguing that there was a mistake that should excuse performance. When only one party to a contract is mistaken as to the terms of a contract, the performance of the contract will not be excused unless the non-mistaken party tries to take advantage of the mistake. Amos was playing in a tournament and reasonably believed he could get the car if he hit a hole in one. No evidence existed that he was trying to take advantage of the situation. The situation would have been entirely different had he not been playing in a tournament.

Hole 12

Hole-in-One Rules:
The ladies' red tees

South Dakota: *Harms v. Northland Ford Dealers, et al.*, 602 N.W.2d 58 (1999)

arms v. Northland Ford Dealers might be considered analogous to a "three ball" golf match.[1] The collegiate golfer, the promoter of the hole-in-one prize, and the country club hosting the tournament each wanted to win the judicial contest.

The odds of hitting an "ace" depend on the golfer's skill level, the difficulty of the shot, and obviously many other variables. No single organization has the official responsibility for collecting hole-in-one data, so the odds of hitting an ace are difficult to predict with any accuracy. The U.S. Golf Register estimates the possibility at 1 in 33,000.

The odds of getting a hole in one are rare, but the odds of a hole-in-one case reaching a state supreme court are even rarer. Suffice it to say, the *Harms* case is unusual.

The Facts

The Dakota Tour is a popular series of golf tournaments played at different South Dakota golf courses during the sum-

---

[1]. In golf, the term "three ball" has a special meaning. It is a form of match play competition where three players play against each other. Think of it as each golfer playing against the other two players.

The Little Book of Golf Law

Moccasin Creek Layout

mer months. It is still played today. The tournament events are open to professional and amateur golfers alike. Although there are prizes, many of the contestants play to have fun and challenge themselves. The omnipresent onslaught of summer gnats are reported to add to the challenge. Some contestants advise that wearing vanilla extract keeps the gnats at bay, while others point out the added benefit of smelling like a freshly baked cake.

Moccasin Creek Country Club in Aberdeen frequently hosts one of the tournament events. It is open to both men and women golfers. In 1995, Northland Ford Dealers, an association of Ford dealerships, sponsored a hole-in-one contest at Moccasin Creek during the annual tour event. The country club agreed to include the hole-in-one contest as part of its tournament. The contest trumpeted to all participants that the first golfer to get

Hole 12: Hole-in-One Rules

an ace on the eighth hole would get the grand prize of a new Ford Explorer from the Ford dealers.

Northland Ford took out a single-premium hole-in-one insurance policy with Continental Hole-in-One, Inc. to insure the award of the Ford Explorer should the improbable ace happen during the three-day tournament. The insurance policy, not surprisingly, contained important terms and conditions. The insurance application contained the following condition, stated in capital letters: "ALL AMATEUR MEN & WOMEN WILL UTILIZE THE SAME TEE."

On the last day of the tournament, Jennifer Harms, a National Collegiate Athletic Association (NCAA) collegiate golfer, defied the odds. She hit a hole in one from the women's red tee box on the eighth hole. One can only imagine the thrill she felt. To hit an ace is thrilling in itself, but to also get a new Ford Explorer while still in college is a dream come true.

When Jennifer finished the round, her parents gave her the bad news: Her miracle shot was disqualified because she did not hit from the men's tees. As a result, Northland Ford refused to give her the hole-in-one prize.

The hole-in-one insurance policy was absolutely clear. For all amateur participants, the minimum required distance was 170 yards. The red tees that Jennifer hit from were less than the required yardage. According to the insurance policy, her ace did not meet the requirements of the policy.

There were some complications, however. The insured, Northland Ford, did not inform either the country club or the participants in the tournament that women were required to play from the men's tees, which met the minimum required distance of 170 yards, in order to be in the hole-in-one contest.

The country club was told, however, about the minimum distances by the insurer, Continental Insurance. The day before the tournament started, the insurer faxed instructions to the club that contained the required minimum distances. The faxed instructions stated: "It is imperative that these yardages are correct each day to keep [Northland's] hole-in-one coverage valid." Nothing in the faxed instructions indicated that different yardages applied to women paricipants.

The country club's tournament information sheet that was given to the golfers didn't say anything about the required minimum distances. In the relevant part, the tournament rules simply said, "Professionals will play from the blue tees. Male amateurs will play from the yellow tees, female amateurs will play from the red tees." The instructions did not say that amateur female players had to hit from the amateur men's tee box to qualify for the hole-in-one prize. In fact, the club's superintendent testified, "I assumed it was a men's prize," and was not told by anyone that women were also competing.

Northland Ford refused to give Jennifer the Ford Explorer. She sued the country club and Northland Ford for breach of contract. The country club and Northland pointed fingers at each other when they cross-claimed against each other. The "threesome" match was on before the trial court.

The trial court granted summary judgment to Jennifer against both defendants. It also granted summary judgment to the country club against Northland Ford. Being on the losing end, Northland Ford appealed both grants of summary judgment. The case landed in the lap of the Supreme Court of South Dakota.

The Law

In order to prevail on a breach of contract claim, a plaintiff must first establish the existence of a valid contract. A contract is a voluntary agreement entered into by two or more parties with

Hole 12: Hole-in-One Rules

the intention of creating enforceable legal obligations. To be enforceable, contract law requires an offer, acceptance, and consideration.

When an offer calls for a contestant to perform an act, such as hitting a hole in one, acceptance occurs when the player enters the contest and hits the hole in one. Performance of the act results in a benefit to the promoter, and this constitutes the required consideration. Of course, the lucky golfer must also comply with the announced contest rules.[2]

The court made short work of Northland Ford's appeal: "No one can seriously dispute that, based on the promulgated contest rules, [Jennifer] Harms earned the prize when she sank the winning shot." The country club and Northland Ford "offered" to award the Ford Explorer to the first golfer to hit a hole in one. Jennifer "accepted" the offer by paying her entry fee and participating in the contest according to the announced tournament rules that required her to play from the women's red tees. Finally, she provided the required consideration when she performed the act of hitting the hole in one.

Additional factors favored the grant of summary judgment to Jennifer. None of the participants knew about the minimum yardage requirements contained in the insurance policy. To

---

2. A case involving the ambiguity of the hole-in-one rules also was decided by the North Dakota Supreme Court. The promotional contest offered a new car to the first participant who "shoots a hole-in-one on Hole No. 8." Every golfer was to play eighteen holes. The legal twist was that the golf course only had nine holes. Participants played the course twice in order to play all 18 holes.

For the first 9 holes, players used the blue tees; for the second 9, players used the red tees. The blue tees were marked 1 through 9 (which matched the hole numbers); the red tees were marked 10 through 18. The plaintiff Grove hit his hole-in-one while playing from the 17th tee. When the car dealership refused to award him the car because he did not make the ace on "Hole No. 8", he sued for breach of contract. The Court found that an enforceable contract existed between golfer and the dealership, and awarded the lucky golfer the prize. Grove v. Charbonneau Buick-Pontiac, Inc., 240 N.W.2d 853 (N.D.1976).

the extent that any ambiguity existed in the contest rules, they should be resolved against Northland Ford, not the contestant. It was their prize contest, after all.

Northland Ford tried to slip out of the deal by arguing that Jennifer had "renounced the prize." How was this possible, you might wonder? Northland Ford argued that by returning to Concordia College, where she was a member of the NCAA golf team, she gave up the right to the prize.

Jennifer hit the hole in one during the summer between her junior and senior years. Under the NCAA rules, she would be ineligible to play her final year at college by accepting the prize. As a result, by returning to play NCAA college golf during her senior year at Concordia, Jennifer manifested her intent to waive the claimed prize.

By electing to play NCAA golf, she waived the right to the prize. She couldn't have her cake (play NCAA golf) and eat it too (claim the prize). Furthermore, after she completed her college career, she should be estopped from changing her election to play collegiate NCAA golf.

The court effectively said, "Wait a minute." A waiver requires a clear relinquishment of an existing right in order to excuse performance. Returning to play NCAA golf during her senior year was not an unambiguous renunciation of her right to claim the prize. The theory of waiver was arguably unpersuasive for another reason. Northland Ford never recognized that she legally won the prize in the first place, so the dealer was hard-pressed to claim that she waived a right whose existence it refused to recognize.

Perhaps more persuasive was the court's reliance on estoppel, which applies when a person unfairly misleads another into detrimental reliance on certain facts or actions. The theory limits "changing your mind to the detriment of another." Northland

Ford rejected the idea that it ever had a duty to Jennifer when she took part in the tournament. Thus, the court reasoned that Northland never relied on her status as an NCAA collegiate golfer. Consequently, her NCAA eligibility was irrelevant.

Who pays the piper (Jennifer)?[3]

The responsibility for paying the prize to Jennifer was not resolved by the court. At trial, the country club prevailed on its motion for summary judgment against Northland Ford. But the supreme court reversed this determination because genuine issues of material fact precluded summary judgment in favor of the country club.

According to the country club, Continental Insurance did not provide it with complete and accurate information about the contest. The only facts it had were the daily yardage distances for amateurs and professionals. Only the insured, Northland Ford, and the insurance company, Continental, knew for certain the relevant details of the policy.

The country club did not seek clarification of the hole-in-one rules, but it set up and administered the contest nonetheless. Whether the club breached its duty by doing so was for the jury to sort out on remand.

On remand, an additional question is apt to loom. Before tackling the question of breach, the existence of an enforceable contract must be proved. The record before the supreme court was thin in regard to identifying the consideration to support an enforceable contract between the country club and Northland Ford. The court seems to assume the existence. But the

---

3. This expression probably comes from the legend of the Pied Piper of Hamelin, in which the piper abducts all the children of the village of Hamelin as punishment for refusing to pay the Piper for catching all the rats. The moral is pretty straightforward: pay your debts or suffer the consequences.

only reference was contained in a single sentence of the court's opinion: "[a] substantial prize offered for a hole in one assuredly enhances a tournament's attraction and presumably increases registration."

Conclusion

In the film *Happy Gilmore*, Happy (Adam Sandler) hits his golf ball a great distance, which is tantalizingly captured in slow motion. The ball bounces on a green, rolls into a hole, and the crowd goes wild. Happy then shouts, "He shoots, he scores! Oh, man. That was so much easier than putting. I should just try to get the ball in one shot every time." Like Happy, Jennifer had the thrill of not putting when she hit her ace on the eighth hole.

The larger lesson is that the participants in hole-in-one contests may want to make sure they know the rules or have ready access to a lawyer. Those hosting and promoting a hole-in-one contest also will benefit from the same advice. In life, as in golf, knowing and following the rules can keep you out of the rough.

Hole 13

Hole-in-One Fraud:
Off to the hoosegow

Federal: *United States v. Krilich*,
159 F.3d 1020 (7th Cir. 1998)

Golf is a game played under the honor system. Unlike most games, golfers are expected to know the rules and call penalties on themselves when they violate the *Rules of Golf*.

Professional golfers are well known for calling penalties on themselves. Other times, golf fans get involved. Some fans watching golf on television seem to have the PGA Tour telephone number on speed dial to report rule violations.

A famous case from the annals of golf involved Robert Tyre (Bobby) Jones, who, golf fans will recall, was a lawyer and competed in golf as an amateur. During the 1925 U.S. Open, in Worcester, Massachusetts, Jones's ball moved ever so slightly in the long grass just after addressing the ball near the 11th green. Nobody else saw the ball move and no prying television cameras captured the incident.

Bobby insisted on calling a one-stroke penalty on himself under rule 18-1. As a result, Jones dropped into a playoff with Willie Macfarlane. Jones then lost to Macfarlane in a 36-hole playoff by one stroke. Although he lost the U.S. Open, he added considerable luster to his legacy as one of the "greatest golfers." When praised for his honesty, he simply said, "You might as well praise me for not breaking into banks. There is only one way to play this game."

Strict adherence to the Rules of Golf differs among amateur golfers and according to circumstances. Many golfers bend or ignore the rules when playing a friendly round with friends. In a tournament or when money is on the line, golfers are expected to follow Jones's example in following the rules.

When a golfer hits a ball into a place that makes swinging at the ball or advancing it difficult, the situation is often called being "in jail." It's golfer slang for being in deep trouble. Being "in jail" is rarely taken literally. But that is what happened in *United States v. Krilich*—the cheater actually wound up in jail.

The Facts

Country Lakes Country Club is nestled among 125 acres of beautiful, gently rolling countryside in Naperville, Illinois. It offers some of the most exciting and challenging public golf in the Chicago area. The ninth hole is an over-the-water par 3. It also has the distinction of being the crime scene, although it wasn't marked off in the traditional yellow crime-scene tape.

Most golfers have a slim chance of hitting a hole in one, but Andy Sarallo's chances were 100 percent. On June 19, 1985, Andy appeared to have hit the perfect shot during a hole-in-one contest on the ninth hole. But appearances are not always what they seem.

After Andy hit his shot, Robert Krilich, who was the sponsor of the hole-in-one contest and an interested observer standing on the ninth green, pulled what appeared to be Andy's ball out of the hole after he hit. But the ball wasn't the one Andy hit.

Krilich performed a magic sleight-of-hand: Krilich palmed one of Andy's golf balls, put his hand into the cup, and displayed the ball. Andy's foursome appropriately jumped up and down

Hole 13: Hole-in-One Fraud

Country Lakes Country Club "Crime Scene"

and shouted for joy. The record does not indicate what happened to the original ball that Andy hit, which is surprising.

The prize for hitting an ace was the choice of a classic 1931 Cadillac or a check for $40,000. But Andy got neither prize because Mayor Sarallo of Oakbrook Terrace, his dad, had rigged the contest with the help of Krilich.[1]

Why the elaborate scheme?

Krilich needed the mayor's support to alter the zoning for an apartment complex he planned and also to orchestrate the fund-

---

1. Mayor Sarallo was also indicted for soliciting the hole-in-one bribe.

ing for a municipal bond offering to build the project.[2] In some places, the time-honored way to accomplish this is by bribing the elected officials in charge.

Krilich and the mayor agreed to use the hole-in-one contest as a disguised way to pay off the bribe for the mayor's support. The scheme, before it unraveled, was a "win-win." Krilich would cover the cost of the bribe by purchasing hole-in-one insurance from the National Hole-in-One Association. The payoff would be funded by the insurance company. The cost to Krilich would be simply the premium he paid for the policy, which would be much less than the cost of the awarded prize.

Krilich wasn't finished, however, with his fraudulent maneuvers. The revenues from the bond issue were placed in trust to ensure they were properly distributed to support the project. The federally insured trustee banks holding the bond revenues were obligated to release funds to reimburse Krilich for appropriate expenses associated with the project as it progressed toward completion.

But Krilich had other pressing personal financial needs for the bond monies, such as making payments on his expensive yacht. Thus, he used the equivalent of a "foot wedge" to get the project vendors on the development project to falsify their invoices, which were then sent to the trustee banks for payment out of the trust accounts.

---

2. The project was to be financed through Industrial Revenue Bonds (IRBs). The bonds would be issued by the city of Oakwood Terrace with the proceeds being used to support Krilich's project. The city would hold title to the underlying project as collateral until the bonds were paid off by the developer. Because the bonds are the obligation of the developer, the city's credit rating generally is unaffected. The arrangement is attractive to investors because the interest paid on the bonds is tax free. It is also attractive to the developer because the bonds are tax exempt and therefore carry a somewhat lower interest rate than privately issued bonds. The developer also benefits because the project collateral is exempt from property taxes because the city has title to the property.

Facing federal environmental problems with the project, which threatened to shut it down, Krilich arranged a meeting with Nicholae Lonescu, the zoning administrator and city engineer. He asked Lonescu to supply an affidavit stating that the project should continue notwithstanding the regulatory problems with the federal environmental authorities. In a decision Lonescu would surely come to regret, he obliged. The same afternoon Lonescu supplied the affidavit, they had a pleasant lunch at a restaurant. After coffee and dessert, Krilich showed his appreciation by passing his lunch partner a "thank you" envelope containing $300.

The Law

Golfers would call Krilich a cheat. The U.S. Attorney had the same view. Krilich was charged with fraud[3] as well as conspiracy to violate the RICO (Racketeer Influenced and Corrupt Organizations) Act.[4]

The federal fraud statute has an extremely broad reach. It applies to *any* statements made for the purpose of influencing in *any* way the action of *any* of the covered institutions in *any* application. It applied because Krilich caused vendors to make false statements in the requisition applications to the federally insured bank trustees. His attorney had numerous arguments, but in the end Krilich was convicted of 14 counts of fraud.

The RICO charge was based on the hole-in-one bribe. Krilich admitted the scheme to bribe the mayor in a proffer to the U.S. Attorney during plea negotiations. Although statements made during such negotiations are generally inadmissible, a defendant may waive this protection. Krilich signed the following conditional waiver:

---

3. 18 U.S.C. § 1014.
4. 18 U.S.C. § 1962(d).

[S]hould [Krilich] subsequently testify contrary to the substance of the proffer or otherwise present a position inconsistent with the proffer, nothing shall prevent the government from using the substance of the proffer at sentencing for any purpose, at trial for impeachment or in rebuttal testimony, or in a prosecution for perjury.

During the trial, several witnesses testified, in response to questions from Krilich's attorney, that the ninth hole is close to the clubhouse and easily observed by the public. The attorney wanted the jury to infer that no one would attempt to fake a hole-in-one result on the ninth green.

On cross-examination, Krilich's attorney got two witnesses to say that they were at the ninth hole when Andy hit the shot, and they didn't think that Krilich was there. The intent was to imply that Krilich did not fake the hole in one, contrary to what he admitted in his proffer.

In response to evidence that Krilich paid a bribe to obtain favorable zoning, his lawyer elicited testimony on cross-examination that no bribe was required because the city attorney thought the new zoning was appropriate. Counsel likewise led witnesses to testify that the procedures followed for altering the zoning were not exceptional. He also had the vice president of his company testify that he was not aware of *any* bribes paid to *any* public official in connection with *any* project—the implication being that if someone so close to Krilich (and the project) was unaware of bribes, there must not have been any.

The court found that Krilich's attorney opened the evidentiary door to allow the use Krilich's inconsistent statements that were made during the plea negotiations. One could sensibly conclude, the court found, that the above testimony was inconsistent with the earlier proffer. As a result, the prosecutor was able to use Krilich's prior admissions.

Not surprisingly, the convictions were affirmed on appeal. The case was remanded for sentencing.

Krilich's conduct was not a victimless crime similar to bending or ignoring the rules during a friendly round of golf. The U.S. Treasury lost approximately one dollar in tax revenue for every dollar Krilich saved. The benefit to Krilich was a reduction in the rate of interest he had to pay to borrow the money for his development project. If interest on the bonds had been taxable, he would have had to pay more to attract investors. Although the National Hole-in-One Association did not have to pay out on the policy, it also was a victim of the scheme.

Conclusion

Agreements with prosecutors are common in federal cases and many state cases. With some exceptions, statements made during plea negotiations are usually accompanied by limited immunity agreements, colloquially known by lawyers as "queen-for-a-day" agreements, in which a prosecutor promises not to use a proffered statement at trial or at sentencing.

But prosecutors generally reserve the right to use such statements as leads to other evidence. They also reserve the right to use them at trial for impeachment purposes and, perhaps more controversially, to rebut any inconsistent factual assertions or arguments made by the defendant or defense counsel. Thus, the proffering witness waives many of the protections afforded by federal rules of evidence or its state law counterpart.[5]

---

5. *See* Federal Rule of Evidence 410 (making statements made in the context of plea discussions inadmissible at trial).

By waiving these protections, Krilich gained a theoretical strategic advantage. His representations were presumably more credible, which strengthened his initial negotiating posture. But the downside to the conditional proffer signed by Krilich is equally clear. Once the evidentiary door was opened, his contradictory statements had a devastating effect on his ability to defend himself. Another downside to conditional waivers is that the statements may lead in unanticipated directions. It may lead to prosecution for obstruction of justice and making false statements to government officials.

Conditional waivers need to be approached with caution, much like a difficult golf shot. In the end, one can say that Robert Krilich turned out to be no Bobby Jones. During his incarceration, he might profit by reading *The Life and Times of Bobby Jones.*

Hole 14

Insurance:
19th Hole drunken assault

Iowa: *Dolan v. State Farm Fire & Casualty*, 573 N.W.2d 254 (1998)

Many golfers enjoy the tradition associated with the 19th hole. This tradition usually involves a trip to the clubhouse bar, or some reasonable approximation, where the order of business is apt to include "settling up" wagers won and lost, some laughs or "what-ifs," and a few drinks. On occasion, some golfers get carried away at the 19th hole, sometimes in handcuffs.

The Facts

Walter Olson had finished at least 12 beers at the 19th hole when he realized that his golf clubs were missing. As you might suspect, at the time of this startling realization he was, to put it politely, intoxicated.

The search was on for the missing clubs. Walter confronted Edward Dolan, an employee who was working at the pro shop, about his missing clubs. When Edward failed to produce the clubs on demand, Walter became physically aggressive. He was mad as hell and wasn't going to lose the missing clubs without a fight. He grabbed Edward's coat and pulled it over his head. In the resulting scuffle, Edward was injured.

The missing clubs were finally found. Walter had forgotten that he put them in his car before proceeding to the bar to slake his thirst. Mental lapses tend to occur after a couple of six-packs. While fortunate to rediscover the missing clubs, Walter was not fortunate enough to avoid the civil lawsuit brought by Edward and the criminal assault charges brought by the state of Iowa.

Edward sued the fractious Walter for negligence about a month after the incident. In November 1993, a jury agreed that Walter was negligent and awarded Edward almost $70,000 in damages. But that wasn't the end of the story; in fact, it was just getting started.

The Law

Walter was defended by an attorney provided by his homeowner's insurer, State Farm Fire & Casualty Co. Although State Farm hired an attorney to defend him, it reserved the right to contest the policy's coverage under the facts. The State Farm attorney was authorized to defend the personal injury claim against Walter, but the attorney had no authority to make representations as to whether the policy actually covered Walter's aggressive and intentional conduct.

Shortly after he was sued for negligence, matters took a turn for the worse for Walter. The state commenced an action against him for criminal assault. Several months after the criminal charges were filed, Walter was found guilty of assault by a jury. His life was unraveling.

Walter saw the handwriting on the wall. He filed for bankruptcy in October 1993 to discharge or avoid any liability to Edward and any other creditors. He was undoubtedly thinking that State Farm might refuse to indemnify him under the reservation of rights provision. Less than a month later, the jury

Hole 14: Insurance

found Walter negligent and awarded Edward close to $70,000 in damages.

Although Walter had declared bankruptcy, Edward did not drop the matter. In March 1994, Edward filed a lawsuit against Walter's insurance company, State Farm, for the purpose of collecting his unsatisfied judgment.

Walter's insurance policy provided that liability coverage and medical payments to others do not apply to: "[A]. Bodily injury or property damage: (1) which is either expected or intended by an insured. . . ." The problem for Edward was that Walter's insurance policy did not cover intentional acts.

The trial court found that State Farm had no responsibility to pay the judgment entered against Walter because the policy excluded coverage for intentional acts. The fact that the jury had found Walter negligent in the original civil action did not control whether the policy exclusion applied. The jury in the original action did not determine whether Walter's actions were intentional. Thus, the finding that Walter was negligent did not prevent State Farm from arguing that his actions were intentional and thus excluded from coverage. The Iowa Court of Appeals affirmed, and Edward took his battle to the Iowa Supreme Court.

The Supreme Court of Iowa found that the jury's finding that Walter was negligent in the civil action did not preclude a subsequent finding that his actions were also intentional and thus excluded from coverage. A person who voluntarily becomes intoxicated does not make his intentional acts unintentional for the purpose of insurance coverage. Because Walter had no right to enforce a claim against State Farm, neither could Edward.

Conclusion

Most liability policies obligate the insurer to indemnify the insured and to provide a defense in litigation. Both duties spring from the agreed terms of the insurance contract. Although both obligations are based on the insurance contract, they are separate and distinct obligations.

An insurer confronted with the demand to defend the insured has essentially three options: (1) to defend the insured under a reservation of rights; (2) to seek declaratory relief to define its obligations under the policy; or (3) to refuse to take over the defense, standing on its interpretation of the policy, at the risk of being later found to have breached its duty to defend. When the insurer defends the insured, the insurer risks being held to have impliedly admitted liability. This risk can be avoided by a reservation of rights, which is what State Farm did. It defended Walter, but then contested coverage.

The supreme court found that Walter's intentional acts were barred by the policy's intentional act exclusion even though the insured was intoxicated at the time of the liability event. When Walter voluntarily became intoxicated, he could not claim that the results were unexpected or unintended. The court reasoned, "[W]e are not inclined to create a situation where the more drunk an insured can prove himself to be, the more likely he will have insurance coverage."

The courts are split on whether intoxication eliminates an insured's capacity to form the requisite intent to commit an intentional act for purposes of the policy exclusion for intentional injury. Courts have generally taken one of two approaches to the issue. *Dolan* is one approach. Other courts have held that intoxication creates what amounts to a "rebuttable presumption" that the insured lacked the capacity to form the intent required to trigger the intentional injury exclusion.

Epilogue

In the end, Walter suffered a criminal conviction, went into bankruptcy, and took a tour of the Iowa civil court system. Edward also lost. He was left with an unsatisfied judgment against Walter because of Walter's bankruptcy and his inability to make a valid claim against State Farm. The fallout from the 19th hole was more than anyone bargained for, except for perhaps the lawyers who were fully utilized. The lesson seems simple: Don't get carried away at or from the 19th hole.[1]

---

1. Some golfers can't wait until the 19th hole before getting into trouble with the law. In 2006, for example, Adam Thompson was charged with felony criminal vehicular operation for driving a golf cart under the influence. (United Press International, "Man faces DWI for golf cart crash," June 10, 2006.) Thompson and Anthony Savage had been drinking heavily during their round of golf. The two golfers allegedly had been slaking their considerable thirst with ample quantities of beer from their personal cooler as well as taking advantage of the Mississippi Dunes Golf Links roving beverage service. As bad luck would have it, there was a cart operation problem. Savage wound up pinned under the golf cart cut, bruised, and with an injured eye. The police were called, and Thompson was charged. Thompson's lawyer argued that the club shared some responsibility for the accident because the cart-girl continued to serve the two golfers after they were visibly intoxicated, something the club disputed. In essence, the claim seemed to be that the golf course was quite clever in putting an attractive seductress with a cart full of booze within Thompson's reach. The Devil made him do it. You be the judge.

The Rules of Golf are noticeably silent on drunken behavior. The etiquette guidelines to the game do cover, however, safety to others and preventing unnecessary damage to the golf course.

Hole 15

Insurance:
Golf cart accidents and policy exclusions

Mississippi: *Dowdle v. Mississippi Farm Bureau Mutual Insurance Co.*, 697 So. 2d 788 (Miss. 1997)

Fred Flintstone, the popular animated character and golfer, is known for bellowing the phrase "Yabba-dabba-doo."[1] Fred drives around the fictional city of Bedrock in a Flintmobile.[2] With a little imagination, the Flintmobile resembles today's golf cart, which is designed to carry two golfers and their equipment.

But one doesn't have to have an imagination to realize that the world of golf carts has been turned upside down with the introduction of the Hovercraft golf cart. In 2013, Bubba Watson demonstrated that the Hovercraft is capable of floating gracefully over a golf course, including water hazards and bunkers. In less than a year, the demonstration has gone viral. It has had more than 9 million hits on YouTube. Golf courses are looking at the possibility of having them available for golfers.

At this point, however, the most commonly used motorized golf cart is a four-wheeled vehicle powered by an electric motor or some type of combustion engine. Its maximum speed, usually

---

1. As perhaps the earliest golfer, Fred recorded the first "eagle" by striking a Pterodactyl with his club in 2000 B.C.
2. A picture of the Flintmobile is available at http://rides.webshots.com/photo/2207795180030961650esbfxk.

around 15 miles per hour, often is controlled by a mechanical governor.

Of the millions of rounds of golf played each year, golfers use a golf cart about half the time. Given their frequency of use, it should be no surprise that golf carts are involved in accidents resulting in personal injury. According to one report, about half of all golf cart accidents involve negligent driving or cart maintenance. The other half involve claims of product liability for defect design or manufacture of the golf cart.

Liability is similar to that imposed on any person who operates a motor vehicle in a negligent manner that causes injury. Negligence may occur in any number of ways, including the driver ejecting a passenger due to an unreasonably sharp turn, crashing the cart while intoxicated, tipping the cart over by following a route not ordinarily taken, or driving in an area prohibited by the golf course.

Depending on the exact cause of the accident, the insured person may sue the golf course as the owner or lessor of the golf cart. When an accident causing injury involves driver negligence, the injured person may sue the driver of the golf cart or the driver's insurance company if the driver has insurance.

Another option is also possible. The injured person may make a claim against his or her own automobile insurance policy under its "uninsured motorist" provision if the driver has no insurance that covers the accident. In such a case, identifying the policy exclusions is essential.[3]

---

3. Identification is also important in golf. A player must be able to identify his or her golf ball before hitting it. If a player cannot, the ball is treated as lost under the Rules. In March 1999, for example, Nick Faldo was disqualified from the Players Championship during the final round when he failed to first identify his ball when it got stuck in a palm tree at the sixth hole. Faldo was incorrectly advised by Corey Pavin that he could drop under the tree for a one-stroke penalty without identifying his ball. Faldo finished the hole and was disqualified. The ball should have been played as a lost ball. Pavin reported that the parting with Faldo after the round was amicable.

Hole 15: Insurance

The Facts

The facts of the case are sparse. Archie Dowdle was injured by the negligent operation of a golf cart driven by Jimmy Berryhill, Jr., who was uninsured. The absence of liability insurance by Jimmy was important. It was also important that the negligent operation was not contested.

Archie lived with his parents and was covered by his father's automobile insurance policy issued by the Mississippi Farm Bureau Mutual Insurance Company. Archie claimed that he was covered by the policy and entitled to recover pursuant to the uninsured motorist provision.

A golf cart arguably meets the common dictionary definition of a motor vehicle—a vehicle with a motor in it. The insurance company was not persuaded that the golf cart was a motor vehicle for purposes of insurance coverage and refused to pay the claim. Archie sued. The trial court found the insurance company was entitled to prevail as a matter of law and granted it summary judgment. The appellate court affirmed. Archie then asked the Mississippi Supreme Court to reverse.

The Law

The issue before the Mississippi Supreme Court was whether a golf cart should be treated as a motor vehicle under the unin-

---

In order to be able to recognize one's own ball, a player should put some type of identifying mark on it. Even when the ball is marked, it is sometimes difficult to identify the ball as the player's own. This problem might occur, for example, when the ball is buried in the heavy rough and the identifying mark cannot be readily seen. In such cases, the player may lift the ball, without penalty, in order to identify it.

In order to lift the ball without penalty, the proper procedure must be followed. Before lifting the ball, the player must tell an opponent or other competitor, mark the ball, and allow that person to observe the identification procedure. Once identified, the ball must be replaced so that no advantage is gained by lifting and replacing the ball. Except to the extent needed to allow for identification, the ball may not be cleaned. Failure to comply with the proper procedure results in a one-stroke penalty.

sured motorist provision of the policy and under the state's Motor Vehicle Responsibility Act. In defining the proper scope of the uninsured motorist coverage of the insurance policy, the court was required to evaluate the contract language and facts in light of the statutory definition of a motor vehicle.[4] To the extent the language of the insurance policy is ambiguous or otherwise unclear, the coverage under the policy will be construed against the insurance company.

The supreme court held that a golf cart is not a motor vehicle for purposes of the insurance policy. The court first looked at the policy definition of "an uninsured motor vehicle." It excluded "equipment designed for use principally off public roads." In addition, the policy defined "automobile" to exclude "all-terrain vehicles or any other recreation vehicle." The court reasoned that golf carts were excluded under the terms of the policy because golf carts are designed primarily for use principally off public roads. It was also a recreation vehicle.

---

4. Not all jurisdictions follow this view. Ohio, for example, treats golf carts as motor vehicles. Ohio law defines "motor vehicle" as "every vehicle propelled or drawn by power other than muscular power or power collected from overhead electronic trolley wires . . . ." R.C. 4511.01(B). Encompassed within the definition of motor vehicle is the term vehicle, which is defined as "every device, including a motorized bicycle, in, upon, or by which any person or property may be transported or drawn upon a highway . . . ." R.C. 4511.01(A). The relevant statutory language does not require actual use on a public highway. It only requires that a person or property "may be" transported on a public highway or that the motor vehicle be capable of transporting people or property upon a highway.

The Ohio Attorney General (AG) has concurred with this statutory interpretation. In 1990, the Ohio AG issued an opinion stating: "A golf cart—i.e. a four-wheeled motor vehicle that is designed and manufactured for the primary purpose of transporting people and equipment on a golf course—is a "motor vehicle" as that term is defined in Ohio Revised Code sections 4501.01, 4503.01, and 4505 .01." OAG 90–043. This 1990 AG opinion was approved and followed in 2008 by a second AG opinion stating "a golf cart is a motor vehicle and may not be driven on public streets and highways unless it meets the statutory requirements that are applicable to motor vehicles, including operating and equipment requirements." 2008 Ohio Atty. Gen. Ops No.2008–030.

The Ohio courts have consistently held that golf carts are motor vehicles. Irvin v. Brown, 2013 Ohio 2883 (Ohio Ct. App. July 1, 2013) (2013 WL 3380928).

Golf carts are used while playing golf and are intended only for limited use on other roadways. Archie's witnesses submitted affidavits saying that the golf carts were used from time to time on the public roads, but the affidavits did not help because the policy excludes equipment used principally off public roads. The court found the language of the policy "clear, unambiguous, and easily understood."

The court also consulted Mississippi's Motor Vehicle statute. It defines "a motor vehicle" as "a vehicle designed for use upon a highway." The golf cart did not fall within this definition. Thus, the statute did not provide a basis for treating a golf cart as a motor vehicle.

The court's reasoning is consistent with the general view that golf carts are not typically used on roads and highways, and thus are outside the financial responsibility and no-fault coverage provisions of automobile insurance. But some cases have treated golf carts as within the definition of a motor vehicle.[5]

Conclusion

The supreme court found that a golf cart was not an uninsured motor vehicle under the language of the uninsured motorist policy. The policy specifically excluded recreational vehicles designed principally for use off the public roads. In addition, the court construed the state motor vehicle statute to exclude golf carts from the definition of a motor vehicle.

Some courts have had difficulty interpreting the scope of

---

5. Del E. Webb Cactus Dev. v. Jessup, 863 P.2d 260 (Ariz. 1993) (holding incidental use of golf carts to cross public roads was "operation" of vehicle sufficient to subject lessor of carts to registration and liability insurance requirements for motor vehicles). *See also,* Coffey v. State Farm Mut. Auto. Ins. Co., 412 N.W.2d 281 (1987) (holding a golf cart to be a motor vehicle when being driven in a private subdivision by an intoxicated driver). *But see* Ebernickel v. State Farm Mut. Auto. Ins. Co., 367 N.W.2d 444 (Mich. 1985) (requiring that an accident actually occur on public road).

the term "motor vehicle."[6] The issue of insurance coverage for golf cart operation is apt to take on continuing importance in the future. One reason is that golf carts are being used increasingly for multiple purposes on and around golf courses and golf course communities.

The possibility of federal action may affect future judicial decisions on the scope of insurance coverage. If the National Highway Traffic Safety Administration succeeds in imposing federal regulations requiring certain golf carts to be equipped with seat belts, turn signals, windshields, and other safety devices, courts may be more willing to classify golf carts as motor vehicles for insurance purposes. You can bet that the insurance companies will keep track of these developments and tailor their exclusions accordingly.

How insurance companies and legislatures deal with Hovercrafts as motor vehicles may be the next generation of litigation involving golf carts.

---

6. Debts are non-dischargeable if they arise out of the debtor's operation of a motor vehicle while intoxicated under the Bankruptcy Code. The federal courts have split on whether motorboats are motor vehicles for purposes of applying the provision. *Compare* Boyce v. Greenway, 71 F.3d 1177 (5th Cir. 1996) (motorboats are not motor vehicles); Willison v. Race, 192 B.R. 949 (W.D. Mo. 1995) (motorboats are motor vehicles).

Hole 16

Insurance:
Hole-in-one insurance scam

Washington: *State of Washington v. Kevin Kolenda d/b/a Hole-in-Won*, case no. 12-1-04505-1 (2012)

This case involves the three-step "dance": (1) create a fake insurance company; (2) sell hole-in-one insurance to small-time tournaments; and (3) stiff the player who has hit the hole-in-one by refusing to pay off.[1]

The Facts

In 1995, Kevin W. Kolenda started a business called Golf Marketing out of Norwalk, Connecticut. Since then, his business has gone through a number of name changes. It currently operates as Hole-In-Won.com Worldwide (hereinafter HIW). HIW offers insurance products to the sponsors of golf events. It uses the Internet, email, facsimile, and telephone to solicit business.

A golf organization putting on a golf tournament often looks for sponsors to offer prizes for specific holes during a tournament, including the prize for anyone hitting a hole in one on a designated hole. If there is an agreement on the premium and other conditions, the golf organization and HIW enter into a

---

1. Country Western Dance fans also use the three step, but for entirely different reasons.

contract. The golf organization pays HIW and, in exchange, HIW agrees to pay a prize amount if someone hits a hole in one during the tournament.

The Office of Insurance Commissioner (OIC) in Washington state is responsible for regulating the insurance industry in the public interest. All insurers wanting to conduct business in the state must meet mandatory requirements, and anyone selling insurance in the state must hold a license issued by the OIC.

According to the OIC, Mr. Kolenda and HIW have not met the requirements to issue insurance, nor does Mr. Kolenda or HIW have a license to solicit or sell insurance. In 2004, the OIC issued a cease-and-desist order (CDO) directing him to stop engaging in illegal actions. The CDO ordered:

> Golf Marketing Worldwide, LLC, Kevin Kolenda, and their officers, directors, trustees, agents, employees, and affiliates to refrain from various activities, among them, the attempted collection of premium monies and the advertising and soliciting by e-mail, facsimile, telephone, mail, website or any other means, taking applications for, procuring or placing for others, any contract providing indemnification for sporting event winnings or losses in Washington or any other form of insurance.

This CDO followed a 2003 complaint filed against Mr. Kolenda with the OIC and its subsequent investigation of him for failing to pay a verified hole-in-one claim.

In 2006, the OIC secured evidence that Mr. Kolenda was continuing to solicit and sell insurance in violation of the 2004 CDO. In 2008, an OIC hearing officer fined Mr. Kolenda $125,000 for violating the CDO, and he was once again ordered to stop soliciting or selling insurance in the state.

The CDO did not deter Mr. Kolenda. In 2010, for example, he sold coverage to pay $25,000 for a hole in one for a golf tournament in Snohomish, Washington. Despite notarized forms attesting to a hole in one, the prize was unpaid despite numerous calls and emails.

Other evidence piled up that he violated the CDO. He contacted, by email or telephone, various organizations offering to provide hole-in-one coverage on behalf of HIW. The HIW contract states: "This is NOT an Insurance Policy or Product." At the risk of stating the obvious, this characterization is not likely to be an effective defense.

The Law

Solicitation by an unauthorized insurer is prohibited under Washington state law.[2] Section 48.15.023 of the Revised Code of Washington provides:

> (1) An insurer that is not authorized by the commissioner may not solicit insurance business in this state or transact insurance business in this state, except as provided in this chapter.
>
> (2)(a) A person may not, in this state, represent an unauthorized insurer except as provided in this chapter. This subsection does not apply to any adjuster or attorney-at-law representing an unauthorized insurer from time to time in this state in his or her professional capacity.
>
> (b) A person, other than a duly licensed surplus line broker acting in good faith under his or her license, who makes a contract of insurance in this state, directly or indirectly, on behalf of an unauthorized insurer, without

---

2. Revised Code of Washington, (RCW) 48.15.020.

complying with the provisions of this chapter, is personally liable for the performance of such contract.

(3) Each violation of subsection (2) of this section constitutes a separate offense punishable by a fine of not more than twenty-five thousand dollars, and the commissioner, at the commissioner's discretion, may order replacement of policies improperly placed with an unauthorized insurer with policies issued by an authorized insurer. Violations may result in suspension or revocation of a license.[3]

Each violation of the above statute is considered a class B felony.

Conclusion

Mr. Kolenda has a history of noncompliance and is subject to numerous cease-and-desist orders and civil penalties in other states. He has been the subject of many complaints nationwide for collecting premiums for hole-in-one insurance and not paying the claims when they are submitted for payment. Similar allegations have been made against him or his business in Alabama, California, Connecticut, Florida, Georgia, Hawaii, Massachusetts, Montana, North Carolina, and Ohio.

Mr. Kolenda has been accused of cheating local golfers out of hundreds of thousands of dollars. Usually disputes about unpaid claims are handled with fines or other administrative action. News reports indicate that he has been extradited to Washington to face criminal charges. Similar criminal charges are pending in other states.

---

3. Id.

Part III

Property

Hole 17

Misappropriation:
The USGA handicap index formula

California: *U.S. Golf Association v. Arroyo Software Corp.*, 60 Cal. App. 4th 607 (1999)

In the early 1890s, a raging disagreement between St. Andrew's Shinnecock Hills Golf Club in New York and the Newport Golf Club in Rhode Island arose over which club's tournament conferred the title of "National Amateur Champion." Out of this dispute, the United States Golf Association (USGA) was created in 1894 to conduct national championships, to administer and promote golf, and to oversee the codification and interpretation of the Rules of Golf, as well as the Rules of Amateur Status.

Among the various services that the USGA provides to an amateur golfer is a handicap index. A USGA index is issued through licensed golf clubs that follow all of the procedures established by the USGA, including a system of peer review. The index allows golfers of different skill levels to compete on an equal basis.

The first version of the USGA handicap formula was published in the late 1890s. A system based on a golfer's best three scores, devised in 1904, was adopted by the USGA in 1911.

Over the years, the formula has been modified. A single, nationwide system was prescribed by the USGA in 1958. In 1987, the USGA adopted new formulas, including the new slope system. Today, approximately 5 million golfers have USGA handicap indexes.

The Facts

A federal trademark identifies the source of goods, and a service mark identifies the source of services. The USGA holds protected service marks under federal trademark law to "U.S.G.A.," "Handicap Index," "Slope," and "Course Handicap."

Arroyo is a computer software company licensed in California. It is not a golf club or golf association authorized by the USGA to issue handicap Indexes. Instead of developing its own handicap formula, Arroyo incorporated the USGA handicap formula as part of its EagleTrak software at little or no cost to the company. EagleTrak was sold to individuals, golf associations, and golf clubs, but there was no system of peer review. Arroyo used the USGA name and service marks in marketing Eagle-Trak.

The USGA repeatedly asked Arroyo to stop its unauthorized use, and when Arroyo refused, the USGA sued. It brought an action for injunctive relief against Arroyo based on common-law misappropriation, unfair competition, and false advertising. It alleged that Arroyo's unauthorized use of the Association's handicap system, formulas, and service marks caused public confusion and devalued its handicap system.

After a bench trial, the trial court granted a permanent injunction preventing Arroyo from misappropriating plaintiff's protected property interests. Arroyo appealed.

The Law

State law defines the boundaries of property protection available under a claim of misappropriation.[1] Misappropriation is based on common-law principles that exist outside the statutory protections available under federal trademark law.

The misappropriation theory typically applies when a court finds that one competitor deals unfairly with another. The analysis is premised on the fact that the complainant has invested time and money on the thing misappropriated, the appropriator has misappropriated the thing at little or no cost, and the complainant has been injured. In essence, the theory operates to prevent the appropriator from unfairly free-riding on the economic investment of another, so-called "reaping where one has not sown."[2]

The trial court found that Arroyo's unauthorized use of USGA's formulas in the EagleTrak software undermined the integrity of the Handicap System, thereby creating the substantial risk of damage to the reputation, standing and viability of the USGA. Arroyo's unauthorized use of these service marks in its advertising, packaging, and instructional materials created a likelihood of confusion by conveying to the general public that USGA had authorized and approved Arroyo's use of the Handicap System. It also found that Arroyo's disclaimers were ineffectual and ambiguous.

Arroyo appealed. The appellate court sustained the trial court on the USGA's claim for injunctive relief based on misap-

---

1. The federal government and states both have the power to regulate intellectual property. The federal government may exercise, however, its constitutional power to preempt state regulation.
2. International News Service v. Associated Press, 248 U.S. 215 (1918) (holding INS liable for the tort of misappropriation under the federal common law). Following this case, a number of states adopted the tort of misrepresentation to protect against unfair commercial practices under state common law.

propriation, unfair competition, and service mark infringement. The USGA had "amply met its burden" of proving that Arroyo's actions violated the USGA's proprietary rights in the Handicap System, formulas, and service marks under the California common law of misappropriation.

Collateral Estoppel

The law of collateral estoppel prevents a party from litigating issues that have been previously decided by a court. When an issue of fact or law has been litigated and the determination is essential to the judgment, the determination is binding in a subsequent litigation between the parties. When the facts and circumstances have changed or are different, collateral estoppel does not apply.

In 1980, the USGA unsuccessfully sued Data-Max to prevent the company from using and advertising the USGA mathematical handicap formula. The USGA argued that it invested time, effort, and money in the creation of the formula, and that the Association was entitled to protection against Data-Max's misappropriation of its handicap formula under state and federal law.[3] The federal district court, applying New Jersey law, ruled in favor of Data-Max, and the USGA appealed.

In *Data-Max*, the U.S. Court of Appeals, Third Circuit, rejected the USGA's claim of misappropriation.[4] It reasoned that New Jersey law required the USGA to establish that Data-Max was in direct competition with it, which it failed to do. Because

---

3. The USGA also argued a violation of federal law. More specifically, it argued the false designation of origin provision of Section 43(a) of the Lanham Act. The USGA asserted that Data-Max's use of the handicap formula violated federal law by misleading the golfing public into thinking that the USGA had endorsed Data-Max's products and services.

4. U.S. Golf Association v. St. Andrews System, Data-Max, Inc., 749 F.2d 1028 (3rd Cir. 1984).

the parties were not in direct competition, the claim for misappropriation of its handicap formula failed.

The California Court of Appeal rejected Arroyo's argument that collateral estoppel applied based on the earlier federal decision in *Data Max*. The court found that the operative facts and controlling law before it were significantly different from those presented in the federal litigation. California law does not require direct competition as an essential element to a claim of misappropriation.

In *Arroyo*, the USGA also successfully alleged the existence of consumer confusion. The company was not only using the USGA's Handicap Index, it was also using USGA's name and service marks to promote the company's software program. This use would lead the public to mistakenly think that the Eagle-Trak system had been approved and complied with the USGA's regulatory requirements.

Preemption

Federal law needs to be clear when it preempts state law. State common-law claims outside the scope of copyright law are not preempted.

The California Court of Appeal affirmed the trial court's holding that the misappropriation claim was not preempted by federal law. Arroyo's argument that the USGA's system should be free of all law restricting its use was a whiff. The appellate court sustained the view that the USGA golf handicap formula was not copyrightable under the Copyright Act, and that federal law did not preempt the misappropriation claim based on state law. Federal copyright law expressly provides that it does not preempt any rights under state law not within the subject matter of copyright law.[5]

---

5. 17 U.S.C. § 301(b).

Conclusion

Arroyo Software Corporation developed a software program that used a golf handicap system created by the USGA. It also used the USGA's name and service marks in advertising and promoting its product. These uses were without the permission of the USGA. When Arroyo refused to stop, it was successfully sued and enjoined by the USGA.

Only a golf club or authorized golf association that issues and maintains USGA handicap indexes in full accordance with the USGA handicap system may use the terms "USGA handicap index," "handicap index," "slope," and "USGA handicap" without risking the wrath of the USGA and a visit to the courthouse.

The USGA claimed that Arroyo "obstructed" its rights. The *Rules of Golf* also deal with obstructions. The guiding principle underlying Rule 24 is that relief from an obstruction should be available because it creates an unfair interference.

An "obstruction" in golf is broadly defined to include anything artificial. It includes such things as cart paths, sprinkler heads, irrigation control boxes, bunker rakes, and discarded beer cans. Excluded from the definition, however, are objects defining the portion of the course considered "out of bounds," such as fences, walls, and stakes.

If the obstruction is movable, the application of the rule is simple: The obstruction may be moved. If the ball moves as a result, the ball is simply replaced with no penalty.[6] If the obstruction is immovable, the situation is more complicated. Relief is available so long as the immovable obstruction interferes with the player's swing or stance. In such a case, the player establishes the nearest point, no closer to the hole, where no

---
6. Rule 24-1.

Hole 17: Misappropriation

interference occurs, and drops within one club-length of that point.[7] In order to avoid administrative difficulties, relief from the immovable obstruction is not generally available when the obstruction interferes with the intended flight of the ball. It would be too difficult to administer a rule based on the proposed flight path of the ball. One exception exists where the unfairness is clear, and that can be remedied without controversy. If the player's ball and the immovable obstruction (such as a sprinkler head) are on the putting green, and it would interfere with the line of the putt, relief is available.

Golf fans may remember "Tiger Woods vs. One Famous Boulder" during the 1999 Phoenix Open. On the 13th hole, Tiger's drive put him behind a boulder that prevented him from having a rip at the par 5 green with his second shot. PGA officials, cognizant of the loose impediment rule (Rule 23), concluded that 12 of the assembled spectators could assist in pushing the "loose impediment" aside because the boulder was not solidly imbedded.[8] The rest of the story is that Tiger went for the green, made a birdie, and finished in third place.

---

7. Rule 24-2.b.
8. Decisions 23-1/2, 23-1/3.

Hole 18

Right of Publicity:
Commercial use of videotaped hole-in-one

Federal: *Pooley v. National Hole-In-One Association*, 89 F. Supp. 2d 1108 (D. Ariz. 2000)

The car-rental company Hertz offered $1 million to the first pro to hit a hole in one on the 17th hole during the 1986 Bay Hill Classic golf tournament. Sheldon G. "Don" Pooley, a professional golfer who played on the PGA Tour and the Champions Tour, obliged by hitting one of the richest shots in golf history during the nationally televised final round.

The $1 million prize was split between Don and the Arnold Palmer Hospital in Orlando, Florida. The money was paid out as promised. But Don's good fortune was not the end of this goodluck hole-in-one story.

The Facts

In 1992, the National Hole in One Association produced an eight-minute video promoting its fundraising services. The video described how the Million Dollar Hole-in-One Shootout worked as a proven fundraiser at golfing events:

> Dynamic, challenging, exhilarating. The hole in one, every golfer's dream. The most dramatic shot in all of golf. . . . We've pioneered a new product—the Million-

Dollar Hole-in-One Shootout. It's the ideal fundraiser for any type of charity. Let us put it to work for you. . . . Major corporations such as Oldsmobile, American Airlines . . . have all used our services. . . . Traditionally, the newer events can raise up to $30,000; however, the more mature, well-managed events can raise up to $50,000. That's a lot of money, but we have the track record to back it up. . . . The National Hole-in-One Association is the only entity in America that can provide tournament insurance, promotion, and execution . . . It's gotta be a vehicle to sell or you have nothing, and that's what it is for us and that's why its [sic] so exciting. . . . You advertise a million dollars and it turns some heads. It's different than any other tournament in the Phoenix area. Most of them have car give-aways. . . . This is the only one that has a million dollars and gives them an opportunity to shoot for that million dollars. We pay the premium and if somebody puts it in the can, its [sic] the insurance companies' ball game . . . This is a win-win situation. The sponsors get tremendous media coverage and we raise a lot of money for the charities.

The marketing spiel had the following irresistible clincher:

Has anyone ever made a million-dollar hole in one? You bet. At the 1986 Bay Hill Classic, Don Pooley electrified a national television audience as he knocked his ball in on the fly for a million-dollar ace. Pooley received half the prize and the other half went to the Arnold Palmer's Children Hospital Charity. And in 1991, an amateur named Ray Wilkerson made the shot of a lifetime and generated national exposure for the title sponsor and charity. . . .

The promotional video included a six-second clip of the televised footage of Don teeing off and then walking up the fairway after hitting his prize-winning hole in one. Although the owner of the video clip authorized its use, Don didn't.

In fact, he was upset by its use and sued the National Hole-in-One Association in Pima County Superior Court for the unauthorized appropriation of his right of publicity, which he argued was protected by the law of Arizona.

The Association removed the case from state court to the federal district court on the ground of diversity jurisdiction. The Association then moved to dismiss the claim on the theory that Arizona did not recognize the right of publicity. The motion to dismiss was denied.

The Law

The case was one of first impression, because Arizona had not previously recognized the right of publicity either judicially or legislatively.[1] Because the right of publicity is based on state law, the federal court was required to figure out whether Arizona law supported the claim that was the basis of Don's lawsuit.

The district court found that, in the absence of persuasive authority to the contrary, Arizona law would follow the Restatements of Law, which are treatises intended to guide judges and lawyers on generally applicable principles of law.

The relevant Restatement was the *Restatement (Third) of Unfair Competition*, which essentially says that a defendant should not be allowed to free-ride on the identity of the

---

1. California, for example, recognizes the right of publicity by statute. The California Civil Code provides, in pertinent part, that "[a]ny person who knowingly uses another's name, voice, signature, photograph, or likeness, in any manner . . . for purposes of advertising or selling . . . without such person's prior consent . . . shall be liable for any damages sustained by the person or persons injured as a result thereof."

plaintiff.[2] The theory is that economic freeriding should not be countenanced.

Section 46 of the Restatement (Third) describes the theory in more detail:

> One who appropriates the commercial value of a person's identity by using without consent the person's name, likeness, or other indicia of identity for purposes of trade is subject to liability for the relief appropriate under the rules stated in 48 and 49 [injunctive and damage relief, respectively].

Although this section of the Restatement clearly recognizes and protects the right of publicity, the district court also looked at what other states say. More than half the states recognize a personal property right in the exclusive use of a person's name and likeness for financial gain.[3] The district court concluded that Arizona also would recognize the right. But that was not the end of the analysis.

Incidental Use

The Association lost the argument that Arizona did not recognize the right of publicity, but it was not out of mulligans. It argued that the use of the six-second clip in an eight-minute videotape was "incidental" under Section 47 of the *Restatement (Third) of Unfair Competition*. It was essentially *de minimus*.

Section 47 provides exception for advertising that is considered an "incidental" use:

> The name, likeness, and other indicia of a person's identity are used for purposes of trade under the rule stated

---

[2]. The right of publicity originally was based on protecting the right of privacy.
[3]. Restatement (Third) of Unfair Competition 46 (1995).

in 46 if they are used in advertising the user's goods or services, or are placed on merchandise marketed by the user, or are used in connection with services rendered by the user. However, use for purposes of trade does not ordinarily include the use of a person's identity in news reporting, commentary, entertainment, works of fiction or nonfiction, or in *advertising* that is *incidental to such uses*.[4]

The rationale underlying the incidental use exception is straightforward. Such a use is thought to have no commercial value, and therefore allowing recovery without some accompanying commercial value would be unduly burdensome. Thus, if the use is deemed incidental, the court should find no violation of the right of publicity.[5]

There was little doubt that the six-second clip was brief in relation to the rest of the videotape. Brevity may be the soul of wit, but the court reasoned that the brief or fleeting use of the plaintiff's name and footage did not render the use incidental. The critical issue was whether the use, albeit admittedly brief, had commercial value.

The Association used the video clip for its commercial advantage. It supported the advertising claim that the Shootout was a "proven fundraiser" by using the video clip. Including the plaintiff's name, image, and accomplishment was an integral part of its commercial advertising strategy. The effectiveness of its spiel was promoted by answering the key question: "Has anyone ever made a million-dollar hole in one?" In the view of the

---

4. Restatement (Third) of Unfair Competition 47 (1995).

5. *See* Aligo v. Time-Life Books, Inc., 1994 WL 715605 (N.D. Cal. 1994) (holding that a four-second appearance of a magazine cover featuring the photo of an unnamed and unidentified plaintiff in a 29-minute infomercial promoting a rock music anthology was an incidental use).

court, the fleeting use was not incidental within the context of commercial value to the Association.

First Amendment

The First Amendment to the Constitution provides: "Congress shall make no law . . . abridging the freedom of speech . . . ." The U.S. Supreme Court has held that this protection applies with equal force to the states through the Fourteenth Amendment.[6] But the Court has yet to provide a clear message or general rule to resolve the conflict between the First Amendment and the right of publicity.[7]

The right of publicity raises First Amendment concerns. The First Amendment allows the use of a person's identity, name, or likeness even when the use would violate the right of publicity as long as the use is for expressive purposes, such as news reporting or artistic purposes.

The critical legal question is, to what extent is the right of publicity restricted by the First Amendment when a commercial purpose, such as advertising, is involved?

The First Amendment applies to commercial speech.[8] The language of the First Amendment ("Congress shall make no law . . . abridging the freedom of speech") does not distinguish

---

6. Most of the provisions of the Bill of Rights are now enforceable against state or local government action by virtue of the incorporation doctrine. This doctrine states that provisions of the Bill of Rights that are fundamental to our system of civil liberties, such as the First Amendment, apply to and limit state and local government through the Due Process Clause of the Fourteenth Amendment. *See* Chicago, Burlington & Quincy Railroad Co. v. Chicago, 166 U.S. 226 (1897).

7. Zacchini v. Scripps-Howard Broadcasting, 433 U.S. 562 (1977) (acknowledging that the right of privacy applies to protect the appropriation of the entertainer's work, but failing to articulate a test for resolving the inherent tension between the right and the First Amendment). *See* Comedy III v. Saderup, 25 Cal. 4th 387 (Cal. 2001) (articulating an influential test for balancing the right of publicity with the First Amendment's freedom of expression).

8. *See e.g.*, Central Hudson Gas & Electric v. Public Service Commission, 447 U.S. 557 (1980).

between commercial and noncommercial speech. Nevertheless, the Court has found that commercial speech receives less protection because it is somewhat removed from the core values protected by the First Amendment.

The Association argued that its use was protected by the First Amendment. It argued that the six-second videotape was simply the recording of a historical fact that occurred in public at a golf tournament, and therefore within the legal umbrella of the First Amendment.

The court didn't buy the argument that the Association was simply using and reporting a newsworthy event. The court pointed out that the Association did not create the videotape in connection with reporting a news account, nor did it use the plaintiff's name to communicate an idea. The use was clearly for advertising purposes and commercial advantage.

The court also reasoned that the Association's use was outside the protection of the First Amendment because the video clip implied a false connection between the plaintiff and the association.

Conclusion

The right of publicity falls within the realm of personal property. The scope of the right is defined by state statute[9] or the common law.[10] Therefore, each state defines the level of protection accorded the right.

As a general matter, the right of publicity encompasses the right to own, protect, and profit from one's name, likeness,

---

9. States recognizing the statutory right of publicity include California, Florida, Illinois, Kentucky, Ohio, Pennsylvania, Texas, and Wisconsin.

10. States recognizing the common-law right of publicity include Arizona, Alabama, California, Connecticut, Florida, Georgia, Hawaii, Illinois, Kentucky, Michigan, Minnesota, Missouri, New Hampshire, New Jersey, Ohio, Pennsylvania, South Carolina, Texas, Utah, West Virginia, and Wisconsin.

voice, or identity and to control the commercial use of that identity. Most successful cases involving the right of publicity require a direct link between the unauthorized use and a commercial purpose.

The most compelling policy rationale for recognizing the right is tied to unjust enrichment. It prevents the unauthorized appropriation of one's good will and identity. No useful purpose is served by allowing a defendant to profit at the expense of the plaintiff. A commercial hitchhiker who seeks to capitalize on another's identity should have to pay the fare associated with obtaining consent, or do without. There should be no free ride on the economic back of another.

Although the right of publicity protects against unauthorized uses, it does not protect against every unauthorized use. Some unauthorized uses may be protected by the recognized incidental use doctrine, and other unauthorized uses may fall within the protection of the First Amendment.

Hole 19

Right of Publicity:
"The Masters of Augusta" painting

Federal: *ETW Corporation v. Jireh Publishing, Inc.*, 332 F.3d 915 (6th Cir. 2003), reh'g denied (Sept. 8, 2003)

Eldrick "Tiger" Woods has guarded his privacy more than almost any professional golfer. He named his yacht "Privacy" for a reason. Following his publicly aired infidelities, which led to his divorce in 2010, much of his private life was publicly exposed. As a result, he fell from grace with some fans and sponsors.

But few can dispute the fact that Tiger has had an unprecedented professional career since becoming a pro golfer in the late summer of 1996. In 1997, at age 21, he became the youngest player to win the Masters Tournament by a convincing 12-stroke margin. By 2005, Tiger had collected four green jackets from his victories at the Masters, a number suitable to outfit a well-dressed foursome of leprechauns on St. Patrick's Day.

Tiger hasn't won the Masters since then, and is no longer as dominant as he was in the early years. In 2013, he was voted by his peers Player of the Year for the 11th time. He continues to add wins to his total record and is just a few tournaments shy of Sam Snead's record for PGA Tour victories. In short, Tiger continues to play golf at an extremely high level.

The Facts

In addition to being one of the world's most recognized golfers and celebrities, Tiger is a major business enterprise. Before playing in his first tournament as a professional, Tiger signed endorsement contracts estimated at $70 million. Although some product endorsers scurried to the sidelines as his personal struggles were aired, there is no doubt that he is still a successful marketing enterprise.

Eldrick "Tiger" Woods, Inc. ("Woods"), Tiger's commercial merchandising arm, holds the exclusive right to manage his publicity rights, including his name, image, likeness, and signature. The company also owns the U.S. trademark "Tiger Woods," which includes the right to use his name in connection with art prints and other memorabilia.

The legal fireworks started in 1998. Rick Rush, who bills himself as "America's sports artist," created a limited-edition painting depicting Tiger's 1997 win at Augusta. Striking various golfing poses, the painting depicted Tiger on the prowl. Also shown in the painting are two caddies (one being Tiger's caddy at the time, "Fluff" Cowan) as well as the Augusta National Clubhouse. The images of other recognized golfing legends—Arnold Palmer, Sam Snead, Ben Hogan, Walter Hagen, Bobby Jones, and Jack Nicklaus—hover in the sky-blue background. The artistic message appears to be that Tiger may someday join this pantheon of golfing greats, a prediction that is undoubtedly accurate. Rush's signature appears in the bottom right-hand corner above the title "The Masters of Augusta."

The publisher of the artwork, and target of the lawsuit, was Jireh Publishing. According to the court documents, it sold 250 serigraphs (prints made by a silkscreen process) for $700 apiece, and 5,000 lithographs (prints made by an ink-impression process) for $100 apiece. The painting and prints were similar

Hole 19: Right of Publicity

to a poster of Woods sold by Nike under a license from Woods. Not surprisingly, there was no dispute that Woods's likeness in Rush's artwork was reproduced and sold to make a profit.

Woods fired a "stinger" at the defendant by suing in the Federal District Court for the Northern District of Ohio for trademark infringement (U.S. Registered Trademark 2, 194, 381), unfair competition, deceptive trade practices, and violation of his right of publicity.[1] However, Tiger's awesome prowess on the golf course didn't translate into a legal victory. The court dismissed the complaint. It found that the use of Tiger's trademarked name was fair use under established principles of trademark law, that Tiger's image in the painting was not protected under the argued theories, and that the Master's painting by Rush was protected by the First Amendment.[2]

The Masters of Augusta
By Rick Rush

The Law

Tiger did not lose graciously; he appealed to the Sixth Circuit Court of Appeals. On June 20, 2003, the court of appeals affirmed the district court, and six weeks later denied his request for a rehearing.

---

1. A "stinger" is a specialty golf shot popularized by Tiger Woods. Instead of using a driver or 3-wood off the tee, Tiger sometimes uses a two-iron to hit a low-boring screamer that goes about 270 yards.

2. U.S. Const. amend. I. "Congress shall make no law . . . abridging the freedom of speech . . . ."

The Sixth Circuit applied three related legal rules. First, it applied an ad hoc balancing approach, which balanced Woods's proprietary right of publicity against Rush's right to free expression. Second, it construed the right of publicity as limited by the analogous fair-use principle used in federal copyright law. Finally, it found that Rush's work satisfied the transformativeness test to bring the work within the protection of the First Amendment. The artwork consisted of much more than a mere literal depiction of Tiger Woods. It was a panorama of Woods's victory, with all the trappings of the tournament presented. In short, it was a portrayal of a historic sporting event that Tiger won.

The right of publicity, the first legal rule applied by the Sixth Circuit, is a type of intellectual property right. The right, which is a creature of state law, has been recognized by the Ohio Supreme Court. Violation of the right gives rise to a cause of action for the commercial tort of unfair competition.

Under this theory, a famous person, such as Tiger Woods, has the general right to exploit his or her name or likeness for financial gain. The *Restatement (Third) of Unfair Competition*, Section 46, which is followed in Ohio, generally defines the right of publicity as follows: "One who appropriates the commercial value of a person's identity by using without consent the person's name, likeness, or other indicia of identity for purposes of trade is subject to liability."

But the right of publicity has limits. As suggested by the *Restatement (Third) of Unfair Competition*, the right is limited by a principle analogous to fair use. Under this principle, the substantiality and market effect is analyzed in light of the informational and creative use of the artist.

In balancing the competing interests between the artist and Tiger, the right to free expression, as guaranteed by the First Amendment, is accorded substantial weight. The court states:

Hole 19: Right of Publicity

After balancing the societal and personal interests embodied in the First Amendment against Woods's property rights, we conclude that the effect of limiting Woods's right of publicity in this case is negligible and significantly outweighed by society's interest in freedom of artistic expression. In this case, we find that Woods's right of publicity must yield to the First Amendment.

Tiger is as aggressive in the courts in attempting to protect his right to publicity as he is in attempting to win every golf tournament. But like everyone else, Tiger does not always win.

Conclusion

An inherent and troubling legal tension exists between the right of publicity and the right of freedom of expression. First Amendment protection is not limited to spoken or written words, but also extends to other mediums of expression, including art. Exercising the right of expression may bump into or interfere with the right of publicity, which gives a person a property right to the exclusive use of his or her name or likeness for financial gain.

At one time, commercial speech was unprotected by the First Amendment. That time has long since passed. Commercial speech receives less protection than other forms of speech, however. The Supreme Court has had difficulty satisfactorily defining commercial speech. The best that can be said is that if the purpose and content of a message are to propose a commercial transaction, it is likely to be considered commercial speech.

The purpose of Rush's art was not to propose a commercial transaction, and the fact that it was sold by Rush for a profit did not require it to be classified as commercial speech. The Sixth Circuit found that the art fell within the full protective shield of the First Amendment. Thus, Tiger's right of publicity claim was required to yield to Rush's First Amendment rights.

Hole 20

Trespass and Nuisance:
Golfer liability

Texas: *Malouf v. Dallas Athletic Country Club*, 837 S.W.2d 674 (Tex. Ct. App. 1992)

Ever thought about buying a house on a golf course? For some, owning a home on a golf course with picturesque views can be annoying and sometimes even dangerous.

All golf courses have areas that are marked "out of bounds" (OB). But this does not prevent golf balls from landing OB.[1] Property owners living next to a golf course may find themselves under a steady barrage of golf balls and players seeking to retrieve them. It is not surprising that errant golf balls do not mix well with windows, cars, and neighbors.

The Facts

Edward Malouf, Harry Hollander, and C.M. Presley not only thought about buying, they did buy. The unhappy trio bought houses adjoining the sixth hole of the Gold Golf Course owned

---

1. Rules, Section II: Definitions. The OB line is determined by the nearest inside point in between two stakes or posts at ground level. Determining the actual line between the stakes or posts requires care. In some cases, it may be difficult to determine whether a ball is actually out of bounds by quickly looking at it. This determination may be challenging because a ball is OB only when all of it is out of bounds. When the ball leaves the course and lands on private property, it doesn't take a cadastral survey to conclude that the ball is OB.

173

and managed by the Dallas Athletic Country Club (DAC). They learned firsthand the hazards of living next to a golf course. Each suffered damage to his car or home from golf balls that were hit by unidentified golfers. Edward's Oldsmobile Cutlass station wagon was damaged, Harry's Porsche was hit, and C.M.'s Ford Mustang and fiberglass awning were both pelted by stray shots.

The trio individually complained to DAC, but they were told that the club's policy was not to reimburse neighbors for damage caused by unidentified third-party golfers. The general manager for the club, Robert Jones, explained that DAC had a procedure for dealing with stray shots that cause damage, which turned out not to be particularly useful.

After receiving a neighbor's complaint, the golf course management would ask players in the likely foursomes whether anyone hit the offending shot. If someone came forward and admitted it, confession presumably being good for the soul, the DAC then would either charge that person for the damage and compensate the complaining neighbor for the loss or put the player and injured party together to sort the matter out. Not surprisingly, this procedure didn't always result in compensating the injured neighbor.

If you can't catch or find the responsible golfer, what do you do? You sue the golf course, which is what the plaintiffs did.

The Law

Every lawsuit needs a legal theory. The trio sued the DAC for their property injuries on the theory of trespass in a justice-of-the-peace court.[2] It ruled in favor of the complaining trio, and

---

2. Plaintiffs also claimed DAC was negligent, but the court rejected this claim because the DAC had acted reasonably to prevent foreseeable harm. Prior to the events that resulted in plaintiffs' claims, the DAC had extensively revised and

Hole 20: Trespass and Nuisance

the DAC then appealed the decision to the Dallas County Court. After a new trial, the county court ruled in favor of the DAC and against the plaintiffs. The unhappy plaintiffs then filed an appeal in the court of appeals, which affirmed the county court.

Under English common law, any intentional and unprivileged entry onto land in the possession of another was considered a trespass. American law follows this approach. The *Restatement (Second) of Torts* sets forth the commonly accepted principles of trespass to land and chattels.[3]

> One is subject to liability to another for trespass, irrespective of whether he thereby causes harm to any legally protected interest of the other, if he intentionally (a) enters land in the possession of the other, or causes *a thing or a third person to do so* . . . .
>
> Trespass to a chattel (personal property) may be committed by intentionally (a) dispossessing another of the chattel, or (b) using or intermeddling with a chattel in the possession of another.

Trespass is an intentional tort. It is commonly distinguished from other torts, such as negligence or nuisance.

Trespass to real property involves the physical invasion of the land. Trespass to personal property involves interfering or meddling with the owner's right of possession of movables, such as the cars. In both cases, the plaintiff must prove that the country club or the golfer intended to commit an act that violated the plaintiff's protected interest.

---

redesigned the layout of fairway number 6, under the guidance of Jack Nicklaus, in order to minimize misdirected shots leaving the course. Golfers were required to aim left, away from the homes on the right. It also installed six-foot photina hedges and a fence as part of the redesign. Adjoining landowners also frequently argue for protection under the law of nuisance.

3. Restatement (Second) of Torts 158 (land), 217 (personal property) (1965)

In the typical trespass case between an adjoining property owner and the golf course, the golf course does not challenge the owner's assertion that the golf balls have landed on the property or caused damage. Both the invasion and the damage are usually undisputed. Therefore, most cases involving the theory of trespass turn on finding the required intent.

The court of appeals found no evidence to support the claim that the golfers who caused the damage intended that their golf balls enter the plaintiffs' property. The record contained no evidence to support the claim that the DAC intended to commit an act of trespass violating the plaintiffs' property rights.

Conclusion

Accidents happen. The golfers who damaged the plaintiffs' personal property intended to hit their golf balls toward hole number six. They did not intend to hit the plaintiffs' cars.

The fact that a ball might "slice" or "hook" onto the plaintiffs' property was an unintended consequence. The failure of the plaintiffs to show intent on the part of the golfers meant that there was no basis for finding the DAC liable. As a result, the appellate court upheld the trial court's finding that the DAC was not liable on the theory of trespass.

When a golf ball hit by a golfer unintentionally causes property damage, it will be difficult to base liability on the theory of trespass, especially when the suit is against the golf course. Other theories of liability might prove more successful.[4]

A trespass to land claim might be successfully brought in certain cases. The essence of the theory of trespass to land is

---

4. *See e.g.*, Sierra Screw Products v. Azusa Green, Inc., 88 Cal. App. 3d 358 (1979) (holding an injunction requiring the owners of the golf course to redesign two golf holes to minimize the nuisance and resulting damage to adjacent landowners from the continuous intrusion of golf balls).

Hole 20: Trespass and Nuisance

interference with the owner's right to exclusive possession and control of the land. If a golfer, for example, enters private property to reclaim an out-of-bounds ball, the golfer has committed a trespass to land, unless consent to recover the ball is expressed or can be implied. Property owners frequently post "keep out" signs to negate the possibility of implied consent. Even if a suit is successful, unless there is some injury that can be quantified, the neighbor may receive only nominal damages.

With respect to the law of trespass, the golf course might be found jointly and severally liable if it can be shown that it somehow aided or ratified the acts of the trespassing golfer. It also might be liable if its employees committed the trespass by entering the adjoining property. Otherwise, the law of trespass is not likely to be much help in a suit against a golf course.

The next time you or someone in your group have the urge to retrieve an out-of-bounds ball on someone's private property, you might remember the law of trespass. It may apply.

Hole 21

Trespass and Nuisance:
Golf course liability

Georgia: *DeSarno v. Jam Golf Management, LLC*, 670 S.E.2d 889 (2008), cert. denied (2009)

G olf courses can be ideal neighbors. Well-maintained fairways, trees, ponds, and environmentally protected areas provide some desirable amenities. But golf courses also can be troublesome daytime neighbors.

Where the Golf Course Ends (and Problems Begin)
There is a place where the golf course ends,
And the neighbor's grass grows soft and white,
And there the golf ball rests from its errant flight,
And there the neighbor burns crimson and bright.[1]

The *Rules of Golf* cover what a golfer should do after hitting a ball out-of-bounds (OB).[2] In some cases, it may be difficult

---

1. Author's adaption of "Where the Sidewalk Ends," by Shel Silverstein.
2. Rules of Golf, Rule 27-1.b. provides a penalty of stroke and distance: "If a ball is out of bounds, the player must play a ball, under penalty of one stroke, as nearly as possible at the spot from which the original ball was last played."
   At the 2013 Masters, the language "nearly as possible at the spot from which the original ball was last played" of Rule 27-1.a. was at the center of a controversy. On the 15th hole, Tiger Woods took a drop under 27-1.a. The Rules Committee initially determined the drop conformed with Rule 27. In a television interview following the round and after he submitted his score card, Tiger said he went two yards farther back and tried to take two yards off the shot. The problem is that two yards farther back was not nearly as close to the spot from which the original ball was played.

to determine whether a ball is actually OB by quickly looking at it, because the entire ball must be out. Other cases are clear. A golf ball that leaves the course and lands on private property is clearly OB. And when damage occurs, the neighbor is apt to "burn crimson and bright" and "seek the first lawyer in sight."

The Facts

Creekside Golf & Country Club in Hiram, Georgia, opened in 1999. In 2003, James and Susan DeSarno decided to build their dream home on a lot next to the ninth hole. The proximity to the golf course was considered an attraction. James played the course on a number of occasions, and was aware that errant balls from the ninth tee box might hit their to-be-developed home. For a time James was a member of the golf course, but like many love affairs, it would not last.

The developer of the land surrounding the golf course agreed to subject those residential lots, including the DeSarnos's lot, to an easement in favor of the course. The easement agreement, which the DeSarnos knew existed, allowed "golf balls unintentionally to come upon the Lot . . . and for Golfers at reasonable times and in a reasonable manner to come upon the exterior portions of a Lot . . . to retrieve errant golf balls." It also provided that "[u]nder no circumstances shall the . . . Golf Course Owner . . . be held liable for any damage or injury resulting from errant golf balls or the exercise of these easements." The easement did not, however, say anything about a golfer's liability for any damage he or she might cause.

The Rules Committee was forced to reconvene. Tiger could have been disqualified by the Rules Committee. It instead waived the penalty of disqualification under Rule 33, and imposed a two-shot penalty. Many think Tiger should have been disqualified. One thing is certain, the ruling will be debated for a long time. For the record, Adam Scott beat Angel Cabrera in a thrilling playoff. Tiger finished tied for fourth place, four strokes behind the leaders Scott and Cabrera.

The dream of living on a golf course turned into a nightmare as Creekside became more and more popular. Business at the course was brisk, with about 30,000 rounds being played there annually.

The problem was that many right-handed golfers were slicing golf balls onto their property. Left-handed golfers were not immune from hooking their shots there too.

The result was the same. The DeSarnos found themselves under a regular barrage of 10 to 15 balls a day. The incoming bombardment over about a two-year period took a toll: 23 broken windows, 26 chips or breaks on the siding of their house, two dents to their car, broken lights, and many near misses to their children. For reasons of safety, the children were banned from playing in their yard.

Enough was enough; the DeSarnos sued for damages. They also asked for injunctive relief to bar golfers from playing the ninth hole as it was currently configured. Their lawsuit named as defendants Jam Golf Management, LLC (the operator of Creekside), Chuck Clancy Golf (the owner of Creekside), Creekside Golf and Country Club, and Jeffery Clancy (the general manager of the course). None of the named defendants were involved in the sale of the lot to the DeSarnos.

The Law

The lawsuit was based on trespass and nuisance. The legal distinction between trespass and private nuisance is clear in theory but quite murky in practice. The law of trespass protects an owner's right to exclude others from real property.[3] It also

---

3. *Restatement (Second) of Torts* 158 reflects the American law with respect to trespass to land:

> One is subject to liability for trespass, irrespective of whether he thereby causes any harm to any legally protected interest of the other, if he intentionally . . . enters land in the possession of the other, or causes a thing or a third person to do so . . . .

protects an owner from interference with personal property by others.[4] The law of private nuisance protects an owner's right to the use and enjoyment of real property.[5] Both trespass and private nuisance are considered intentional torts, which means that the plaintiff must prove that the defendant intended the act that invades or interferes with the protected interest. Because many of the underlying facts are common to both theories, they are frequently alleged in the same lawsuit.

Creekside has the affirmative right under the terms of the easement to use the burdened land for errant shots without liability. The language describing the right was an obvious problem for the plaintiffs. To avoid it, they argued that the extremely large number of errant balls hitting their property constituted an excessive use of the easement, and therefore the actual use of the easement exceeded the scope of the easement.[6]

The general rule is that an easement holder may use the easement so long as the use is not excessive. In determining whether the use is excessive, courts look to the intent of the parties who created the easement. Unless otherwise indicated by the evidence, courts usually presume that the parties intended that the use of the easement may evolve to accommodate reasonably foreseeable changes.

The court reasoned the easement expressly allowed Creekside to use the DeSarnos's property as a landing zone for

---

4. *Restatement (Second) of Torts* 218 reflects the general view with respect to trespass to chattels:

> One who commits a trespass to a chattel is subject to liability to the possessor of the chattel if, but only if, (a) he dispossesses the other of the chattel, (b) the chattel is impaired as to its condition, quality, or value . . ..

5. *Restatement (Second) of Torts* 821D provides that a private nuisance is "a nontrespassory invasion of another's interest in the private use and enjoyment of land."

6. In rare cases, a court may declare an easement forfeited for misuse, but this is an extraordinary remedy that is available only in the most egregious cases. There is no evidence that the plaintiffs attempted to argue forfeiture.

errant balls and exonerated it from liability. The DeSarnos had actual notice of the easement. They therefore had no reason to complain about the existence and use of the easement.

Excessive use, the court reasoned, was not related to the number of times the easement was used by balls landing on the property. So long as the easement was not limited, which it wasn't, Creekside and its golfers could use the property as an unintentional "landing zone" without the fear of liability. The number of times an express easement is used does not automatically transform the use into legally objectionable conduct. Therefore, the court found that no claim of trespass or nuisance could be maintained. Except for the golf balls they salvaged, the plaintiffs were left empty handed.

Conclusion

Several points are worth noting. First, the plaintiffs' property was expressly burdened by a written easement that provided under no circumstance shall the golf course be held liable for any damage or injury resulting from errant golf balls. The court reasoned that the expressed easement allowed conduct that otherwise might be considered a trespass or private nuisance.[7] Had the easement been limited and the limit exceeded, the outcome presumably would have been different.

The plaintiffs could not avoid the burden imposed by the easement by arguing lack of notice. They had actual knowledge of the easement. Even if they did not have actual knowledge, the easement was recorded in the chain of title to their property, and this would be considered legal notice.

---

7. *See* Sierra Screw Products v. Azusa Green, Inc., 88 Cal. App. 3d 358 (1979) (upholding plaintiff's nuisance claim, issuing an injunction requiring the defendant to redesign two golf holes to minimize the nuisance, and rejecting the defendant's claim of an implied easement for the intrusion of golf balls on the plaintiff's property).

Second, the case says nothing about the liability of the golfers who hit the errant shots. To the extent that the plaintiffs pursue them as legal quarry, several challenges exist. The most obvious practical challenge is to identify the offending golfers and to bring them to ground as defendants. The finger-pointing refrain "it wasn't me" can be anticipated.

Assuming the plaintiffs can identify the golfers, the next challenge is to formulate a legal theory that will allow recovery. The easement allows golfers at reasonable times and in a reasonable manner to come on the exterior portions of their property to retrieve errant golf balls.

The plaintiffs have additional obstacles to chasing the offending golfers. The two theories, trespass and nuisance, are intentional torts. Successfully arguing that the offending golfer has committed an intentional tort would be a challenge, because in all likelihood the golfer didn't intend to hit the ball OB.

The fact that a ball unintentionally hooks or slices onto their property is likely to be considered an accident. Of course, the plaintiffs might argue negligence, but the defense of assumption of the risk (buying a house adjacent to the golf course) is likely.

Ultimately, the DeSarnos are left with taking defensive measures, such as installing screens, nets, trees, or other defensive greenery. Of course, such measures may reduce the desirability of having a dream home next to a golf course.

Hole 22

Trespass and Nuisance:
Assault and battery

Rhode Island: *Hennessey v. Pyne*,
694 A.2d 691 (1997)

The Facts

Returning home from church on a pleasant Sunday morning in mid-September, Eileen Hennessey paused to smell the flowers in her front-yard garden. Her morning reverie was abruptly ended when she was hit in the head by a golf ball. Sometimes it can be dangerous to stop and smell the flowers.

Eileen lived next to the Rhode Island Louisquisset Golf Club. Her condominium was located on the crook of the dogleg on the 11th hole. From the teeing ground, the hole swerved slightly to the left. Her back yard was about 14 feet from the edge of the out-of-bounds marker and approximately halfway down the fairway from the teeing ground.

Eileen testified that she did not see the ball coming because trees blocked her view of the 11th hole teeing area. The golf course's assistant pro, Michael Pyne, hit the wayward shot, which was modestly described in court documents as having "veered slightly left." His airmailed shot clearly had the wrong address.

Eileen had had trouble with golfers and their errant shots before. At her deposition, she testified that golfers regularly peppered her condominium with golf balls. For approximately

five years, during the heaviest part of the playing season, she said that her condominium was hit about ten times a day. Eileen claimed that sometimes her condominium was hit twice in the same day *by the same golfer*. Presumably, these repeat offenders were simply following the Rules of Golf on out-of-bounds, which is reload and hit again.[1]

She was not alone in her knowledge of the problem. Michael Pyne, the assistant pro and author of the misfired shot, knew about the location of the condominiums and of the propensity for the club's golfers to strafe them with misfired golf shots.

Eileen tried to protect herself and her property from damage caused by errant golf balls. She installed Plexiglas™ in various windows of her home because of the frequency with which golf balls pelted the exterior and broke her glass windows.

Eileen Hennessey sued Michael Pyne on a variety of theories, including assault and battery.

---

1. *Rule 27-1.b.* Ball Out of Bounds. If a ball is out of bounds, the player must play a ball, under penalty of one stroke, as nearly as possible at the spot from which the original ball was last played. This rule would require Michael to play another ball from the spot (or as nearly as possible to that spot) from which he clobbered Eileen. He would be subject to several penalties under the rules (stroke and distance) as well as having to defend himself in a lawsuit.

The Law

Although various theories of liability were argued, the assault and battery claim is interesting. Why did the Supreme Court reject it? In short, the facts did not support the theory.

Claims of assault and battery may be pursued by private parties as torts or prosecuted by the state as crimes.[2] Broadly speaking, a tort is a civil wrong, other than a breach of contract, which a court will remedy by awarding damages. Eileen sued in tort because she wanted money.

Assault and battery are two different types of intentional torts. It is common to speak of assault and battery in one smooth breath because the facts that give rise to the claims often support both theories. However, they are separate legal theories that require a plaintiff to prove different elements in order to prevail.

The law of assault protects a person from the apprehension or fear of harmful or offensive contact. The defendant must intend that the plaintiff fear or apprehend the contact. In addition, the defendant's act must create a reasonable apprehension of immediate harmful or offensive contact to the plaintiff because the law does not protect one against exaggerated fear of contact.

In order for the plaintiff to be in reasonable apprehension, he or she must obviously be aware of the defendant's threatening act. Eileen was not aware of Michael's presence on the teeing ground, nor did she fear any injury from the errant golf ball that ultimately hit her. Recall that Eileen was in her front yard. Thus, she was unable to establish the critical fact that she had any reasonable apprehension of imminent bodily harm from

---

2. The criminal law definitions of assault sometimes emphasize the intent to injure and the risk of escalating violence instead of the apprehension of a battery. As a result, criminal assault cases are not necessarily sound precedent for civil tort cases.

Michael's conduct. In addition to this problem, Eileen failed to prove that Michael had the necessary intent needed to establish a compensable claim under the law of assault.

In contrast to assault, battery is harmful or offensive contact with the plaintiff's person that is caused by an act of the defendant who intended to produce such a result. The law of battery protects individuals from intentional and nonconsensual contact. It protects a person's body, as well as anything closely associated with the person and identified with the individual's personal dignity, such as the clothing a person is wearing.

In the words of the court, a battery is "an act that was intended to cause, and in fact did cause, an offensive contact with or unconsented touching of or trauma upon the body of another, thereby generally resulting in the consummation of the assault. . . . Intent to injure a plaintiff, however, is unnecessary in a situation in which a defendant willfully sets in motion a force that in its ordinary course causes the injury." The key words are "act that was intended." Thus, the plaintiff's burden is to prove that the defendant intended the harm.

Eileen argued that Michael intentionally hit the golf ball that struck her, and thus his act was a battery. Her reasoning was not persuasive to the court. Although Michael clearly intended to hit the ball, there was no evidence that he intended to hit *her* with it.

In short, Michael's intent was limited to committing a battery on the ball, and perhaps on the fairway, by taking a divot, followed by a battery to the green when his ball landed, followed by a possible one-putt battery on the hole. But his intent was limited to these types of inconsequential batteries.

While it was indisputable that Michael's teeing off on the ball willfully set in motion a force, namely hitting the ball, that force did not "in its ordinary course" cause Eileen's injury. Indeed, if the ball had traveled in its ordinary course after having been hit by Michael, one can safely assume that the ball would have found the fairway rather than Eileen Hennessey's head.

Conclusion

The Supreme Court of Rhode Island found that the trial court was correct in dismissing Eileen's claim of assault and battery. It also rejected her nuisance claim and her husband's loss-of-consortium claim, but that's another story.

But Michael was not out of the woods, where in truth he would have been better off. The Supreme Court found that the trial court should not have dismissed her claim of negligence and that she should be given the opportunity to prove negligence. The matter was remanded to the trial court because the record was incomplete on the issue of negligence.

The record does not indicate certain important facts that might materially affect her negligence claim. These include: How many yards was the golf hole from the tee? How many strokes were par for the hole? What golf club was used by Pyne on the tee? What was the exact distance of Hennessey's front-yard garden and condominium from the tee? Was he trying to cut the corner? It is also unclear from the record whether Michael actually saw, or could have seen, Eileen from where he addressed the ball on the tee. Finally, the record does not indicate whether Pyne shouted "fore" or attempted to give any warning either before or after he saw his tee shot heading off the course and toward Hennessey's condominium.

Although I do not know how Eileen fared on her negligence claim on remand, I am reasonably certain that she wasn't looking to Michael for golf lessons.

Hole 23

Golf Course Private Easement:

Abandonment

California: *Bernardo Heights Country Club v. Community Association of Bernardo Heights* (D024460), Fourth Appellate District (April 6, 1998)

The *Rules of Golf* deal with the subject of abandonment. Under Rule 27, a player may hit a provisional ball when the player thinks the ball has gone out of bounds or is lost outside a water hazard.[1] If the ball is either found or in bounds, the player must abandon the provisional ball and play the original ball.[2] As much as a player might like to abandon a bad shot, the player is stuck with playing the original ball. If a player doesn't abandon the provisional ball, the player is penalized for playing the wrong ball.[3]

Abandonment is encountered in another situation. A player is allowed five minutes to search for a ball. If the ball isn't found

---

1. Rule 27-2 (Provisional Ball). Before hitting the provisional ball, the player must inform an opponent that he or she is hitting a provisional ball. The USGA decisions interpreting the Rule give examples of statements that do not satisfy the Rule. Comments such as "I'm going to re-load" or "I'd better hit another one" do not comply with the Provisional Ball Rule.

2. Rules, Definition, "Lost Ball." The ball is deemed lost if the player has made a stroke at a provisional ball. This definition is the legal equivalent of abandonment. Thus, if the provisional ball is hit a second time before finding the original ball or determining it to be in bounds, the provisional ball is the ball in play.

3. Rule 15-3 (Wrong Ball). The penalty for playing the wrong ball is different for match play (loss of hole) and stroke play (two strokes).

193

The Little Book of Golf Law

within that five-minute search window, the Rules declare that the ball is lost. This is legal equivalent of forced abandonment.[4]

Abandonment under the *Rules of Golf* has different consequences than under the law abandonment. In addition, the legal theory of abandonment stresses the intent of the owner, where intent plays less of a role in golf.[5]

The Facts

The Bernardo Heights Country Club ("Country Club") is a private golf course situated near San Diego, California. The course is located within the planned residential community of Bernardo Heights. As is common with many planned developments, the developer, in this case Genstar Development, Inc., created a homeowner's association ("Association") to operate and maintain the community in accordance with the provisions contained

---

4. Rules, Definition, "Lost Ball." A ball is deemed lost if not found or identified within five minutes after beginning to search for it.

5. A player is not required to look for a wayward ball. In this sense, intent may be thought to come into play—the intent to forgo looking for the ball. But if some helpful soul finds the wayward ball, the player is required to play the original ball if it is found within the five minute search window. In this case, the provisional ball must be abandoned regardless of intent.

Hole 23: Golf Course Private Easement

in a master declaration of covenants, conditions and restrictions (CC&Rs).

The CC&Rs govern all the property in the Bernardo Heights development, including the golf course. In what many might consider Dickensian tangled legalese, the CC&Rs provided:

> All of the property in the Community shall be owned, held, conveyed, encumbered, used, occupied and improved subject to the easements, liens, covenants, conditions and restriction *stated in this Community Declaration* (italics added for emphasis). . . . All of the easements, liens, restrictions and covenants [are] equitable servitudes and shall run with the title to said real property and shall be binding on all parties having or acquiring any right, title or interest therein or thereto and shall be for the benefit of each Owner of any portion thereof and inure to the benefit of and binding upon each successor in interest of such Owners.

In 1986, Genstar Development sold the golf course to the Bernardo Heights Country Club. Between the signing of the deed to the Country Club and its subsequent recording, Genstar granted the Association several reserved "in gross" (personal) easements over the slope-areas adjoining the golf course. In simple terms, this meant that the Association had a legal right to use the slopes. The golf course had the legal title to the slopes, but the slopes were subject to the Association's easements or right of use.

At the time the easements were conveyed to the Association, Genstar wore the legal hat of both the grantor and the grantee. Why? Because Genstar, as the developer, controlled the Association. The Association did not assume majority control until 1988, some two years after the sale to the Country Club.

The easements were for the purpose of providing irrigation and maintenance of the slopes. From the Association's perspective, both a benefit and burden attached to the easements. On the one hand, the Association received the benefit of aesthetically pleasing and stable slopes, some of which were adjacent to and viewed by individual homeowners living within the residential community. The easements also allowed the Association to go on the property owned by the Country Club to maintain and irrigate the slopes.

On the other hand, the Association was burdened with the financial obligation of maintaining and irrigating the easements. In 1992, the Association said this cost was running about $20,000 a year. In 1994, the Association determined that the cost of maintaining and irrigating the easements exceeded its benefit. In short, the Association wanted out of this financial burden.

The Association filed a legal notice to abandon the easements, and pursuant to it stopped maintaining and irrigating the slopes. If the abandonment was effective, the Country Club would have had to assume these financial obligations, which it resisted.

With the developer Genstar out of the picture, the Country Club sued the Association to enforce the easements. It wasn't going to let the Association off the financial hook without a fight.

The Law

Under principles of contract law, a properly executed contract normally binds only the parties to the contract. A contract normally does not bind third persons who are not parties to the contract. You might think of it in terms of not being bound by a bet on the golf course unless you agree to it.

Hole 23: Golf Course Private Easement

In matters involving real property, this principle has been adjusted to meet society's needs. It is often desirable to create obligations that are binding on parties who were not parties to the original contract. Thus, for example, if a real estate developer agrees with a purchaser that the property should be used only for residential use, normally it is important that the residential use restriction also apply to all subsequent purchasers of the property. The parties want the property to be used for residential purposes regardless of who may own it in the future.

Real property law has a way of allowing this. If the promise legally binds whoever owns the land, it is said by lawyers to "run with the land." This phrase is descriptive of the fact that the promise binds subsequent purchasers. To ensure that subsequent purchasers have notice of the promise and are not surprised by unknown obligations, the agreement is recorded in a master declaration of CC&Rs, which is available for public inspection by any subsequent purchaser.

The Association was aware of its obligation so there was no surprise as to its obligations. It just wanted out of them.

Abandonment of an easement occurs when the holder of the easement manifests the intent to abandon it. The Superior Court of San Diego County granted the Association's motion for summary judgment affirming its right to abandon the easements. The trial court also found that the deeds of easement did not create covenants or equitable servitudes. Moreover, even if the deeds did, they were not legally binding on the Association.

The Country Club appealed to the Fourth Appellate District, which affirmed the judgment in an unpublished opinion. The Country Club argued that the Association could not legally abandon its obligation to maintain the slopes because the "deeds of easement" created a binding covenant or equitable servitude. Simply put, the Country Club argued that the legal rules concerning abandonment of an easement did not apply, and that the Association couldn't simply abandon its obligations.

The appellate court rejected this argument. It reasoned that the conveyances creating the interests were personal to the Association, and thus did not resemble covenants or equitable servitudes that bind third parties. The court reasoned:

> Because the deeds of easement did not create a covenant running with the land or an equitable servitude binding on the members of the Community Association and their successors in interest, Community Association was entitled to treat them as that which they purported to be deeds of easement subject to extinguishment by release and abandonment.

The court examined the documents creating the easements and found that nothing in them foreclosed abandonment. It further held that the Association properly recorded the notices of abandonment as to each of the slope easements. The court relied on the traditional theory that an easement may be terminated through abandonment.[6] Once the easements were extinguished, this left the Country Club with the unencumbered title to the slopes and the Association without any continuing obligation to maintain or irrigate them.

Conclusion

An easement may be terminated by abandonment. In order to abandon the easements, the Association had to affirmatively manifest the intent to relinquish its entitlement, which the Asso-

---

6. The court of appeal observed that "[t]he issue of whether the deeds of easement evidence a contract between the parties is not before us in this appeal." It was not addressing Genstar's liability, if any.

Hole 23: Golf Course Private Easement

ciation did when it filed the notices of abandonment. The courts uniformly hold that nonuse of an easement does not result in termination. Thus, the Association could not simply discontinue maintaining and irrigating the sloped areas in the hope of ending its obligations.

A real covenant or equitable servitude may be terminated by a written release from the benefit holder, but one cannot unilaterally slip out from under a burden. Therefore, had the court accepted the Country Club's characterization of the Association's interest as a covenant or equitable servitude, which it did not, the Association would not have been able to unilaterally abandon the burden of maintaining and irrigating the slopes without legal consequence. The Country Club would have been entitled to claim damages or injunctive relief for the Association's breach.

Part IV
Intellectual Property

Hole 24

Patent Infringement:
Doctrine of equivalents

Federal: *Wilson Sporting Goods v. David Geoffrey & Associates d/b/a/ Slazenger*, and *Dunlop Slazenger Corp. aka Dunlop Sports Corp.*, 904 F.2d 677 (Fed. Cir. 1990), cert. denied, 498 U.S. 992 (1990)

Today golfers can purchase golf balls featuring titanium, tungsten, or magnesium powders mixed into the cover or core. Before these and other advances in technology found their way into the market, golf ball manufacturers focused on improving balls by varying the dimple design on the cover of the ball.

After the golf ball leaves the face of the golf club, the ball is controlled by essentially two forces: gravity and aerodynamics. These forces control the flight of the ball no matter how strongly the golfer protests or otherwise invokes the name of God.

The dimples on a golf ball affect the drag and lift of the ball and influence both distance and control. The general effect of dimples is dramatic. A well-hit, smooth golf ball would travel about half as far as a golf ball with dimples.

A dimpled ball produces less drag than a smooth ball. The dimples on the ball create a thin, turbulent boundary layer of air around the surface. This layer decreases the size of the turbulent wake following the ball and reduces drag.

Dimples also affect lift. The spin of the ball makes the air pressure on the lower half of the ball higher than on the upper half, and this creates lift. This spin contributes about half of the lift. The other half is provided by the dimples.

The dimple pattern on the cover of the golf ball aids aerodynamic optimization. Golf ball dimples may be numerous or few, and can vary in shape, width, depth, location, and other features. The science behind dimple design is complicated, but the basics of drag and lift are straightforward.

The Facts

Wilson Sporting Goods is a major sporting goods company that sells a wide range of products, including golf balls. Wilson, which sells such well-known balls as ProStaff and Ultra, holds a patent for a dimple configuration issued by the U.S. Patent and Trademark Office (PTO).

Dunlop is a golf ball competitor of Wilson. Dunlop's Slazenger golf balls are distributed through David Geoffrey & Associates (DGA), and its Maxfli golf balls are sold through various distributors.

The patented location of the Wilson dimples was designed to create a symmetrical distribution to enhance the flight performance of the ball.[1] The dimples described in the Wilson patent are arranged by dividing the cover of a spherical golf ball into 80 imaginary spherical triangles. The dimples (typically

---

1. Claim 1 of the Wilson patent 168 reads:

    1. A golf ball having a spherical surface with a plurality of dimples formed therein and six great circle paths which do not intersect any dimples, the dimples being arranged by dividing the spherical surface into twenty spherical triangles corresponding to the faces of a regular icosahedron, each of the twenty triangles being sub-divided into four smaller triangles consisting of a central triangle and three apical triangles by connecting the midpoints [of the sides] of each of said twenty triangles along great circle paths, said dimples being arranged so that the dimples do not intersect the sides of any of the central triangles.

Hole 24: Patent Infringement

several hundred) then are placed into strategic locations in the triangles.[2]

In 1988, Wilson separately sued Dunlop and DGA in the U.S. District Court of South Carolina. Wilson accused Dunlop of infringing specific claims of its 168 patent. It also made a general accusation of infringement against DGA. The dispute

---

2. For those interested in the technical aspects, the triangles are constructed as follows. First, the ball is divided into an imaginary icosahedron (Fig. 1). The golf ball is completely covered by 20 imaginary equilateral triangles, five of which join tips at each pole of the ball and 10 of which surround its equator. Second, the midpoints of each of the sides of each of the 20 icosahedral triangles are located, marked as "X's" on Figure 2. Third, the midpoints are joined, thus subdividing each icosahedral triangle into four smaller triangles. The central sub-triangles are referred to in the patent claims as "central triangles" ("A" in Figure 3), whereas the three sub-triangles surrounding each central triangle are referred to as "apical triangles." The latter are so named because each of them contains an apex or tip of the larger icosahedral triangle. The resulting 80 imaginary triangles on the golf ball are shown in Figure 3. Critically important are the light lines which join the midpoints. As can be seen from Figure 3, they form the arcs of circles on the ball which pass completely around the widest part of the ball. There are six such circles, referred to in the patent as "great circles."

Figures 1, 2, and 3

In discussing the technology associated with Wilson's claim, the court of appeals observed:

All of the claims of the 168 patent require this basic golf ball having eighty sub-triangles and six great circles. Particular claims require variations on the placement of dimples in the triangles, with one common theme—the dimples must be arranged on the surface of the ball so that no dimple intersects any great circle. Equivalently stated, the dimples must be arranged on the surface of the ball so that no dimple intersects the side of any central triangle. See Figure 4, below. When the dimples are arranged in this manner, the ball has six axes of symmetry, compared to prior balls which had only one axis of symmetry.

Figure 4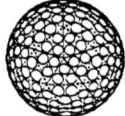

This was Wilson's view of the prior art, which was disputed by Dunlop. The parties agreed, however, that every golf ball has at least one great circle which is not intersected by dimples. It is the "mold parting line," a seam around the ball which is created where the two halves of the mold used to make the ball are joined.

205

between Wilson and Dunlop and DGA focused on the location of the dimples on the surface of the cover and not their shape or width.

In the Wilson-Dunlop suit, a jury determined that the Wilson patent was valid, and that the Dunlop golf balls (the Maxfli Tour Limited MD, the Maxfli Tour Limited HT, the Slazenger Interlock 480 Surlyn, and the Slazenger Interlock 480 Balata) infringed the Wilson patent. Wilson also prevailed in its suit against DGA on the theory of collateral estoppel.

Dunlop and DGA appealed to the Federal Circuit where the cases were consolidated. The court found that the Wilson claims were not infringed under the doctrine of equivalents. The U.S. Supreme Court declined to grant review.

The Law
The Basics of Patent Law

The U.S. Constitution authorizes Congress to establish a patent system to promote the progress of science and useful arts by giving authors and inventors the exclusive right to their respective writings and discoveries for a limited time. Pursuant to this authority, Congress has established a statutory system for the issuance and protection of patents. A federal patent gives the patentee the right to prevent others from making, using, or selling the patented invention without the patent holder's consent. Patents are now protected from infringement by federal law for a period of 20 years from the date of filing, not issuance.

To get a patent, the applicant must apply to the PTO. The patent application must describe the invention by written specification. This specification is a critical part of the patent process because it gives the public, as well as the patentee, notice as to what is protected. The written specification typically consists of various standard parts, such as a background, a summary, and

Hole 24: Patent Infringement

one or more claims, which delineate the elements and limitations to the invention.

To be patentable, the invention must be distinguishable from the prior art by being both novel[3] and non-obvious.[4] It must be an advancement beyond the prior art, which is generally defined as the knowledge available at a given time to a person of ordinary skill in the art. If it is not, the invention is not entitled to patent protection. The determination of whether a patent is obvious, and thus not protected, is one of the most litigated issues in patent law.

A patent infringement claim may be formulated as a literal infringement or as an equivalent infringement. When the invention is a device, the plaintiff-patentee must establish that the infringer makes, uses or sells a device that includes each of the elements identified in the patent. Proving a literal infringement is often difficult when minor variations to the invention have been made by the alleged infringer. Clever infringers often attempt this ploy to avoid the grasp of a literal infringement.

But the law anticipates such cleverness. When it is not possible to prove a literal claim, the plaintiff still may be entitled to patent protection. If the infringing product appropriates the essence of the patented invention, the doctrine of equivalents may step in to give the patentee protection from infringement.

Although Dunlop raised various issues on appeal, the critical question for the court was the correct application of the doctrine of equivalents. The Federal Circuit found that the range of asserted equivalents made by Wilson encompassed the prior art. In other words, the Wilson patent would have been obvious in view of the prior art.

---

3. 35 U.S.C. §§ 102(a), 102(e) & 102(g). A patent is not obtainable if the invention is not new.
4. 35 U.S.C. § 103.

The Prior Art

Patent law precludes an inventor, such as Wilson, from obtaining a patent if the difference between the patented ball and the prior art is such that the ball would be obvious to one of ordinary skill in the art of golf-ball design. Dunlop successfully defended the infringement claim by showing that the Wilson patent was invalid for being unpatentable in light of prior art, notwithstanding issuance of the patent by the PTO.

To determine whether Wilson's claim was protected, the Federal Circuit embarked on a historical review of golf-ball patents and design. The court found that the most pertinent prior art was a 1932 British patent granted to a Mr. Pugh. His invention was described in the following way:

> A method of distributing a pattern with substantial uniformity over the surface of a sphere, such as a golf ball, which consists in . . . form[ing] equilateral triangles in the case of the . . . icosahedron . . . , dividing the sides of the triangles so found into the same number of equal or substantially equal parts and finally joining corresponding points in each pair of sides of each triangle by a series of arcs of great circles, substantially as described.

The court also observed that the prior art included several patents issued to Uniroyal for a ball sold in the 1970s. The Uniroyal ball, the court found, was an icosahedral ball having six great circles with 30 or more dimples intersecting the great circles by about 12 to 15 thousandths of an inch. It was beginning to look like Wilson's patent was obvious.

The Doctrine of Equivalents

The judicially created doctrine of equivalents operates to prevent a canny infringer from avoiding the law by adopting minor changes and substitutions as a means of avoiding a patent. When the accused product "performs substantially the same overall function or work, in substantially the same way, to obtain substantially the same overall result as the claimed invention," the doctrine of equivalents allows the patentee to pursue an infringement claim even though there is no literal infringement.

The Federal Circuit applied a hypothetical claim test to determine whether the Dunlop ball was substantially equivalent to the Wilson ball. The hypothetical essentially tests whether the prior art available at the time Wilson patented its ball precluded the infringement claim. To show infringement by equivalence, Wilson had to prove that the hypothetical claim would have been patented notwithstanding the prior art. If the hypothetical claim would not have been allowed, Wilson would lose. In short, if Wilson could not have gotten a patent in the first place, it cannot get backdoor protection through the doctrine of equivalents.

The Federal Circuit explains the test this way:

> The specific question before us, then, is whether Wilson has proved that a hypothetical claim, similar to [its] claim 1 but broad enough to literally cover Dunlop's balls, could have been patentable. . . . Thus, the issue is whether a hypothetical claim directed to an icosahedral ball having six great circles intersected by 60 dimples in amounts up to 9 thousandths of an inch could have been patentable in view of the prior art Uniroyal ball . . . .
>
> We hold that these differences [from the prior art] are so slight and relatively minor that the hypothetical claim—which permits twice as many intersecting dimples, but with slightly smaller intersections—viewed as

a whole would have been obvious in view of the Uniroyal ball. As Dunlop puts it, there is simply 'no principled difference' between the hypothetical claim and the prior art Uniroyal ball. Accordingly, Wilson's claim 1 cannot be given a range of equivalents broad enough to encompass the accused Dunlop balls.[5]

Conclusion

The dimples on the Dunlop balls were similar to the patented Wilson dimples. This similarity was not enough, however, to constitute an actionable infringement. As the proponent of the doctrine of equivalents, the burden was on Wilson to prove that the range of equivalents was not ensnared by the prior art, which it failed to do.

The Federal Circuit applied a hypothetical claim analysis to assess whether the asserted scope of equivalents was permissible in view of the prior art. Infringement exists under the doctrine of equivalents if the accused product performs substantially the same overall functional work in substantially the same way. But even if this occurs, no infringement exists if the scope of the equivalency of what is literally claimed encompasses the prior art.

Following the *Wilson* case, the U.S. Supreme Court added guidance on the doctrine of equivalents in *Warner-Jenkins Co. v. Hilton David Chemical Co.*[6] To ascertain whether inven-

---

5. Dunlop's balls are icosahedral balls with six great circles, five of which are intersected by dimples. The balls contain 432 to 480 dimples, 60 of which intersect great circles in amounts from four to nine thousandths of an inch. In order for a hypothetical claim to Dunlop's balls, its limitations must permit 60 dimples to intersect the great circles by at least nine thousandths of an inch.
6. Warner-Jenkins Co. v. Hilton David Chem. Co., 520 U.S. 17 (1997) (holding that the doctrine of equivalents must be applied to the individual elements of the claim, not to the invention as a whole).

Hole 24: Patent Infringement

tions are equivalents, a comparative assessment may be made. It cautioned that courts must exercise care in actually making this comparative assessment in order to avoid unintended consequences. A broad application of the doctrine has the potential of impermissibly expanding a patent beyond its original boundaries and harming the potential for further innovation.

Innovation is important to the financial success of golf ball manufacturers. Their quest to secure patents on golf balls that travel longer, straighter, and with improved accuracy around the green is similar to a golfer's quest for the magic of a hole in one.

Hole 25

Patent Infringement:
Novelty and obviousness

Federal: *Callaway Golf Co. v. Acushnet Co.*, 576 F.3d 1331 (Fed. Cir. 2009), reh'g and reh'g en banc denied (2009), cert. denied, 130 S. Ct 1525 (2010)

Product innovation is important to the golf ball industry for a simple reason: It allows manufacturers to market and sell more golf balls. A manufacturer has a strong economic incentive to protect its golf ball innovations by patenting them. But having a patent is not enough. A manufacturer also must be willing to enforce the patent against unauthorized use, which can mean costly and time-consuming patent infringement litigation.

Golf balls are manufactured using a variety of specialized materials and designs calculated to appeal to a wide range of player abilities, from the beginner to the professional. The search for a golf ball that gives the player more control and greater distance can be expensive as well as confounding.[1] It can also leave the golfer longing for the simple pleasures of the 19th hole.

---

1. The search for a better ball seems endless. Golfers who have played golf for any length of time realize that Pogo, the central character in the long-running comic strip, had it right when he said, "Yep, we have met the enemy and he is us."

Although a wide variety of golf balls are available, all but a small fraction of balls sold today comply with the *Rules of Golf* and its accompanying Appendix III. The rules identify specifications for maximum weight,[2] minimum size,[3] spherical symmetry,[4] initial velocity,[5] and overall distance[6] when tested under specified conditions. These standard specifications provide a surprising and complex opportunity for golf ball manufacturers to look for and patent their innovations.

The Facts

Callaway and Acushnet are well-known competitors in the golf ball market. Callaway sued Acushnet in federal district court for patent infringement of its Sullivan patents. Callaway's lawsuit alleged that Acushnet's Titleist Pro V-1 branded balls infringed its multilayer, polyurethane-covered patented golf balls.[7]

Acushnet defended by arguing that Callaway's patents were not valid. More specifically, it claimed the Callaway patents were not novel[8] and were obvious.[9] The litigation between these

---

2. No heavier than 1.62 ounces.
3. No smaller than 1.68 inches in diameter. In the early days of golf, there was no standard hole size. It's said that the current size of 4-1/4 inches evolved purely by chance from the size of a pipe used to reinforce a crumbling hole at St. Andrews, Scotland.
4. Not designed, manufactured, or intentionally modified to have properties different from those of a spherically symmetrical ball. Polara Golf manufactures balls with a self-correcting technology feature designed to promote straighter ball flight. Because they are aerodynamically asymmetrical, they do not meet the USGA standard and are not approved for tournament play.
5. The Initial Velocity Test procedure, which is on file with the USGA, uses a test machine and a hierarchy of statistically designed tests. According to this procedure, the velocity of the ball shall not be greater than 250 feet per second, subject to a maximum tolerance of 2 percent.
6. The standard for the combined carry and roll for a conforming ball is also on file with the USGA.
7. Callaway Golf v. Acushnet, 523 F. Supp. 2d 388 (D. Del. 2007).
8. 35 U.S.C. § 102(a), (e). An invention must be new to be patentable. Anticipation bars a patent that was already publicly known at the time of the invention.
9. 35 U.S.C. § 103 (a). The patent statute also bars patents for obvious inventions.

industry titans went on for years and was the subject of a number of written judicial opinions.[10]

Patent Claims

The patent claims of an inventor are essential to analyzing the validity of a patent.[11] The U.S. Patent and Trademark Office (PTO) evaluates the claims contained in the patent application in deciding whether to issue a patent.

Comparing the claims against prior work in the field is important to deciding whether to issue a patent. In considering a patent application or reexamining it, the patent examiner is required to consider all the information previously disclosed to

---

10. The Callaway and Acushnet litigation is reminiscent of Jarndyce v. Jarndyce, the long-running litigation described by Charles Dickens in his classic novel *Bleak House*.
11. Claim 1 of the 293 Sullivan patent (which is generally representative of Callaway's other patent claims) states:

1. A golf ball comprising:
a core: an inner cover layer having a Shore D hardness of 60 or more molded on said core, said inner cover layer having a thickness of 0.100 to 0.010 inches, said inner cover layer comprising a blend of two or more low acid ionomer resins containing no more than 16% by weight of an alpha, beta-unsaturated carboxylic acid; and an outer cover layer having a Shore D hardness of 64 or less molded on said inner cover layer, said outer cover layer having a thickness of 0.010 to 0.070 inches, and said outer cover layer comprising a relatively soft polyurethane material.

The term "Shore D hardness" in the above claim refers to a hardness standard published by the American Society for Testing and Materials. An indentor is forced into the material tested, in this case the golf ball. Shore D hardness uses a size D indentor.

At trial, the parties disagreed on whether a hardness test should be applied to the cover layer of the ball or to a sample cover layer off-the-ball. The district court held that the hardness test should be applied on-the-ball. Acushnet challenged this finding on appeal, but the Federal Circuit agreed that the test for determining hardness was on-the-ball. The Callaway (Sullivan) patent claim referred to a "cover layer" having a specified hardness, and not generally to the material or sample used on the cover. In addition, the claim related to the assembled ball, and not simply to the cover in isolation or off-the-ball. Moreover, no cover layer existed until the ball was actually assembled, which favored an on-the-ball interpretation. Finally, Acushnet's own experts admitted that they generally measure hardness on-the-ball.

The Little Book of Golf Law

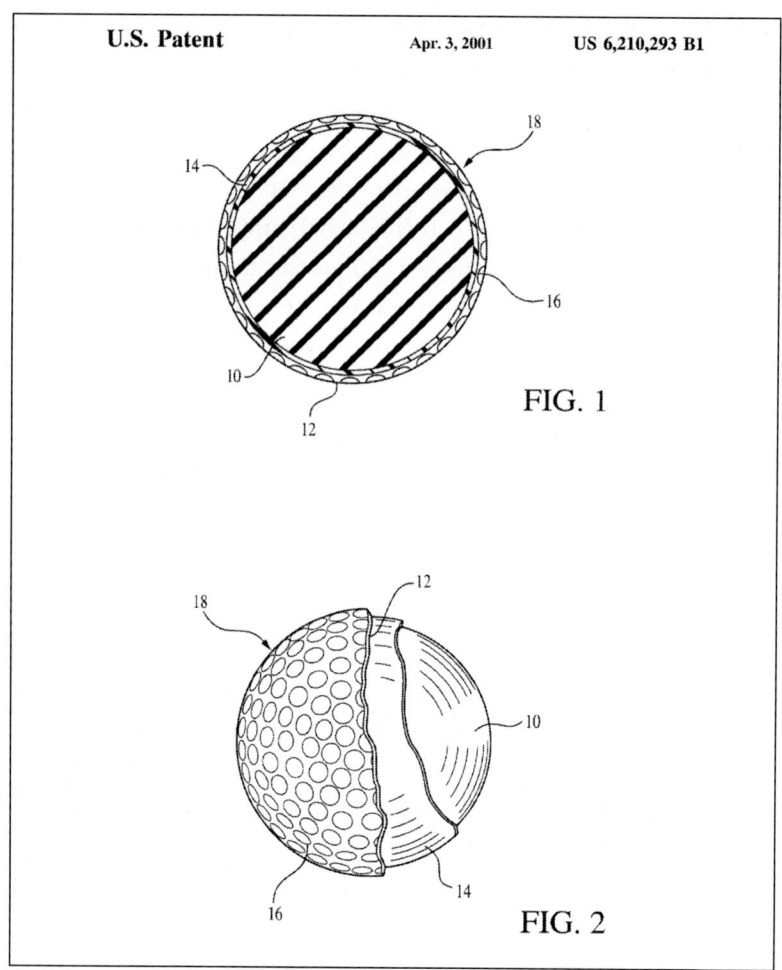

Callaway Patent Drawing

the public in any form about the patent-seeking invention. This body of information, called the "prior art," is used by the examiner to determine whether the invention is novel and unobvious.

The fact that a patent has been issued by the PTO is not controlling when the patentee files an infringement lawsuit. A court may decide that the patent does not meet the requirements of patent law. Alleged infringers often argue this as a defense to the claim of infringement. Thus, a careful consideration of the claims set forth in the patent compared to the prior art is critical to the claim of infringement.

Modern Golf Ball Technology

Some understanding of golf ball technology is useful to understanding the Dickensian legal battle between Callaway and Acushnet.

Cut a golf ball in half, and you'll typically find that it is either a two-piece or three-piece ball. Two-piece balls have a solid or "wound" core that is surrounded by an outer layer. Solid cores are made of rubber and consist of a solid piece or multiple layers. In contrast, wound cores are made of elastic windings around either a solid or liquid-filled core. Three-piece balls have a core, inner cover layer, and outer cover layer.

During the 1980s and 1990s, manufacturers experimented with many variations of two-piece and three-piece golf ball covers and cores. The goal was to find an innovative design that would promote distance without sacrificing playability around the green.

The technical challenge was that distance and playability are governed by competing laws of physics. Distance is gained by using a harder cover, whereas playability is improved by using a softer cover.

A ball with a softer cover generally was preferred by low handicappers and professionals for its playability in providing, among other features, more backspin and bite. One trade-off was less distance. Another trade-off was that a softer cover was easily cut or scuffed, which is less important to the professional who gets free golf balls or the player for whom money is no object. Most recreational golfers favored golf balls with harder covers, because they were more cut-resistant and provided better distance.[12] For the recreational golfer, the downside was less playability and control.

The search for the Holy Grail of golf ball design and innovation was a ball that promoted both distance and playability. This challenge was described in the background section to Callaway's patents (the Sullivan patents).[13]

> [A] great deal of research continues in order to develop a golf ball cover composition exhibiting not only the improved impact resistance and carrying distance produced by the 'hard' ionomeric resins, but also the playability (i.e., 'spin', 'feel', etc.) characteristics associated with the 'soft' balata covers, properties which are still desired by the more skilled golfer.[14]

Callaway believed its patents were the Holy Grail.

The background time line

2001/2003   The PTO issues Spalding Golf four U.S. patents (the Sullivan patents) for Spalding's multilayer golf balls.[15] Spalding suffers hard times and goes bankrupt. Its assets, including the Sullivan patents, are purchased by Callaway.

---

12. A ball is unfit for play if it is visibly cut, cracked, or out of shape. A ball is not unfit for play, however, solely because mud or other materials adhere to it, its surface is scratched or scraped, or its paint is damaged or discolored. If the ball is unfit for play while playing a hole, the player may substitute another ball as long as the proper procedure is followed. Any ball may be replaced after completing the hole being played. RULES OF GOLF, Ball Unfit for Play, 5-3.

13. The Sullivan patents included U.S. Patent Nos. (6,506,130), (6,503,156) (6,210,293) and (6,595,873). The parties agreed that patent 6,210,293 was representative of all the claims asserted by Callaway.

14. U.S. Patent No. 6,210,293.

15. Under patent law, the date of filing is the effective date for assessing questions of prior art. The filing date for the Sullivan patents preceded Acushnet's introducing the Pro V1-branded balls.

Hole 25: Patent Infringement

2006   Callaway files suit against Acushnet, the parent company of Titleist, in federal district court in Delaware. Callaway alleges that the Titleist Pro V1-branded golf balls infringe its patents. The Titleist balls are the number-one selling ball on the market.

Before the trial starts, Acushnet petitions the PTO to reexamine the validity of the Callaway patents. The PTO does and declares the patents invalid.

During the trial, the district court rules that the PTO's reexamination decision that the patents were invalid should not be revealed to the jury. The court grants part of Callaway's motion for summary judgment. The court finds the patents satisfy the novel requirement.[16] But the legal battle before the court continues on the factual issue of obviousness.

2008   The district court finds that all but one of Callaway's claims satisfy the legal requirements of novelty and non-obviousness. The court finds that a person of ordinary skill would not have been motivated to put a polyurethane cover on a ball with the expectation that it would yield the level of hardness in the Callaway patents. It also finds the preexisting patent information (prior art contained in the previously issued Nesbitt patent) did not render the Callaway patent obvious. It grants Callaway a permanent injunction against Acushnet's manufacturing and distributing its Pro V1s.[17]

In 2009, Acushnet appeals the district court's decision findings of novelty and non-obviousness to the Federal Circuit,

---

16. Callaway Golf Co. v. Acushnet Co., 523 F. Supp. 2d 388 (D. Del. 2007).
17. Callaway Golf Co. v. Acushnet Co., 585 F. Supp. 2d 600 (D. Del. 2008).

which has jurisdiction over patent appeals. Acushnet also challenges the district court's evidentiary ruling that the PTO's decision on the invalidity of Callaway's patents was inadmissible. The Federal Circuit takes up the controversy.

The Law

The U.S. Constitution authorizes Congress to establish a patent system "to promote the Progress of Science and useful Arts, by securing for limited Times to Authors and Inventors the exclusive Right to their respective Writings and Discoveries." The general goal of granting a patent is to promote new and useful inventions.

Pursuant to this grant of constitutional authority, Congress created the statutory framework for granting and protecting patents. The U.S. Code, Section 101, sets forth the general categories for patentable subject matters:

> Whoever invents or discovers any new and useful process, machine, manufacture, or composition of matter, or any new and useful improvement thereof, may obtain a patent therefor, subject to the conditions and requirements of this title.[18]

To receive a patent, the applicant must apply to the PTO. The patent application must distinctly identify what is new and useful about the invention. The application consists of various standard parts, such as a Background, a Summary, and one or more Claims that delineate the elements and limitations to the invention.

This application process gives the PTO the information it needs to decide whether to issue the patent. It also gives the public notice as to the claims being made for the patent, which

---

18. 35 U.S.C. § 101.

Hole 25: Patent Infringement

is important to avoiding an infringement lawsuit. A properly issued federal patent gives the patent holder (patentee) the right to prevent others from making, using, or selling the patented invention without consent for a period of 20 years.[19] The patent is presumed valid, but its validity may be challenged in litigation.

A patentable invention must be distinguishable from the prior art by being both novel[20] and non-obvious.[21] It must be an advancement beyond the prior art, which is generally defined as the knowledge available at a given time to a person of ordinary skill in the art.

Novel (or Unanticipated)

To be novel, the invention must be new, which means that it must not already have been publicly used or published. An invention does not meet the novelty requirement if the prior art anticipates the invention.

Anticipation as a bar to patentability requires that every element of the claimed invention be found in a single prior art reference (earlier patent or publication). This occurs when a single prior art ("host") document describes every element of the invention in a way that would be obvious to a person of ordinary skill in the subject.

Materials not explicitly contained in a single host document may also render an invention anticipated if those prior art materials are incorporated by reference. The incorporating host document must identify with sufficient particularity what material is incorporated and where the material is found.

---

19. 35 U.S.C. § 154(a).
20. 35 U.S.C. §§ 102(a), 102(e) & 102(g). A patent is not obtainable if the invention is not new.
21. 35 U.S.C. § 103.

The Federal Circuit describes these legal principles as follows:

A patent claim is invalid due to anticipation (lack of novelty) if, within the four corners of a single, prior art document . . . every element of the claimed invention [is described], either expressly or inherently, such that a person of ordinary skill in the art could practice the invention without undue experimentation. However, [m]aterial not explicitly contained in the single, prior art document may still be considered for purposes of anticipation (lack of novelty) if that material is incorporated by reference into the document. To incorporate matter by reference, a host document must contain language clearly identifying the subject matter which is incorporated and where it is to be found; a mere *reference* to another application, or patent, or publication is not an *incorporation* of anything therein . . . . Put differently, the host document must identify with detailed particularity what specific material it incorporates and clearly indicate where that material is found in the various documents.

Whether material is incorporated by reference into a host document is a question of law that is reviewed *de novo* on appeal. The district court granted Callaway summary judgment on its motion that the Sullivan patents were novel (not anticipated).

The Federal Circuit disagreed. It held that the Nesbitt patent (prior art) identified with specificity both what material was incorporated by reference (foamable polymeric compositions suitable for golf ball cover layers) as well as where it could be found (the Molitor 637 patent). Nesbitt incorporated the entire list of foamable compounds disclosed by Molitor as appropriate materials for use in golf ball cover layers. As a result, the Federal Circuit reversed the grant of summary judgment in favor of Callaway and remanded the matter to the district court.

Callaway argued that even if the district court erred on the incorporation issue, its determination of novelty was still appropriate. The Federal Circuit was reluctant to consider the issue beyond incorporation. Its holding reversing the grant of summary judgment and remanding the matter to the district did not prevent Callaway from arguing the broader point on remand. One did not need a crystal ball, however, to see which way the wind was blowing.

Obviousness

Section 103 also precludes inventions that are obvious:

> A patent may not be obtained though the invention is not identically disclosed or described as set forth in section 102 [novelty], if the differences between the subject matter sought to be patented and the prior art are such that the subject matter as a whole would have been obvious at the time the invention was made to a person having ordinary skill in the art to which said subject matter pertains.[22]

Whether an invention is obvious is one of the most commonly litigated issues in patent law. Although novelty and obviousness overlap, the overlap is not perfect. Obviousness is determined from the point of view of a person having ordinary skill in the art. Only that prior art that is reasonably pertinent is relevant to the inquiry. Some differences from the prior art must exist. Otherwise, the invention would be considered obvious and not patentable.

The Federal Circuit found that the jury's determination on

---

22. 35 U.S.C. § 103(a).

obviousness was irreconcilably inconsistent. The jury found that the broader claim (claim 4) of the Callaway patent was valid, but that the narrower claim (claim 5) was invalid for obviousness without offering any reservation or qualification. The irreconcilable inconsistency prompted the Federal Circuit to remand the issue of obviousness for a new trial.

The PTO's reconsideration

A federal court evaluating the validity of a patent is not limited by the PTO's determination or materials considered by it in issuing the patent. On appeal, Acushnet challenged the district court's ruling that the PTO's reexamination decision that the Callaway patents were invalid could not be introduced into evidence.

The Federal Circuit offered several explanations for upholding the district court on this point. First, it found that the reexamination decision by the PTO was both non-final and non-binding. Thus, it had little relevance to the jury's independent deliberations in the district court on the issue of obviousness. Allowing the PTO's subsequent decision into evidence also had the potential to prejudicially confuse the jury.

Second, although Callaway opened the evidentiary door by referring to the three PTO patent examiners who granted the patent in its opening statement, the district court ruled that Callaway could not repeat this information during the trial to bolster its claim that the Callaway patents were somehow valid. The Federal Circuit accepted the view that any possible prejudicial effect from the statement was effectively minimized by requiring that the statement not be repeated. It was *de minimus non curat lex*.[23]

---

23. "The law does not concern itself with trifles." When a technical violation of the law occurs according to the letter of the law, if the effect of the violation is non-prejudicial or too small to be of consequence, the violation will be ignored.

Finally, Acushnet did not make a timely objection to Callaway's opening statement being unfairly prejudicial when the statement was made at the trial.

Conclusion

The holding by the Federal Circuit was not the end of the litigation. In 2009, requests for a rehearing and a rehearing en banc were made and denied. In 2010, a petition for certiorari was also made and denied by the U.S. Supreme Court.

In 2011, Callaway suffered another setback. On remand to the district court, Callaway's motion for a judgment as a matter of law was denied. After further proceedings, the district court entered a judgment in favor of Acushnet.[24] Callaway filed another notice of appeal in the Federal Circuit.

After years of litigation, Callaway and Acushnet finally came to an agreement in 2012 that allows each party to make balls and clubs under the other's patents without any monetary settlement being paid.

Several points about the struggle are worth noting. One is that the golf ball industry is big business and manufacturers will go to extreme lengths to protect their intellectual property.

Another is that a patent issued by the U.S. Patent and Trademark Office is presumed to be valid, but that doesn't mean it will be found to be valid by a federal court. The validity of the patent is often challenged in a lawsuit for infringement on the theory that the patentee failed to meet the requirements for the issuance of the patent.

The African saying "when the elephants fight, the ants suffer" is appropriate. The consumer ultimately pays for the fight between the titans in the form of higher prices.

---

24. Callaway v. Acushnet, 778 F. Supp. 2d 487 (D. Del. 2011).

Hole 26

Golf Equipment and the *Rules of Golf*:
The battle over grooves

Federal: *Gilder, et al. v. PGA Tour, Inc.*,
936 F.2d 417 (9th Cir. 1991)

The multibillion-dollar golf equipment industry has changed over the years with the steady march of technology. Golf shafts are no longer made of hickory, but of composite materials that are lighter and stronger. Driver heads have gone from beech to persimmon to today's space-age materials. Wooden golf balls used in the 15th century are found only in museums. In the 1800s, the gutta-percha ball replaced the traditional feather-filled ball. Today's golf balls consist of layers of synthetic materials, such as surlyn or urethane blends.[1]

Although fans may marvel when a golf commentator announces that a Tour player has launched a drive more than 330 yards, they may attribute it, at least in large measure, to technology.

Golf is protective of its traditions. In the 1960s, Sam Snead's cure for the "yips" was putting croquet-style. Officials quickly banned the technique as contrary to tradition. Today, a proposed ban on "anchored putting" is center stage.

---

1. *Rules of Golf*, Appendix III provides that the diameter of the ball used today must not be less than 1.680 inches. Until 1990, balls smaller than this standard were allowed in tournaments under the jurisdiction of the R&A. The ball was called the "British ball" and was known for being effective for playing into the wind.

The enemy of tradition is change. With change comes conflict. In 2010, the PGA Tour season had barely begun at the Farmers Open at Torrey Pines in San Diego when a controversy erupted over application of the United States Golf Association (USGA) "groove" rules. Beginning January 1, 2010, the section of the *Rules of Golf* dealing with the design of clubs went into effect.[2]

The rules specify that the grooves on the face of irons shall meet the following:

The width of the groves shall not exceed 0.035 inches (0.9mm) . . . The distance between the edges of adjacent groves must not be less than three times the width of the grooves, and not less than 0.075 inches (1.9mm).[3]

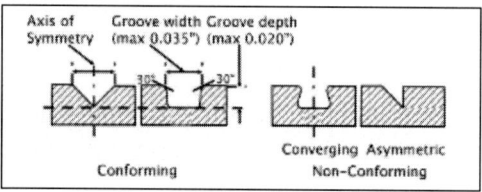

This means that there must be a 3:1 ratio in grooves placement to be conforming. In simpler terms, the space between each groove must be three times the width of the groove. Therefore, if the width of the groove is the maximum allowed (.035 inches), then the space between the grooves must be not less than .075 inches.

In addition to these provisions, "the grooves must not have sharp edges or raised lips." These design rules impact golfers as well as manufacturers.[4] For Tour players, nonconforming irons cannot be used in PGA Tour–sanctioned events. Nonconfor-

---

2. Rules of Golf, Appx. II.
3. Rules of Golf, Appx. II, 5-c.(i).
4. Recreational golfers can continue using nonconforming irons until 2024. Prior to that date, the principal effect will be finding pre-2010 irons that are unaffected by the rule change.

Hole 26: Golf Equipment and the *Rules of Golf*

mance has broader consequences. Golf equipment manufacturers are forced by consumers to adjust their production practices to meet the USGA's requirements.

But what was behind the change in the groove requirements? The 2010 rules were adopted because the USGA was concerned that some tour players were using irons with grooves that were too close together in order to get more spin on the ball. Getting more spin allowed those players to play shots more effectively from the rough, and this allowed them to minimize the penalty for not hitting their ball in the fairway. The USGA thought this advantage wasn't consistent with the traditions of the game, which emphasize skill and competence. At the core, this was a conflict between tradition and technology.

At least four tour players, including Phil Mickelson and John Daly, didn't like the new groove rules. They responded by using vintage Ping Eye 2 wedges, which did not meet the 2010 groove rules. Some of their competitors were offended and publicly groused that using the vintage wedge was cheating, which is extremely strong language in the world of golf. The charges of cheating and the prospect of slander lawsuits catapulted the dispute to front-page news.

A premium exists in knowing the *Rules of Golf*.[5] During the Wells Fargo Championship in 2012 at Quail Hollow, for example, Tiger Woods, known for his remarkable play both on and off the course, hooked his tee shot into the trees and his large traveling gallery. After an extensive search, his ball couldn't be found.[6]

---

5. Sometimes ignoring the rules is permitted. A "Billigan" is a "tribute" to former president Bill Clinton, who is well known for his substituting bad shots with reloads or Billigans whenever he is so disposed.

6. In 2006, Tiger hit a shot over the ninth green at the Bridgestone Invitational. It hit the cart path and seemingly bounded onto the roof. It was never found. It turned out that someone on the kitchen staff, who was delivering pies, thought the ball was thrown at him as a prank and drove off with it. Tiger was given a free drop. Woods went on to win the event.

Was it a lost ball, which would require Tiger to return to the tee under a penalty of a stroke and distance? No. Tour officials concluded that it was virtually certain that the ball had been moved (stolen) by an "outside agency" (a sticky-fingered fan). Therefore, Tiger was entitled to a free drop, as near as possible to where the ball landed, with no penalty. Although Tiger missed the cut, had he survived the cut and won the tournament, the ruling might have gotten more press.

In any event, those four players using the nonconforming vintage Ping Eye 2 wedges relied on *Gilder v. PGA Tour, Inc.*

The Facts

In the early 1980s, USGA rules allowed manufacturers to design clubs with square (U) shaped grooves. Karsten Manufacturing Corporation, the maker of Ping golf clubs, built and sold clubs consistent with those rules.

The square grooves worked well, but they also came with a consumer-use problem. The grooves, which produced great backspin, had a tendency to shred the golf-ball covers. This shredding problem was great for companies selling golf balls, but not so great for the Ping brand. The solution Karsten developed was to slightly round or bevel the edges of the square groove to remove part of the bite that caused the shredding.

Rounding the edges of each groove on the face of the iron had the effect of making each one a tiny bit wider. It also made the distance between the adjacent grooves on the face of the iron a tiny bit smaller—estimated to be less than the thickness of a business card. Although Karsten solved the shredding problem, the beveling solution created a problem with the USGA.

Karsten maintained that the irons complied with the USGA's groove rules. The USGA disagreed. The disagreement focused how to conduct the measurement under the rules. The measure-

Hole 26: Golf Equipment and the *Rules of Golf*

ment-compliance issue had nothing to do with extra spin or the shape of the grooves, although that concern was lurking in the background.

At the time, no explicit USGA standard existed for measuring the distance between the edges of the adjacent grooves. Karsten argued that the beveling did not affect the measurement of the grooves because the distance should be measured between the groove edges by projecting upward from the vertical walls of the groove. The USGA said the measurement should be done differently. It used the 30-degree measurement rule, which is the standard used today. The measuring disagreement can be put in simple terms: The Ping club grooves were legal using Karsten's approach to measuring, but were nonconforming under the USGA's approach.

The disagreement drew wide attention. The PGA Tour, which in reality simply consists of the touring pros, got involved. The PGA Tour's complaint focused on the performance of the square grooves being manufactured by Karsten. It argued that the high spin rate associated with the clubs changed the character and nature of the game. To support its position, the PGA Tour conducted a survey of Tour players. Sixty percent of the respondents thought that square grooves should be banned. The PGA Tour also commissioned two university studies to look at the matter. Both studies concluded that square-shaped grooves imparted more spin to the golf ball than the traditional V-shaped grooves.

Notwithstanding the fact that the USGA tests did not show a significant difference to ban square grooves, the PGA Tour announced a rule forbidding the use of square grooves in PGA Tour events. The real reason for the PGA Tour's opposition is not certain.

One theory is that the PGA simply was flexing its muscle to

fight off technological change, which it believed was adversely changing the nature of the game. Another theory is tied to money, the use of pro endorsements, and anticompetitive action. Karsten Ping clubs were popular with the playing public without tour player endorsements, and thus the company didn't use many PGA Tour players to endorse the Ping product line. By outlawing the popular club on the PGA Tour, the Tour could effectively promote manufacturers of equipment product lines more that were more agreeable to Tour player endorsements. A final theory is that the PGA Tour believed the square grooves changed the character and nature of the game.

Karsten was confronted with the PGA Tour's ban of its irons as well as with USGA's nonconforming determination. Being stymied, Karsten pulled out the legal rule book. It sued both the PGA Tour and the USGA in federal court.

The Law

Karsten's suit against the PGA alleged violations of federal[7] and state antitrust laws.[8] It also alleged interference with Karsten's professional business relationships. More specifically, it claimed that the PGA Tour ban decreased sales and harmed its reputation in the marketplace.

The complaint also charged the PGA directors with breaching their fiduciary duties. It sought to hold them personally liable for their alleged tortious conduct, which was an aggressive legal move.

The suit against the USGA challenged the method used to measure the grooves, which effectively banned the Ping Eye 2 clubs for use in USGA tournaments starting in 1990 and in all

---

7. Sherman Anti-Trust Act, 15 U.S.C. §§ 1, 2.
8. Arizona Anti-Trust Law, ARIZ. REV. STAT. § 44-1401 *et seq.*

amateur tournaments starting in 1996. Karsten maintained that the USGA's 30-degree measurement rule was arbitrary. It argued the groove beveling was minor, hypertechnical, and had no effect on performance.

The Karsten-USGA Settlement

Before the case went to trial, Karsten and the USGA agreed to an out-of-court settlement. Karsten agreed that the Ping Eye 2 design would be changed in the future to comply with the USGA's system of measuring grooves. Karsten also agreed to stop manufacturing clubs the USGA considered nonconforming.

The USGA agreed that all old-production clubs it claimed violated the rules were grandfathered for continued use as conforming. This provision protected the 2 million or so sets of the clubs that had been previously sold. The square-grooved clubs that surfaced and exploded in controversy during the 2010 Farmers Open were manufactured between 1985 and 1989 and were legally grandfathered under the terms of the settlement.

The wording of the settlement said that the dispute "was of a technical nature," and was not a condemnation of square grooves. The settlement also indicated that the parties agreed that "there was no competitive advantage to a user of the clubs." This provision is subject to varying interpretations. One interpretation is that the provision means no competitive advantage exists between the nonconforming Ping clubs and the conforming Ping clubs with square grooves. Another interpretation is that square grooves *per se* do not provide players with a competitive advantage, which was the PGA's complaint. The first interpretation seems more reasonable, because the existence of square grooves wasn't the focus of disagreement between Karsten and the USGA. Until resurfacing in 2010, the Karsten-USGA settlement receded into the background.

Gilder v. PGA Tour

The groove dispute was alive and well, on another front. Several PGA Tour players sued the PGA. The plaintiff listed first on the pleadings against the PGA was Robert (Bob) Gilder, a golfer who joined the Tour in 1973.[9] He testified that being forced to change clubs as a result of its ban would hurt his game, which in turn would affect his endorsement income. George Lanning, a left-handed golfer and also a Tour player, testified that Karsten made the only quality left-handed clubs on the market, and that he might lose his exemption card if forced to change clubs.

Karsten presented expert testimony by an economist. He testified that the grooves did not have a negative effect on the PGA, and cited the fact that the percentage of prize money that Ping Eye 2 players *won* was actually less than the percentage of players who *used* the Ping Eye 2 clubs. Thus, the Ping Eye 2 clubs did not give the players who use them a playing advantage. He also testified that the Ping golf clubs did not help the players using the clubs to get on the green in less than regulation, which is the number of strokes left after subtracting the two strokes on the putting green from par for the hole.

The expert also testified that the ban of U-groove clubs had a financial impact because a positive correlation exists between the equipment PGA professionals use and the equipment recreational golfers buy. As a result, Karsten experienced a drop in its market share of golf club sales and other products because of the PGA ban. In the economist's opinion, Karsten would experience harm to its reputation if forced to manufacture an iron conforming to the new PGA measuring rule. Players forced to use other irons might not perform as well, which could impact their livelihood.

---

9. His record of achievement on the pro golfing circuit includes wins on the PGA Tour, the Japan Tour, and the Champions Tour.

Hole 26: Golf Equipment and the *Rules of Golf*

The PGA had its own experts, who disagreed. Tom Kite, for example, testified that square grooves diminished the skill factor of the game because the clubs offset the traditional advantage of being able to hit the ball in the fairway of the golf course.[10] In addition, the commissioner of the PGA testified that granting a preliminary injunction against the PGA would have dire consequences for the organization. He testified that it threatened the organization's ability to promulgate rules for PGA tournaments.

After an evidentiary hearing, the district court held that Karsten and the Tour plaintiffs had demonstrated that (1) they had a reasonable chance of success on the merits; (2) they would suffer irreparable injury if the injunction were not imposed; (3) the balance of hardships tipped sharply in favor of the plaintiffs; and (4) serious questions for trial needed to be sorted out.

The PGA appealed the issuance of the preliminary injunction to the Ninth Circuit. It challenged the district court's reasoning on balancing the hardships and the serious questions for trial.

The Ninth Circuit affirmed the district court's decision. It found that the plaintiffs had demonstrated that they would suffer an immediate threatened injury. The ban had the potential to affect the Tour plaintiffs' earnings, ability to maintain Tour eligibility, and economic endorsement potential. The court reasoned that the difficulty in quantifying the plaintiffs' injuries did not make them any less real.

The Ninth Circuit also found that the harm to Karsten was equally supported by the record. Without a preliminary injunction against the ban, Karsten would be required to redesign its clubs, retool its manufacturing process, and abandon its well-established square-groove market.

---

10. Tom Kite is a well-known golfing professional with close to 40 wins on the PGA Tour, European Tour, and Champions Tour.

235

The arguable harm to the PGA Tour was to its reputation as a governing body and to the ability to promulgate rules binding its members. This harm, the court recognized, might be substantial. Nevertheless, Karsten and the professional player plaintiffs demonstrated a harm to their reputation as well as a severe financial injury. Thus, the district court did not abuse its discretion in finding that the balance of hardships tipped sharply in favor of Karsten and the Tour plaintiffs.

The Ninth Circuit also found that the district court did not abuse its discretion in determining that serious questions exist which should be resolved at a trial on the merits of the respective claims.

In the end, the issuance of the preliminary injunction, which was affirmed by the Ninth Circuit, simply preserved the status quo. So what is the rest of the story?

The litigation with the PGA went on for another three years. The PGA fought Ping's $200 million suit, even after the preliminary injunction blocked the tour's ban on square grooves. Karsten found a number of Tour players to sponsor. The PGA settled the matter six days before the Karsten suit was to go to trial. How much money changed hands, if any, is not clear.

Some think that other pro Tour sponsors were behind the square-groove ban. Perhaps other equipment manufacturers were simply ganging up on Karsten. Reports of the settlement say that the PGA and Karsten agreed to respect the USGA's rulemaking authority. But because Karsten had previously agreed to that in its settlement with the USGA, the practical effect was to simply concede something that was already settled. More significantly, the PGA dropped its rule against square grooves, which was the fundamental complaint it had against Karsten.

The battle may not be over. One report states that there is

a provision buried in the Tour's Settlement Agreement that would allow the PGA Tour to essentially override the USGA equipment provision "if it were shown to be necessary for the Tour." This provision may be the trapdoor to more employment for the lawyers.

Conclusion

The irons with square grooves manufactured by Karsten between 1985 and 1989 and previously considered illegal by the USGA have been grandfathered for use by the settlement agreement between Karsten and the USGA. Importantly, those clubs were not considered to be nonconforming because they had square grooves. Rather, the technical disagreement focused on how to measure the grooves on irons with square grooves that were beveled. The problem was generated because the USGA's measuring rules were not clear at the time. They are now.

The older Karsten grandfathered irons may be played legally today, although public pressure has resulted in their practical disappearance on the Tour. The recent claims that those players using the older Ping Eye-2 clubs were acting contrary to the spirit of the rules or acting illegally seems wrong. The USGA signed the settlement agreement allowing their use, and one should not simply ignore the history surrounding the dispute.

Square grooves are legal as long as they comply with the *Rules of Golf* set out in Appendix II. Such irons were briefly banned from the PGA Tour. The purported justification for the ban was based on claims related to performance. But experts differ on this. Compared to V-shaped grooves, square grooves provide either no competitive advantage or slightly higher spin rates from the rough. Although both views are supported by technical studies, square-groove irons are regularly used today.

Hole 27

The Right of Publicity:
"Grip it and rip it"

Federal: *John Daly Enterprises, LLC v. Hippo Golf Co.*, 646 F. Supp. 2d 1347 (S.D. Fla. 2009)

John Daly is a professional golfer known for his long drives, rough-and-tumble lifestyle, and loud, psychedelic golfing outfits and clothing line. Many golf fans associate his aggressive style on the golf course with the phrase "grip it and rip it."

"Big John" has had his share of difficulties both off and on the course. He admits that he has had a rocky relationship with some equipment manufacturers because of his personal problems.[1] With some fans, he continues to be a favorite underdog whenever he tees it up.[2]

---

1. In 1999, for example, his drinking and gambling problems led to his loss of a multimillion-dollar endorsement contract with Callaway Golf.

2. Big John has posted a number of important wins on the PGA Tour, European Tour, and other golfing events. His playoff victory over Costantino Rocca at the 1995 British Open and being named PGA Tour Comeback Player of the Year in 2004 stand out.

Daly also has been cited by the PGA numerous times. As of 2010, the PGA cited him 11 times for "conduct unbecoming a professional" and another 21 times for "failure to give best efforts." He has been fined by the PGA more than $100,000 for his behavior. He has also picked up international fines. During the 2012 UBS Hong Kong Open, for example, Daly launched his putter into the trees after being upset by fans using cell phones and cameras, which led to a fine by the European Tour.

The Facts

John Daly Enterprises owns all of Big John's intellectual property rights, including the three trademarks.[3] The following is the signature and lion swing registered trademark:

---

3. U.S. Trademark Reg. 2,559,785 (John Daly signature and Lion swing design), U.S. Trademark Reg. 3,138,914 (John Daly signature), and U.S. Trademark Reg. 3,200,989 (Lion head design). The latter two trademarks were registered after Hippo discontinued selling merchandise and equipment bearing Daly's signature on January 31, 2005

Hole 27: The Right of Publicity

Hippo Golf is a golf equipment manufacturer. It entered into a sponsorship contract with John that made him the principal spokesman for Hippo during the period January 1, 2001, through December 31, 2003. The contract guaranteed him $50,000 per quarter in return for making public appearances and displaying the Hippo logo on his outfits and equipment during golf events.

John and Hippo entered into a second contract in 2002 for the licensing of his name, likeness, and marks for Hippo's use in the sale of their products. This contract, like the spokesman's contract, also ended on December 31, 2003.

Daly's personal battles with alcohol, gambling, and assorted other problems led Hippo to part company with him when their contracts were up. Because Hippo had product inventory based on Daly's endorsement, Hippo was given until March 31, 2004, to dispose of all its inventory of Daly-branded merchandise.

By the fall of 2004, John appeared to be on the verge of a professional comeback. He was named PGA Tour Comeback Player of the Year, was 19th on the tour's money list, and was under a sponsorship contract with the golf equipment company Dunlop. His improved good fortune ultimately led, however, to litigation with Hippo.

Hippo continued to sell merchandise and equipment bearing John Daly's signature without his permission for 10 months after the March 2004 grace period in their contract ended. The company also continued to use John's name and picture on its website without his permission. The website displayed his name and picture under the heading "PLAYERS PREVIOUSLY ASSOCIATED WITH HIPPO."

The website contained the statement:

> The twice major winner and golfing superstar, John Daly, will continue to be synonomous [sic] with Hippo.

Renowned as the longest hitter in the professional game, Daly truly had the power of Hippo behind his game, working closely with the Hippo design teams over the years to produce some of the most technologically advanced woods to hit the golf market.

Although this advertising may have been a hit in the golf market for Hippo, it created a marketing problem. John was then under a contract with Dunlop to promote its equipment. John was also miffed by the fact that he was not receiving any licensing royalties from Hippo because their contract had ended.

As a result, John found a lawyer and sued Hippo for violation of federal trademark law, unauthorized use of his name and likeness under Florida law, and breach of their licensing contract. He moved for summary judgment, which the court granted in part.

The Law
Federal Trademark Law

Under federal trademark law, no infringement exists without the use of the trademark or something similar to it.[4] The "likelihood of consumer confusion" is a legal key that unlocks the question of liability. The use of a colorable imitation of a protected trademark by an infringer that results in likely consumer confusion is the basis for finding liability.[5]

---

4. The Lanham Act, 15 U.S.C. § 1114.
5. 15 U.S.C. § 1114(1) provides:

"Any person who shall, without the consent of the registrant—(a) use in commerce any reproduction, counterfeit, copy, or colorable imitation of a registered mark in connection with the sale, offering for sale, distribution, or advertising of any goods or services on or in connection with which such use is likely to cause confusion, or to cause mistake, or to deceive."

As a general matter, the federal courts use a variety of factors to determine whether consumer confusion is likely. Because the trademark statute does not identify the factors to be used in determining whether consumer confusion exists, the courts often look to the *Restatement of Torts* and *Restatement (Third) of Unfair Competition* for legal guidance.

John Daly's trademark covered his signature and lion swing design.[6] Infringement of a federally registered trademark does not require use of the actual mark. The court had no difficulty in finding that the use of only part of his trademark, his signature, on Hippo's merchandise would likely result in consumer confusion given Daly's then-current endorsement of the Dunlop merchandise. Weighing various factors, such as the distinctiveness of the trademark, the similarity of the trademarks, and market sharing, was unnecessary to determine the existence of consumer confusion, presumably because the likely confusion was so clear.[7]

State Law: The Right of Publicity and Breach of Contract

In some states the right of publicity applies only to individuals who are well known. Big John was undoubtedly well known as a golfing celebrity. Florida law prohibits the unauthorized publication of any person's name, portrait, photograph, or other likeness for commercial or advertising purposes. Thus, the protec-

---

6. The Daly trademark applies to the following: Clothing, Golfing Apparel and Accessories, Namely, Shirts, T-shirts, Sweatshirts, Pants, Shorts, Jackets, Sweaters, Gloves, Socks, Footwear, Shoes, Sweat Bands, Rainwear, Hats, and Headwear (Int. Cl. 28); Sporting Articles, Namely, Golf Bag Covers, Golf Bag Tags, Golf Bags, Golf Ball Markers, Golf Ball Retrievers, Golf Balls, Golf Club Heads, Golf Club Inserts, Golf Club Swing Aids, Namely, Long Drive Power Enhancers, Golf Clubs, Headcovers for Golf Clubs, Golf Gloves, Golf Irons, Golf Putter Covers, Golf Putters, Golf Putting Aids, Namely, Practice Clubs, Golf Tees. JOHN DALY™2559785.

7. The question of damages was left to be established at trial.

tion afforded by the statute applies to any person and not just those who are well known.

The statute is designed to protect the autonomy and privacy of an individual by preventing others from commercially exploiting a person's identity. When an individual is well known by the public, the law also serves to prevent consumer confusion about an individual's association or endorsement of a product.

The unauthorized publication law has statutory and judicially recognized limits. The prohibition on use does not apply to news reporting, commentaries having a current and legitimate public interest, and limitations similar to the first-sale doctrine of copyright law.[8] In addition to statutory exceptions, the protection against unauthorized publication also is limited by state and federal constitutional law.[9]

Hippo argued that the statement appearing on its website was simply a true factual statement. Although this undoubtedly was factually correct, the court parried the argument. The prob-

---

8. *See e.g.*, FLA. STAT. ANN. 540.08 (West). Section 540.08 (4) (b) provides:

"The use of such name, portrait, photograph, or other likeness in connection with the resale or other distribution of literary, musical, or artistic productions or other articles of merchandise or property where such person has consented to the use of her or his name, portrait, photograph, or likeness on or in connection with the initial sale or distribution thereof.

9. For example, Tiger Woods lost his right of publicity claim against Rick Rush, a sports artist in ETW Corp. v. Jireh Publishing, Inc., 332 F.3d 915 (6th Cir. 2003). The case involved a painting by Rush featuring three literal likenesses of Tiger in different poses in the foreground, with the Augusta National Clubhouse behind him and the likenesses of other famous golfing champions looking down on him. The Sixth Circuit found the painting worthy of First Amendment protection. It was a panorama of Woods's historic 1997 victory at the world-famous Masters Tournament, and conveyed a message about the significance of his achievement through images that suggested he would eventually join the ranks of the world's best golfers.

In balancing the competing interests of the artist and Tiger, the Sixth Circuit observed:

"After balancing the societal and personal interests embodied in the First Amendment against Woods's property rights, we conclude that the effect of limiting Woods's right of publicity in this case is negligible and significantly outweighed by society's interest in freedom of artistic expression. *Id.* at 938.

lem was the commercial exploitation of Daly's name and likeness to promote Hippo's golf equipment without his consent. Its commercial promotion was not within the realm of fair use and constituted a violation of Florida law.[10] The use was simply a blatant attempt to capitalize on the fame of a well-known golfer.[11]

The breach of contract claim was based on the fact that Hippo sold Daly branded equipment without paying him during the inventory sell-off grace period, which ended on March 31, 2004. Hippo admitted its contract liability, but disagreed with the calculation of damages. It maintained that all the royalty payments had been paid, and that Daly had in fact been overpaid by about a thousand dollars. This was simply a factual dispute that could not be properly decided on the motion for summary judgment.

The court granted Daly summary judgment on the issue of liability for his federal, state, and contract claims. But it also found that genuine issues of material fact remained on the question of damages, which would have to be resolved at trial.

Conclusion

The federal court granted John Daly's motion for liability against Hippo on his federal trademark infringement claim and also on

---

10. The Florida statute does not mention fair use as a defense, which does not mean that it may be available as a common-law defense. Federal copyright law may provide states recognizing such a defense with guidance to determine the meaning of fair use. Copyright law requires a court to consider the following factors in finding fair use: (1) the purpose and character of the use, including whether such use is of a commercial nature or is for nonprofit educational purposes; (2) the nature of the copyrighted work; (3) the amount and substantiality of the portion used in relation to the copyrighted work as a whole; and (4) the effect of the use upon the potential market for or value of the copyrighted work. 17 U.S.C. § 107.

11. The damages associated with this violation would have to be determined at trial because the value of Daly's name and likeness depended on the facts yet to be established.

his state statutory right of publicity claim and breach of contract claim. As material issues of fact concerning damages existed, damages would be determined at trial.

On this issue of federal trademark infringement, the court recognized that Daly's trademark covered his combined signature and lion-like swing logo. Although the Hippo merchandise featured only Daly's signature, this partial use of the trademark was enough to establish an infringement. The use of the signature was a colorable imitation of his registered mark and was likely to cause consumer confusion.

Florida law statutorily prohibits the unauthorized publication of a person's name, portrait, photograph or other likeness for commercial purposes. The federal court found Hippo sought to capitalize on the value of John Daly's name and likeness in promoting its product line after its endorsement and licensing agreements ended. Hippo's use constituted unauthorized commercial exploitation in violation of state law and was not protected by a fair use defense.

Hippo admitted Daly's liability for breach of contract. But it disagreed with the calculation of damages. Thus, the amount of the damages would have to be determined at trial. How much he finally received is not part of the public record.

Hole 28

Copying Famous Golf Holes:
Legal "gimmies"

Federal: *Pebble Beach Co. v. Tour 18 I, Ltd.*,
155 F.3d 526 (5th Cir. 1998)

Mother nature provides the basic palette for the design of a golf course.[1] Golf course architects then expend considerable time, resources, and creativity in altering the landscape to meet their design goals. They do this by changing the contour of the land, scattering water and sand hazards and other obstacles with abandon in order to challenge the skill of the good golfer and make life maddeningly difficult for the rest.

The Facts

The Texans behind the Tour 18 project (Dennis Wilkerson, Barron Jacobsen, and Jim Williams) wanted to build an 18-hole public golf course just outside Houston, Texas. They knew the key to success was a good design and aggressive marketing.

One problem was money. Hiring a prominent golf course

---

1. The influence of natural topography on golf course design is illustrated by the Old Course at St. Andrews. As early as the 15th century, golfers at St. Andrews followed a customary route through the terrain dictated by Mother Nature and maintained by roving sheep that kept the grass trimmed and fertilized. The original course had 11 holes. Because some of the holes were considered too short, the route was reduced to nines holes. It was then played twice, which is why it is customary to play 18 holes during a round of golf.

architect would be costly and would not guarantee the success of the project. They needed a legal "gimme."[2] Instead of hiring a renowned course architect, the entrepreneurial trio hit upon an innovative idea—they would simply copy the holes from famous golf courses around the United States and name their compilation course "Tour 18." Although imitation may be the sincerest form of flattery, every student beyond a certain age knows that copying can invite trouble.

As innovations go, the idea of replicating famous golf holes was, to their way of thinking, great publicity and financial suc-

---

2. In golf, a "gimme" is a shot that is conceded without actually being played. The conceded shot counts, however, for purposes of scoring. A gimme is sometimes used during match play when the gimme would not change the outcome of the hole, but is not allowed under the rules during stroke play. A gimme is commonly used as a courtesy by players during casual play. It is sometimes referred to as an agreement between two golfers, neither of whom can putt very well.

Hole 28: Copying Famous Golf Holes

cess. It would be their private oil patch. Avid golfers the world over would be familiar with the prestige and difficulty of the famous holes and would flock to the course. Some of the holes they copied have their own place in the world of golf: the "Blue Monster," "the Lighthouse Hole," and "the Church Pews." The course opened for business in late 1992.

The trio chose the copied holes based on several criteria, including the fame of the course, the fame of the hole itself, and their ability to replicate the hole after considering the geography, topography, and natural vegetation of their Texas tract.

They considered hundreds of golf holes for inclusion. The famous holes making the final cut included:

Tour 18 Hole	Original Hole and Location
1	Harbour Town # 18 (*Hilton Head Island, S.C.*)
2	Bay Hill # 6 (*Orlando, Fla.*)
3	Pinehurst No. 2, # 3 (*Pinehurst, N.C.*)
4	Inverness # 18 (*Toledo, Ohio*)
5	Augusta National # 11 (*Augusta, Ga.*)
6	Augusta National # 12 (*Augusta, Ga.*)
7	Augusta National # 13 (*Augusta, Ga.*)
8	LaCosta # 4 (*Carlsbad, Cal.*)
9	Sawgrass # 17 (*Ponte Vedra, Fla.*)
10	Desert Inn # 10 (*Las Vegas, Nev.*)
11	Disney # 6 (*Orlando, Fla.*)
12	Colonial # 3 (*Ft. Worth, Tex.*)
13	Pebble Beach # 14 (*Pebble Beach, Cal.*)
14	Oakmont # 3 (*Oakmont, Pa.*)
15	Shinnecock Hills # 8 (*Long Island, N.Y.*)
16	Merion # 11 (*Philadelphia, Pa.*)
17	Oak Tree # 8 (*Edmund, Okla.*)
18	Doral # 18 (*Miami, Fla.*)

The Little Book of Golf Law

The following depicts the Tour 18 holes that were challenged by the plaintiffs:

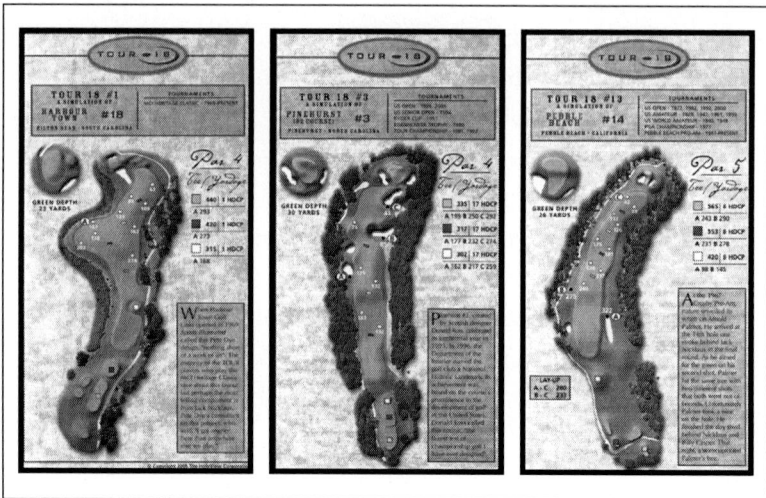

In addition to copying the layout of above famous golf holes, the trio also used the service marks[3] of the golf courses in their advertising. This use allowed them to capitalize on the publicity associated with the famous holes. To give golfers a heightened sense of enjoyment, signs at each of the copied holes told the golfers which replicated hole they were playing.

The Texas boys aggressively marketed Tour 18 as a golfer's dream. Just think of it: Golfers were given the chance to play replicated golf holes that affected the outcome of tournaments such as the U.S. Open, the Masters, the Tour Championship, and the PGA Championship.

Advertisements were placed in local and national publications, such as the *Houston Chronicle*, *Golf Digest*, *Golf Hous-*

---

3. Service marks and trademarks are those words, symbols, phrases, or designs that the public associates with a single source of goods and services. The Lanham Act, a federal statute, protects against service mark and trademark infringement.

Hole 28: Copying Famous Golf Holes

ton, *Corporate Golfer*, and in other promotional golf brochures and newsletters. Golfers were seductively promised a unique experience: "Imagine yourself playing on carefully simulated holes from some of the greatest golf holes in America. This collaboration of incredible replicas offers players a memorable experience of walking in the footsteps of some of the great legends before them."

One Tour 18 brochure captured the dream this way:

> Imagine yourself facing the awesome challenge of Augusta's famous Amen Corner, or contemplating Harbour Town's #18 complete with the red-and-white-striped lighthouse to line up your tee shot, then finishing off with Doral's "Blue Monster" but before that, you'll be faced by some of the most renowned golfer's challenges, like . . . Pinehurst #3. . . and many others. No this is not a dream, this is Tour 18. Tour 18 is the only golf course of its kind in the world. Each hole is a careful simulation of one of America's most famous golf holes. . . . Each hole features something unique . . . [a]nd with a little imagination you can almost smell the salty air and hear the seals barking as you play Pebble Beach's #14.

Though one might need an active or perhaps alcohol-fueled imagination to "almost smell the salty air" and "hear the seals barking" in a Houston suburb, Tour 18 was a financial success. In its first year alone, the golf course rewarded its resourceful owners with $1.7 million in profits. Not about to let their idea go to seed, the trio quickly opened a second Tour 18 in nearby Flower Mound, Texas. They were Texans and thinking big. Plans were quickly hatched to expand the Tour 18 concept to Arizona, Georgia, and Virginia.

The owners and operators of Pebble Beach Golf Links,[4] Pinehurst No. 2,[5] and Harbour Town Golf Links[6] were neither impressed by Tour 18's success nor flattered by the imitation. They responded by filing suit in federal court, seeking both damages and a permanent injunction against Tour 18. The plaintiffs alleged, among other things, that Tour 18 violated federal and state law first by using their names (which they claimed were protected service marks) without their permission in Tour 18 advertising, promotions, and on-site signs and also by copying their golf-hole designs without permission.

More was at stake to the plaintiffs than bruised professional pride. Tour 18 was a public golf course that charged each golfer $75 in greens fees. By comparison, it was a bargain. Why pay a premium when you can get a bargain? A golfer would have had

---

4. Pebble Beach is a California general partnership. It owns and operates five golf courses: Pebble Beach Golf Links, The Links at Spanish Bay, Spyglass Hill, Peter Hay Golf Course, and Old Del Monte Golf Course.

5. Resorts is a North Carolina corporation that is owned by Club Corporation of America. Resorts owns and operates a golf resort, Pinehurst, in North Carolina that includes seven golf courses, numbered 1 through 7.

6. Sea Pines is a South Carolina corporation. It owns and operates Harbour Town Golf Links as part of its golf and tennis resort on Hilton Head Island.

Hole 28: Copying Famous Golf Holes

to pay $245 in greens fees at Pebble Beach, $164 at Pinehurst, and $145 at Harbour Town—which by today's prices is a bargain. To the plaintiffs, golfing was big business, and they were not about to let an upstart Texas golf course trade on the goodwill and prestige of either their names or their golf-hole designs.

The plaintiffs' legal claims were clouded by facts relevant to the law of intellectual property. Pebble Beach did not own a trademark, copyright, or patent for the design of its copied 14th hole, and did not include it in any of its advertising materials. Similarly, Pinehurst did not own a trademark, copyright, or patent for the design of the copied third hole, and also did not include it in its advertising.

Unlike Pebble Beach and Pinehurst, Harbour Town's 18th hole is prominently featured in all its advertising materials. The 18th at Harbour Town is widely known to television fans because of the distinctive red and white lighthouse in the background. Harbour Town does not own the lighthouse. But Tour 18's replicated lighthouse was nearly identical to Harbour Town's signature neighboring lighthouse.

In a lengthy opinion, the federal district court found Tour 18 liable for service mark infringement, trade dress infringement,[7] unfair competition in violation of the Lanham Act, common-law unfair competition, and dilution under Texas law. But that opinion was not the end of the story, because Tour 18 appealed to the Court of Appeals for the Fifth Circuit. The appellate court saw the matter differently.

---

7. The Lanham Act protects unregistered "trade dress" when certain requirements are met. The term "trade dress" refers to overall appearance of a product, including its size, shape, color, or color combinations. The trade dresses at issue were the shapes of the plaintiffs' holes, their length and width, the placement and shape of bunker and water hazards, and so on. Harbour Town made the additional trade dress claim that the design and appearance of the red-and-white-striped lighthouse used by Tour 18 violated its trade dress.

The Law

The federal law of intellectual property is conventionally divided into copyrights, patents, and trademarks. Included within the category of trademark law are the subcategories of service marks and trade dress. Federal trademark law does not preempt state regulation, which is the reason the plaintiffs' complaint asserted a violation of both federal and state law.

Copyright

Some readers may be surprised to learn that the design of a golf hole is not protected under federal copyright law.[8] Copyright law protects original works of authorship once they are fixed in any tangible medium of expression.[9] Once the work is protected by the copyright, the owner has the exclusive right to make and control copies of the work. Thereafter, any unauthorized use of the copyrighted work constitutes an infringement and exposes the infringer to liability.[10]

The design of a golf hole does not meet the copyright definition of a protected architectural work. Congress has defined the term "architectural work" as "the design of a *building* as embodied in any tangible medium of expression, including a

---

8. *See* Raphael Winick, *Copyright Protection for Architecture After the Architectural Works Copyright Protection Act of 1990*, 41 Duke L.J. 1598, 1613 (1992) ("Golf courses, gardens, tunnels, bridges, overpasses, fences, and walls are only a few of the structures designed by architects that would not fit the common definition of building."). For purposes of understanding Tour 18, the golf course exclusion was critical.

9. Works of authorship are broadly encompassing and include the following identified categories: (1) literary works; (2) musical works, including any accompanying words; (3) dramatic works, including any accompanying music; (4) pantomimes and choreographic works; (5) pictorial, graphic, and sculptural works; (6) motion pictures and other audiovisual works; (7) sound recordings; and (8) architectural works. 17 U.S.C. § 102 (a).

10. The potential remedies include: 1) an injunction (17 U.S.C. § 502); 2) damages and profits (17 U.S.C. § 504); and 3) attorneys' fees and costs (17 U.S.C. § 505). In extreme cases, criminal sanctions may apply (17 U.S.C. § 506).

building, architectural plans, or drawings. The work includes the overall form as well as the arrangement and composition of spaces and elements in the design, but does not include individual standard features." This definition limits the category of architectural works to the design of buildings, such as houses and shopping centers.

In addition, copyright law requires that the design aspects of a protected work must not be considered as utilitarian or useful. Courts frequently state that copyright protection does not extend to functional aspects of the work, which is another way of saying the utilitarian or useful aspects. If the design elements of a golf hole reflect a merger of aesthetic and functional aspects, the work may not be copyrightable. Consequently, without the benefit of a design patent, the claimant does not obtain a protectable interest in the useful article depicted by those plans.

Service Mark and Unfair Competition

The primary federal trademark statute is the Lanham Act.[11] A trademark identifies the source of the goods, whereas a service mark identifies the source of the services. As a general matter, the same legal rules apply to both. The dual goals of the law are to protect consumers from confusion and the producers of goods and services against unfair competition. The underlying theory of unfair competition is the inequitable diversion of business outside the arena of normal competition. Protection of the holder's reputation, even when there is no diversion of trade, is also an important concern of the Lanham Act.

A plaintiff must first show that it has a valid service mark worthy of protection, and then prove that the defendant's use of

---

11. 15 U.S.C. §§ 1051 *et seq.* (popularly referred to as the Lanham Act).

the mark is likely to cause consumer confusion. Unregistered service marks are entitled to protection under limited circumstances.

Pebble Beach and Pinehurst owned registered service marks for the names "Pebble Beach" and "Pinehurst" issued by the U.S. Patent and Trademark Office. In contrast, Sea Pines did not own a federally registered service mark for the name "Harbour Town." Therefore, it sought protection as an unregistered service mark claimant to the name and to the lighthouse image that was part of its logo. In essence, it claimed that the name "Harbour Town" and the symbolic lighthouse used in its marketing qualified as a service mark. The appellate court found that the plaintiffs were on the fairway—each plaintiff had a service mark worthy of legal protection.

But just being on the fairway in golf isn't enough. The next issue was whether there was a likelihood of consumer confusion. The court found that Tour 18's advertising practices were likely to confuse purchasers. But, one might reasonably ask, how could any golfer be confused? Even the most confused golfers, such as those who regularly can't remember how many strokes they have taken on a hole, ought to remember they were playing golf in Texas, not in some other state.

There are various kinds of confusion. The court reasoned that the possible confusion did not pertain to where the golfer was playing golf, but rather in the belief that Tour 18 had secured permission and approval from the plaintiffs to use their service marks in advertising and to use their names on each golf hole. The plaintiffs used both witness testimony and survey evidence to show actual confusion by players. The potential for this type of sponsorship or endorsement confusion was exacerbated by the similarity and overlap in advertising campaigns by the plaintiffs and the defendant, the fact that the plaintiffs and

Hole 28: Copying Famous Golf Holes

the defendant both provided golf services, and the defendant's intent to take advantage of the plaintiffs' reputation, goodwill, and service marks.

The plaintiffs were making progress, but obstacles lay ahead. The federal law allows a defendant to assert certain legal defenses. Tour 18 argued two defenses, comparative advertising and effective use of disclaimers.

An imitator may lawfully use another's product for purposes of comparative advertising so long as the consumer will not be confused. Tour 18 argued that it had used the plaintiffs' service marks only to inform its golfers as to the source of the copied golf holes. Therefore, Tour 18's use of the plaintiffs' service marks was for comparative advertising purposes and thus lawful.

The court reasonably wondered what comparative advertising purpose was served by Tour 18's use of plaintiffs' service marks on the Tour 18's restaurant menu, including the Harbour Town sandwich, the Pinehurst tuna salad, and the Pebble Beach French toast. Moreover, the court noted that Tour 18's prominent use of the plaintiffs' service marks in its brochures, signs, advertisements, and scorecards showed that Tour 18's purpose was not to inform its golfers. In the end, the court rejected its defense because of the existence of consumer confusion.

Tour 18 also argued that its disclaimers effectively eliminated confusion. In order for the disclaimer defense to work, Tour 18 had to show that its disclaimers were prominently displayed. But this defense was also rejected by the court. Tour 18 presented no evidence that the disclaimers it used were actually effective in eliminating confusion. Moreover, most of its advertisements did not contain any disclaimers, and those that did were obscure and in minuscule print, and thus neither conspicuous nor prominent.

Although the plaintiffs prevailed on the service mark claim, it should be clearly understood that the court's finding did not require Tour 18 to alter any of the holes it had copied.

Trademark: Trade Dress Infringement

Trade dress, which is a special type of trademark, refers to the total visual image or overall appearance of a product, including its size, shape, and so on. The trade dress can be goods, services, or a combination of both.

The purpose of trade dress protection, like trademark protection, is to secure for the owner of the trade dress the goodwill of its business and to protect the ability of consumers to distinguish among competing products. In order to accomplish these objectives, the trade dress must be used as a source identifier for the goods and services.

In order to be a source identifier, the trade dress must be distinctive—it must identify and distinguish the goods or services from other goods and services. The mark may be either inherently distinctive or acquire distinctiveness by becoming known to the public in the marketplace.

Pebble Beach and Pinehurst claimed that the defendant's copying of their golf hole designs were trade dress infringements. Harbour Town had an additional argument: It claimed that Tour 18's copying of the lighthouse was a trade dress infringement.

The court found that nothing about the Pebble Beach or Pinehurst golf holes served as a source indicator. In fact, the court found that the designs were mere variations on common golf hole designs. The hole designs were neither inherently distinctive nor had they acquired a secondary meaning, primarily because the advertising by Pebble Beach and Pinehurst did not focus on these holes. Therefore, it rejected their trade dress infringement claims.

In contrast, Harbour Town's 18th hole was found to be distinctive. The lighthouse had come to serve as a source indicator for the hole in the mind of the public. Golfers seeing the red-and-white-striped lighthouse at Tour 18 would think of the Harbour Town golf course. Having found the design distinctive, the next question was whether there was the likelihood of consumer confusion. Since the court had already found the likelihood of confusion with regard to the service mark infringement, the court used the same reasoning on the claim of trade dress infringement. The likelihood of consumer confusion was that the use of the lighthouse by Tour 18 was endorsed by Sea Pines.

The court's service mark analysis suggests the difficulties lying ahead for plaintiffs claiming trade dress infringement. Almost all golf holes combine common features, such as bunkering and split-level greens. Thus, it may be difficult to establish the necessary level of distinctiveness to serve as a source indicator. The requisite level of fame needed to establish secondary meaning is also likely to be problematic for establishing any protection for most golf holes.

Conclusion

The Tour 18 business strategy was built on replicating famous golf hole designs and packaging them together as a unique experience. After chipping over some legal hazards, the strategy paid off. The Tour 18 course in Humble, Texas, at the center of the dispute was sold to the Arnold Palmer Golf Management, which operates and manages it today.

The court found no evidentiary support for the award of damages. Tour 18 was enjoined, however, from using the service marks "Pebble Beach" and "Pinehurst" in all contexts except use in comparative advertising that contained prominent and clear disclaimers. Although not enjoined from using the Pebble Beach or Pinehurst golf hole designs, Tour 18 was enjoined from using a lighthouse that was confusingly similar to the trade dress lighthouse of the Harbour Town 18th hole. Since Tour 18 could no longer copy Harbour Town's 18th hole, there was no need for comparative advertising. Therefore, Tour 18 was permanently enjoined from using the Harbor Town service mark for any purpose.

As a practical matter, Tour 18 stands for the proposition that little protection is available to prevent the copying of famous golf hole designs. The plaintiffs in Tour 18 were the golf course operators and not the architects. Unlike the golf course owner and operator, a golf course architect has an arguable false advertising claim under the Lanham Act that the copied hole inherently misrepresents the original design of the architect.[12]

---

12. The plaintiffs in Tour 18 brought a Lanham Act false advertising claim under section 43(a)(1)(B). They alleged that the word "copy," used in advertisements to describe the holes, misled consumers into believing the holes were exact copies. The federal district court rejected the claim because the plaintiffs failed to provide any evidence to support the argument.

Hole 29

Resale of Trademarked Golf Balls:
Finders keepers, losers weepers

Federal: *Nitro Leisure Products, LLC v. Acushnet*, 341 F.3d 1356 (Fed. Cir. 2003)

In the pantheon of movies about golf, *Tin Cup* is considered a film classic.[1] In the film, Roy "Tin Cup" McAvoy (Kevin Costner) is a former golf prodigy struggling with his personal demons on the road to making a professional comeback. In a scene toward the end of the movie, Roy is in a three-way tie for the championship of the U.S. Open on the last day of the tournament.

Excitement builds as Roy plays the par-5 18th hole. Roy refuses to play it safe by laying up short of the water hazard and goes for the green. Heartbreaking disaster follows as Roy hits ball after ball into the water hazard, throwing away his chance for victory.

---

1. This scene is based on an actual event involving Gary McCord, a well-known television golf commentator and professional golfer. During a 1987 tournament, his water hazard derring-do cost him 15 strokes on a hole.

Threatened by disqualification for being down to his last ball, the "Golf God" relents. His shot clears the water and rolls into the hole. His love interest, Dr. Molly Griswold (Rene Russo), assures him a place in golf history is secure: "Five years from now nobody will remember who won or lost, but they're gonna remember your 12." Indeed, nobody forgets such golf calamities.[2]

Most moviegoers undoubtedly never thought about all those new balls Roy hit into the water hazard. In real life, some golfers carry ball retrievers to recover their pond balls. Many seem to take unusual pleasure in fishing for as many balls as they can reach. These balls probably get reused.

But the recovery and reuse of lost pond balls is also big business. Rarely does one see a professional golfer fishing for a ball he or she has contributed to the watery depths. But, rest assured, there is gold in those lost balls. Golf courses often employ divers or use other recovery systems to retrieve "pond balls" before recycling them for future sale. The more water hazards, the more finders benefit from the Scottish proverb "finders keepers, losers weepers."[3]

---

2. Art often mimics life. During the 1999 British Open, Jean Van de Velde made a decision that still reverberates through the halls of Carnoustie Golf Links. Three strokes in the lead and needing only a 6 on the par-4 18th hole, Van de Velde squandered the championship by clanging one shot into the bleachers, another into the water hazard, and one into a bunker before making a triple-bogey 7. Paul Lawrie holed his shot from the same bunker to force a playoff, which Lawrie ultimately won.

3. The *Rules of Golf* state that a ball not found within five minutes after the search has begun is considered lost. A penalty of one stroke is imposed for a lost ball. Under Rule 27-1.c., the unfortunate golfer must return to the spot from which the original ball was last played. This is referred to as a stroke and distance penalty.

If the ball is subsequently found after five minutes have elapsed, the ball is no longer legally lost because it still belongs to the golfer. Yet, the ball is still treated as lost under the *Rules of Golf*, so the stroke and distance penalty applies. This makes sense, because otherwise some players might never give up the search for their missing ball. Most golfers have occasionally encountered folks who are unaware the need to give up the search.

Hole 29: Resale of Trademarked Golf Balls

Are balls that have been fished out of the water up to par? *Golf Digest* did a study some years ago that demonstrated that the performance of water balls decreases with the type of ball and the passage of time the ball has been immersed in the water. For three-piece balls, the study reported a 6-yard loss of distance after spending eight days in the water, a 12-yard loss after three months, and a 15-yard loss after six months. For two-piece balls, they found about a 6-yard loss after eight days in the water, about a 9-yard loss after three months, and after six months in the water, the ball inexplicably averaged one yard farther than the ball that had been in the water three months.

Although interesting, the study usually doesn't help the buyer or fisher of water balls because one can't accurately determine how long the ball has been in the water hazard.

The Facts

The company Nitro is in the business of selling used balls at a discounted rate. The used golf ball market is big business, because many golfers focus just on price. In 2001, for example, Nitro sold close to $5 million in refurbished balls.

Most recycled balls are retrieved from water hazards. Nitro offers two categories of reclaimed balls. The first category includes those that are in relatively good condition. These lost balls are simply cleaned up and repackaged for sale.

The second category requires more extensive refurbishing and includes balls with stains, scuffs, or other blemishes. The refurbishing process includes removing the balls' trademark and model markings, the clear coat layer, and the base coat of paint. The balls are then repainted, clear-coated, and the original trademark is reaffixed. Nitro stamps the ball "USED & REFUR-BISHED BY SECOND CHANCE" OR "USED & REFURBISHED

The Little Book of Golf Law

BY GOLFBALLSDIRECT.COM." Some, but not all, of the refurbished balls also bear the Nitro trademark.

Nitro's refurbished balls are packaged in containers displaying the following disclaimer:

> ATTENTION USED/REFURBISHED GOLF BALLS: The enclosed contents of used/refurbished golf balls are USED GOLF BALLS. Used/Refurbished golf balls are subject to performance variations from new ones. These used/refurbished balls were processed via one or more of the following steps: stripping, painting, stamping and/or clear coating in our factory. This product has NOT been endorsed or approved by the original manufacturer and the balls DO NOT fall under the original manufacturer's warranty.

Would you rather be a plaintiff or a defendant? Nitro decided that it was better to be the plaintiff, so the company sued Acushnet in federal district court in Florida for unfair competition. Undoubtedly, the decision to initiate litigation followed threats from Acushnet that Nitro was violating its intellectual property rights under state and federal law. In response to Nitro's Florida lawsuit, Acushnet then sued Nitro in federal district court in California. After some jurisdictional wrangling, the California federal action was transferred and the legal disputes consolidated in Florida.

Acushnet moved for a preliminary injunction in the consolidated action on the theory that Nitro's refurbishing process, which involved repainting and reaffixing Acushnet's Titleist trademark, produced a ball that bore no resemblance to a new Acushnet ball in performance, quality, or appearance. Acushnet also claimed Nitro was violating its trademark.

Hole 29: Resale of Trademarked Golf Balls

The Florida district court denied Acushnet's motion for a preliminary injunction on the theory that the differences between Acushnet's new golf balls and Nitro's refurbished balls were no so great as to cause the likelihood of consumer deception, confusion, or mistake.[4] Acushnet appealed the denial of the preliminary injunction to the U.S. Court of Appeals for the Federal Circuit.

The Law

The federal Trademark Law (Lanham Act) is design to protect both the trademark holder and the consuming public. Liability is imposed for unauthorized commercial use of the trademark that is likely to deceive, cause confusion, or result in mistake. The central legal question before the Federal Circuit was whether the district court applied the correct infringement test.

Acushnet argued that a materially different test should be applied. It maintained that because the refurbished balls were materially different from the original Titleist balls, the consuming public was deceived when Nitro re-stamped the refurbished ball with the Titleist trademark. In addition, any inferior performance of the balls bearing the Titleist trademark would be attributed to Acushnet, not Nitro.

The landmark case on the use on trademarks on repaired or refurbished products is the Supreme Court decision in *Champion Spark Plug Co. v. Sanders*.[5] The Court in *Champion* found

---

4. The decision to seek a preliminary injunction is a strategic one. Although it does not determine the merits of the underlying claim, success in getting one creates a strong incentive to settle the dispute. Fed. R. Civ. P. 65 governs motions for preliminary injunctions, but does not provide the standard that should be used in granting or denying the motion.
   The court required the moving party, Acushnet, to show the likelihood of success on the merits in order to prevail on its motion for a preliminary injunction. Other federal courts express the standard differently.
5. Champion Spark Plug Co. v. Sanders, 331 U.S. 125 (1947).

that used and repaired goods may be sold under the trademark of the original manufacturer without deceiving the consumer. Therefore, the sale of repaired and reconditioned Champion spark plugs under the Champion trademark did not constitute an infringement providing the defendant attempted to restore the original condition of the goods "so far as possible" *and* made full disclosure of this fact to the consumer. Restoration "so far as possible" protects the manufacturer's interest, and full disclosure protects the consumer's expectation.

The Federal Circuit found the *Champion* case controlling. The court relied on the crucial factual finding that the alteration of the balls was not so extensive that it would be misleading to bear the original trademark. To the extent that the refurbishing is so extensive that the ball should be treated as a different product, then the use of the Titleist trademark would cause consumer confusion.

The continued use of the original Titleist trademark on the refurbished balls did not constitute a trademark infringement that should be preliminarily enjoined. Providing the consumer gets a ball with the expected characteristics and is not misled, and the brand of the trademark owner is not eroded by being identified with an inferior quality, the Lanham Act does not prohibit the truthful use of another's trademark.

There are limitations to applying these legal principles. In 1995, for example, Acushnet discovered that Birdie Golf Ball Company was stripping, repainting, and remarking pond balls that bore various Acushnet trademarks, including Titleist and Pinnacle. Unlike the facts in *Nitro,* many of the balls were not manufactured by Acushnet, even though the balls were re-stamped bearing the Acushnet trademark.

Acushnet filed a complaint and motion for a temporary

restraining order in *Acushnet v. Birdie Golf Ball Co.*[6] It succeeded in getting the restraining order and seized the printing plates and thousands of refurbished golf balls falsely bearing the Acushnet trademark. Upon entering the facility to effectuate the seizure, it was learned that the title "Birdie Golf" was not related to scoring one under par on a hole, but to the fact that tropical birds were flying free within the building and doing what comes naturally. The federal district court permanently enjoined Birdie Golf from re-stamping non-Acushnet balls and enjoined Birdie from claiming in its advertising and promotional materials that the refurbished balls were in perfect condition. Clearly, Birdie Golf had crossed the line drawn by the Supreme Court in *Champion*.

Conclusion

The Federal Circuit upheld the Florida district court's decision denying Acushnet's request for a preliminary injunction. This was not a decision on the merits. Acushnet still has the chance in a motion for summary judgment or at trial to show that the refurbished Nitro balls cause consumer confusion. But the marking and packaging of the refurbished balls by Nitro make the likelihood of Acushnet succeeding questionable.

Trademark owners enjoy significant protections. But as *Nitro* illustrates, the ability of a trademark holder to prevent the trademark being used on refurbished or reconditioned golf balls is limited. The "likelihood of consumer confusion" standard, judged from the perspective of the reasonable prudent purchaser in the resale market, lies at the core of trademark protection.

---

6. Acushnet v. Birdie Golf Ball Co., 95-7030-CIV-Gonzalez (U.S. Dist. Ct. for the Southern Dist. of Fla.). Case report provided by Peter D. Vogl, partner, Orrick, Herrington & Sutcliffe, LLP.

An alternate theory to trademark infringement is dilution. Federal law protects trademark dilution, which is defined as "the lessening of the capacity of a famous mark to identify and distinguish goods and services."[7] The advantage of this theory is that it does not require a showing of a likelihood of consumer confusion. The problem with applying the theory in *Nitro* is the fact that Acushnet did not show that there was any actual dilution of its trademark.

---

7. 15 U.S.C. § 1127.

Part V

Environmental Law

Hole 30

The Federal Endangered Species Act (ESA): "Can't we all just get along?"

Federal: *Wild Equity Institute, et al. v. City and County of San Francisco*, 2012 WL 14581178 (N.D. Cal. April 26, 2012)[1]

Most folks consider themselves environmentalists. After all, who can be against the environment? The federal Endangered Species Act (ESA) is one of the country's most robust environmental laws. This case shows that the ESA goes beyond protecting those animals that are only cuddly or cute and illustrates the process of navigating through its requirements.

The Facts

Sharp Park and its public golf course are located in Pacifica, California. It is owned and operated by the City and County of San Francisco. The golf course, which opened in 1931, was landscaped by John McLaren and designed by famed architect Dr. Alister Mackenzie.[2] The course is considered part of the early

---

1. The Wild Equity Institute was joined as a plaintiff by the Sierra Club. The San Francisco Public Golf Alliance intervened as a defendant.
2. Dr. Mackenzie was the architect of several world-renowned golf courses, including Augusta National and Cypress Point.

Above: The San Francisco Garter Snake. At right: The California Red-Legged Frog

movement to make golf available to the American working class and has earned its reputation as the "Poor Man's Pebble Beach."

Many of the features of the golf course, such as green contours, tees, and bunkers, have lost their original detail with the passage of time. For example, storms have destroyed several of the original holes. Notwithstanding the many changes to the course, it is still considered a historical treasure. It has been designated a "historical resource" by the San Francisco Planning Department. The golf course also is considered historically and culturally significant by the City of Pacifica, the Pacifica Historical Society, and the Cultural Landscape Foundation. The United States Golf Association has called it "one of America's most precious public golf courses."

In addition to being lined with stately cypress and pine

Hole 30: The Federal Endangered Species Act

trees, the 18-hole, par 72 golf course offers fabulous views of the Pacific Ocean. The Sharp Park wetlands complex, which is to the west and southwest of the golf course, consists of Laguna Salada, the Horse Stable Pond, and a connecting channel between these freshwater ponds. The surrounding wetlands, with reeds, cattails, and tulles, provide the home to a variety of birds, amphibians, and reptiles. Sharp Park's lagoons and wetlands provide the habitat for the California Red-Legged Frog (Frog) and the San Francisco Garter Snake (Snake).

So what is the problem?

The golfers and the Frog and Snake all like the golf course environs. Both the Frog and the Snake are protected species by the federal Endangered Species Act (ESA). The environmental plaintiffs argue that the golf course routine operations and activities violate the ESA.

During the winter rainy season, water levels rise in the Park's water bodies and flood portions of the golf course. To avoid this flooding, flood waters are pumped through pipes in the seawall to an outfall on the beach. The plaintiffs specifically allege that the water management practice of pumping of water to reduce the flooding of the golf course exposes the Frog egg masses to the air, causing their fatal desiccation, and thereby jeopardizing the Frog's population. They also claim that the pumps trap Frog tadpoles, causing their death. According to the plaintiffs, the pumping may be great for the golfers, but bad for the protected species.

The plaintiffs also claim that routine activities, such as lawn mowing and golf cart usage, harm the Snake and Frog by running over them or otherwise "harassing" them. This also violates the ESA.

The plaintiffs allege that the defendants' operations and activities have "taken" these protected species in violation of the ESA. Their lawsuit asks the federal court for declaratory relief and a preliminary injunction to stop the defendants from continuing to violate federal law.

The Frog

In 1996, the federal Fish and Wildlife Service (FWS) listed the Frog as a "threatened" species under the ESA.[3] The FWS found that the Frog was "likely to become an endangered species within the foreseeable future throughout all or a significant portion of its range." It found that the species had suffered massive declines in recent decades, and was found in only a few select coastal drainage areas. The listing as "threatened" brought the Frog within the ESA's umbrella of protection.

Some additional detail about the Frog is useful to understanding the ESA complaint. The amphibian's breeding typically starts during the rainy season. The egg masses laid by the female are attached to vegetation near the surface of the water to maximize growth potential and to minimize exposure to aquatic predators. If left undisturbed, the eggs hatch in 6 to 14 days. The tadpoles typically metamorphose into frogs several months later. According to the plaintiffs, pumping water off the golf course adversely affects the Frog and its habitat.

The Snake

The Snake is a harmless and multicolored serpent that can be identified by its reddish-orange head with red, black, and turquoise blue racing stripes on its sides and back. If you are a herpetologist or just like snakes, it's a beauty.

Unlike the "threatened" Frog, the Snake has been designated as an endangered subspecies since the ESA list was first

---

3. 16 U.S.C. § 1532(20); *see* 61 Fed. Reg. 25,813 (1996).

Hole 30: The Federal Endangered Species Act

established in 1973. According to plaintiffs, it is the most endangered serpent in North America. The Snake populations remain in only a few fragmented locations.

The Snake is primarily a frog-eater, which is good for the Snake but bad for frogs, including the California Red-Legged Frog. In 2004, four Snakes were captured and released at Horse Stable Pond in Sharp Park. In 2008, two Snakes were observed in Sharp Park near Horse Stable Pond. Since then, no sightings of the Snake in Sharp Park have been reported.

The Law

The ESA contains a variety of protections designed to save species from extinction.[4] The secretary of the interior is authorized by the ESA to designate and protect a species if the FWS finds the species "threatened" or "endangered." Only those species in these two categories are protected.

The ESA makes it unlawful for any person to "take" an endangered or threatened species. The term "take" is statutorily defined to mean "harass, harm, pursue, hunt, shoot, wound, kill, trap, capture, or collect, or attempt to engage in such conduct."[5]

The FWS regulations further define the term "harm" to include any "significant habitat modification or degradation where it actually kills or injures fish or wildlife by significantly impairing essential behavioral patterns, including breeding, feeding or sheltering."[6] This prohibition extends to both endangered and threatened species, and includes any "egg or offspring." The courts have held that the "take" prohibition also includes the reasonably certain threat of imminent harm to a protected species.

---

4. The Endangered Species Act of 1973, 16 U.S.C. § 1531 et seq.
5. 16 U.S.C. § 1532(19).
6. 50 C.F.R. § 17.3.

Not all "takings" are prohibited. Under Section 10(a) of the ESA, the FWS may issue an Incidental Take Permit (ITP) that authorizes the taking of a protected species that would otherwise be unlawful.[7] Fans of the board game Monopoly might liken this as the equivalent of a "get-out-of-jail" card.

An ITP may be granted if the taking is incidental to an otherwise lawful activity and the applicant has submitted an acceptable habitat conservation plan (HCP). The HCP requires a description of the impact resulting from any take, the reasons why alternatives are not being utilized, and what steps the applicant will take to minimize and mitigate impacts of its actions. Its goal is to minimize the taking to the maximum extent practicable, to ensure that the taking will not appreciably reduce the likelihood of the survival of the species in the wild, and to ensure that the plan is adequately funded.

Shortly after being sued, the defendants asked the U.S. Army Corps of Engineers (ACE) for a permit to implement the proposed Sharp Park Pump House Safety and Infrastructure Improvement Project (Project). The Project required a federal Clean Water Act (CWA) permit.[8] Before the ACE could legally issue the required CWA permit, it had to consult with the FWS.

Persons requesting a federal permit that may affect a species protected by the ESA must submit to a consultation between the appropriate federal wildlife agency (FWS) and the federal permitting agency (ACE).[9] This federal interagency consultation is required by the ESA. It is designed to prevent the permitting agency (ACE) from taking action that could jeopar-

---

7. 16 U.S.C. § 1539.

8. CWA Section 404 (33 U.S.C. § 1344) provides the principal federal protection of wetlands. No one can discharge dredged or fill materials into a wetland without obtaining a permit from the ACE. Identified activities requiring a permit are described in the federal regulations. See 33 C.F.R § 323.2(f).

9. 16 U.S.C. § 1536 (7)(a).

dize the continued existence of the protected species or result in the destruction or modification of the species' habitat.

The consultation process begins with the permit applicant preparing a Biological Assessment (BA). The BA provides important details about the Project and how it relates to other water management on the Sharp Park Golf Course. It also identifies planned conservation measures intended to avoid and minimize the effects to listed species.

Once the FWS received the BA, the formal consultation process between the ACE and FWS began. As a result of the required consultation, the district court appropriately put the temporary brakes on the litigation.

In October 2012, the FWS completed the consultation and issued its Biological Opinion (BO).[10] The BO analyzed the effects of the ongoing golf course maintenance and operations, the restoration actions and the proposed construction activities. The opinion concluded that the "Project, as proposed, is not likely to jeopardize the continued existence of the California red-legged frog or San Francisco garter snake."

As part of the BO, the FWS also issued an Incidental Take Statement (ITS) that covered golf course maintenance and operations as well as construction and restoration activities. The ITS specified the terms and conditions that had to be met in order to avoid violating the ESA. The defendants and ACE were required to comply with various nondiscretionary terms and conditions intended to ensure the long-term safety of the Frog and Snake.

In 2012, the district court lifted its temporary stay.[11] The court was persuaded that the FWS's action rendered the plain-

---

10. C.F.R. § 402.14(h).
11. Wild Equity Inst. v. City & Cnty. of San Francisco, 2012 WL 6082665 (N.D. Cal. Dec. 6, 2012).

tiffs' case moot, which meant that there was no longer a case or controversy. The ITS issued by the FWS authorized the incidental take of the Frog and Snake by the golf course operation and maintenance activities as well as by its construction and restoration projects. It found that compliance with the terms and conditions would avoid what otherwise would be an unlawful taking of the Frog and Snake under the ESA.[12]

The court also found the terms and conditions of the ITS to be self-effectuating, which meant that the defendants were required to follow the terms and conditions or face the prospect of additional litigation for noncompliance.

Conclusion

Plaintiffs complained that the operations and activities at the Sharp Park Golf Course violated the Endangered Species Act (ESA). They argued that operation of pumps to manage the water bodies at Sharp Park, the golf cart use, and the routine maintenance operations, such as mowing, resulted in illegal "take" of two protected species, the California Red-Legged Frog and the San Francisco Garter Snake.

The plaintiffs asked the federal district court to issue a preliminary injunction to prevent the alleged continued violation of the ESA, which would have temporarily shut down the golf course. In 2011, the court denied the plaintiffs' motion because they failed to establish irreparable harm, one of the necessary requirements for a preliminary injunction. But the case was not over.

The court stayed moving forward with the litigation after the defendants notified it that the ACE was engaged in consultation with the FWS to assess the proposed Sharp Park Pump

---

12. 16 U.S.C. § 1536(o)(2).

House Safety and Infrastructure Improvement Project (Project). This federal interagency consultation was required by the ESA.

As part of the consultation process, the FWS issued a Biological Opinion (BO) and Incidental Take Statement (ITS). The BO concluded that the "Project, as proposed, is not likely to jeopardize the continued existence of the California red-legged frog or San Francisco garter snake." The ITS, which covered golf course maintenance and operations, stated that compliance with various nondiscretionary terms and conditions intended to ensure the long-term safety of the Frog and Snake would avoid violating the ESA.

Epilogue

In 2012, the favorable BO and ITS prompted the defendants to file a motion asking the court to dismiss the plaintiffs' lawsuit as moot. The principal question under both the constitutional "case or controversy" and prudential versions of mootness is the same: whether the circumstances have changed since the filing of the lawsuit so as to prevent the court from affording the plaintiffs meaningful relief.

The plaintiffs challenged the motion, arguing that the BO and ITS did not moot the matter because the Army Corps of Engineers had not yet issued the section 404 permit. They also claimed that the ITS included language indicating it does not take effect until the Corps acts by issuing a permit.

The district court rejected both these arguments. It found that the ITS shielded the defendants from liability provided they complied with its terms and conditions. The court found that the "language in the ITS clearly contemplates that the document is self-effectuating." As a result, the district court dismissed the plaintiffs' lawsuit.

The decision usefully clarified that a federal permit applicant may rely on "take" authorization provided by an FWS before the ACE has issued its permit as long as the applicant is required to comply with the BO and associated ITS. The finding that the ITS can be self-effectuating is particularly helpful to applicants faced with a time lag between issuance of an ITS and a permit issued by the ACE or other federal action agency. To the extent the defendants do not comply with the terms and conditions of the ITS, the plaintiffs can always sue for noncompliance.

Although the defendants prevailed on their substantive claim, popping champagne corks was premature. On May 13, 2013, the court granted close to $400,000 in attorneys' fees and costs to the plaintiffs. Why?

The Endangered Species Act provides that in a citizen suit, a court "may award costs of litigation (including reasonable attorney and expert witness fees) to any party, whenever the court determines such an award is appropriate."[13] When the plaintiffs achieved the desired result because the lawsuit brought about a voluntary change, the court reasoned that it should apply the "catalyst theory" to determine the plaintiffs' request for fees and costs. Plaintiffs successfully argued that the outcome they sought—that the defendants stop taking the protected species without authorization of the FWS—occurred as a result of their lawsuit.

The decision closed an important chapter in the attempt to shut down the historic Sharp Park Golf Course for violating the Endangered Species Act. But the threat of additional litigation for noncompliance with the ITS is always possible.

---

13. 16 U.S.C. § 1540(g)(4).

Hole 31

Forfeiture:
Clubbing wildlife is a no-no[1]

Hawaii: *State v. Terry Pupus*,
LNR T1, LNR T2 (1997)

J ust as windows and errant golf balls don't always mix well, golfers and wildlife may not play well together. Golfers who carry food in their golf bags or carts are a magnet for marauding wildlife, such as crows, gulls, and squirrels. These villains love to snatch a tasty morsel and scamper or fly off, often with an angry player in pursuit.

---

1. Clubbing other golfers, or anyone else for that matter, invites trouble with the law. In 2013, for example, Glenn Lott used his five-iron to register his frustration over the scorekeeping of his playing partner. The frustration peaked at the unlucky 13th hole of the Westwynd Golf Course in Michigan. Apparently Glenn didn't appreciate being asked several times what he had on the previous hole. According to the police report, Glenn broke his club over the victim's arm and then used his newly acquired shiv to stab the scorekeeper. The hapless victim wisely made a break for it in his golf cart. But with escalating fury, Glenn hopped in another cart and chased him, screaming "I'm going to get him." Glenn Lott was arrested and charged with aggravated assault with a deadly weapon. At his arraignment, he was directed to have no contact with the victim, no firearms, and no golf courses. The lesson: Sometimes it's better to let a golfer keep his or her own score. Cora Van Olson, *Detroit-area golfer hits partner with clubs, stabs arm with broken shaft*, www.trutv.com/library/crime/blog/2013 (last visited July 4, 2013).

In April 2007, ownership of a golf ball retrieved from a water hazard resulted in a fight on the sixth hole of the Oceanside Municipal Golf Course in Southern California. The resulting melee landed one golfer in the hospital with severe facial trauma. Michael Babin, a bishop and minister, and his son were charged with felony assault. The bishop said that the criminal case has not affected his ability to preach to his nondenominational Christian church. Krista Davis, *Minister to be arraigned in assault at golf course*, SAN DIEGO UNION TRIBUNE, Apr. 3, 2007, at B3.

Right:
Protecting the Environment.
Below:
Sandalwood Golf Course Layout.

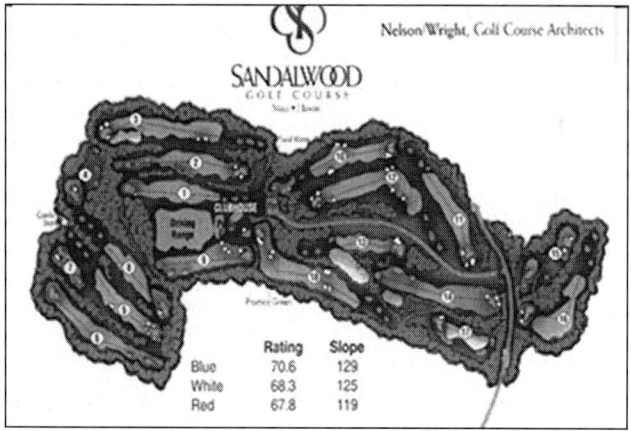

The Facts

The state bird of Hawaii, however unlikely, is a goose. More specifically, it is the Nene, known to bird lovers as *Nesochen sandwicensis* or *Bernicata sandwicensis*.[2] This species is the lone survivor of a community of grazing waterfowl that inhabited the Hawaiian Islands long before the coming of the Polynesians.

Scientists speculate that the Nene was once nearly identical

---

2. HAW. REV. STAT. § 5-17 (1997) designates it the state bird.

Hole 31: Forfeiture

to the Canada goose, but after thousands of years of evolution, they are now quite distinct. Because the Nene's wings are relatively weak, they do not fly as much as other geese. They are now considered indigenous.

The Nene is also an endangered species. Consequently, the Nene is protected from harm by both state and federal law.[3] Approximately 800 to 1,000 Nene geese live in the wild throughout the Hawaiian Islands, with about 250 of the birds inhabiting the island of Maui.

The Kahili Golf Course, formerly Sandalwood Golf Course, opened to the public in 1991. It is located in the Waikapu Valley on Maui, and is set into the West Maui mountain range and has a commanding view of the Pacific Ocean. From the blue tees, the course is somewhat more than 6,400 yards. In addition to being a challenging golf course, it is also home to a small group of wild Nene.

Golf is a challenging game. It can bring out the best in a person or the worst. In Terry Pupus's case it was the worst. Terry presumably was having a particularly bad day of golf in July of 1997. After teeing off on the 16th hole, he encountered three Nene grazing near the teeing ground.[4] In a fit of rage, undoubtedly triggered by a bad round or irked by the mischievous *Menehunes* trolling the golf course, he unexpectedly attacked the birds.[5] Using his driver, a Callaway Big Bertha, he clubbed to death one of the three birds, a four-month-old male. The dead Nene was two to three pounds and stood a foot high. According to official records, the bird was born in early 1997 and raised

---

3. The trumpeting sound of the Nene goose may be heard at http://www.thewildones.org/Animals/nene.html.
4. The term "tee box" is commonly used by players to describe the place where they make their tee shot. The *Rules of Golf* refer to the area as the "teeing ground."
5. *Menehune* are the legendary mischievous "little people" of Hawaii who are similar to pixies or trolls.

at the Maui Bird Conservation Center before being released into the wild and settling in the Sandalwood area.

Pupus struck the bird with blows described by a golfer paired with the goose slayer as "Jose Canseco–style swings." In the onslaught described by the witness, the bird suffered eight fractures, its wing was fractured in several places, and its neck was broken. Immediately after killing the bird, Pupus drove off in his golf cart to resume play, unaware that he would have an upcoming date with the law.

The Law

Pupus was prosecuted by the state on charges of cruelty to animals and for violating the state indigenous wildlife act.[6] Although Terry claimed he "accidentally" hit the bird, eyewitness testimony contradicted his questionable version of the facts. Terry was found guilty as charged, fined $4,000, ordered to perform 300 hours of community service, and placed on a year's probation. Not surprisingly, the court said that it had no sympathy whatsoever for Mr. Pupus.

In surely what was a surprise to this frustrated golfer, the prosecuting attorney also argued that Pupus should forfeit *all* his golf clubs (Big Bertha's criminal associates, if you will).

The law of forfeiture has a long pedigree in both English and American law.[7] The central idea of the law is that the property itself has committed the crime and should be relinquished to the state.

---

6. Haw. Rev. Stat. § 711-1109 (1997); Haw. Admin. R. § 13-124-(3). My thanks are extended to Detective Daniel J. Minan, formerly with the Criminal Investigation Section, Hawaii County Police Department, for his detective work on this caper and for providing these citations.

7. The U.S. Supreme Court reviewed the constitutional limitations to the law of forfeiture in Bennis v. Michigan, 516 U.S. 442 (1996). The Court held that a wife's interest in an automobile used by her spouse to commit a crime did not prevent its forfeiture, notwithstanding her innocence.

Hawaii law authorizes the forfeiture of an item used in the commission of a crime. It provides, in part, that one commits the offense of cruelty to an animal if the person intentionally, knowingly, or recklessly cruelly beats any animal. The court rejected full forfeiture of all his clubs as unduly punitive, ordering instead that only the weapon used in the attack be seized and forfeited. Pupus got his clubs back, minus his Big Bertha, which was the weapon used to kill the bird. It is not clear what ultimately happened to the forfeited weapon.

Conclusion

The game of golf is intended to be enjoyable. The *Rules of Golf* include etiquette guidelines to aid in achieving this goal. Players are expected to conduct themselves in a disciplined manner, demonstrating courtesy and sportsmanship at all times. Intentionally clubbing or killing wildlife is a no-no.

State v. Terry Pupus reminds one of "The Rime of the Ancient Mariner," by Samuel Taylor Coleridge. The mariner, now played by Pupus, is hounded by disaster after senselessly murdering an albatross, now played by the deceased Nene. The disaster for Pupus was the public humiliation associated with being found guilty of violating the law of Hawaii. The hope is that Pupus, like the mariner, ultimately realized the gravity of his action and accepted responsibility for it.

Epilogue

John Henry (Tripp) Isenhour regularly appears on the Golf Channel and is a former PGA Tour player. In 2007, Tripp had an unhappy run-in with the law for killing a protected migratory species.

While he was filming "Shoot Like a Pro," Tripp became angry at the squawking of a red-shoulder hawk. The bird, which was about 300 yards from Tripp, caused him to do another take of the film segment because of the screeching. Tripp went on the attack. He drove his cart closer to the bird and started hitting balls at the noisemaker.

He gave up trying to stop the interference, but the drama wasn't over. Whether the bird was annoyed at Tripp or wanted to make up is not clear. What is clear is that the bird made the mistake of flying within about 75 yards of Tripp. According to news reports, Tripp allegedly said "I'll get him now." On about his sixth try, Tripp hit the hawk in the head and killed it.

Tripp was charged by the state of Florida with cruelty to animals and for killing a migratory bird. Tripp pleaded "no contest" to the charges and accepted responsibility for his act. The terms of his plea agreement included a year's probation, four hours of anger management classes, and 100 hours of community service. Tripp was able to get the community service hours reduced to 60 hours by paying a $2,000 penalty.

News from Scotland indicates that problems with wildlife have an international dimension. In 2011, the British Broadcasting Corporation (BBC) reported that Donald Forbes, who was no Doctor Doolittle, had beaten a fox nearly to death after he saw it trying to steal a biscuit (chocolate cookie) from his golf bag. After the assault, another group of golfers found the fox screaming in agony and put it out of its misery.

Donald's defense that "he was only trying to scare it away" belied eyewitness accounts and didn't go well with the public or the police. The fox was a "popular fixture" at the club and was voluntarily fed by some club members. To make matters worse, the villain was reportedly tame. Poignant photos show this wily quadruped, prior to its demise, standing next to someone's foot.

Hole 31: Forfeiture

Donald was charged under the Wild Mammals (Protection) Act with animal cruelty, fined, and suspended from the Aberdeen Golf Club for nine months. He was also required to forfeit the weapon, his golf club.

Hole 32

Water Quality:
Golf course use of reclaimed water

California: City of Santa Barbara Against the Use of Potable Water by the Tsukamoto Sogyo Company, Department of Water Resources Control Board, Decision 1625, Feb. 15, 1990[1]

In the United States, the demand for clean, reliable water is constantly increasing. In the western states, effectively dealing with and managing water supply is a permanent part of the public debate. The challenge has now spread to other parts of the country. Mark Twain captured the importance of water to the West when he said, "Whiskey is for drinking, and water is for fighting about." This case is about a fight over usable water.

Golf courses compete with other users for access to scarce water supplies. Golf courses use water for many purposes, including general irrigation of fairways and greens, the maintenance of riparian habitats, and in lateral hazards and water hazards.[2] The golf industry has known for some time that the avail-

---

1. Available at http://www.waterrights.ca.gov/hearings/decisions/wrd1625.pdf.
2. Golf balls can perform amazing disappearing acts when water is involved. Rule 26 covers the situation when a player hits a ball into a water hazard, including a lateral water hazard.
   The color of the stakes or lines used to mark the hazard is significant. Yellow stakes or lines are used to mark a water hazard, whereas red is used to delineate a lateral water hazard. The reason it makes a difference is that the options available to a player are different depending on the type of hazard.

ability of usable water is essential to the viable operation of golf courses. Paying more for water increases the cost to play golf, and thus ultimately hits the industry as well as the golfer in the pocketbook.

Responsibly managing water supplies has led to an increased interest in the use of reclaimed or recycled wastewater for purposes other than drinking. The first national symposium on the use of recycled water for golf course irrigation was held in the late 1970s, and its proceedings have become an important reference work on this topic.

Since those early days, there has been a continuing interest in golf and the environment, and not without justification.[3] The

---

A player has three options when a ball is hit into a water hazard, such as a pond or lake. A player may simply play the ball as it lies from within the water hazard under no penalty, apart from getting wet as a result of splashing around. Whether this option is available as a practical matter is going to depend on the actual facts. The second option is to play another ball from the spot from which the original ball was hit under a penalty of "stroke-and-distance." In the film classic *Tin Cup*, Roy "Tin Cup" McAvoy, played by Kevin Costner, used this option when he repeatedly hit his ball into the water hazard. The final option, under a penalty of one stroke, is that the player may drop another ball anywhere "behind" the water hazard along an imaginary line drawn from the hole to the point where the ball last crossed the margin of the hazard.

Two additional options are available when the ball is hit into a lateral water hazard. A ball may be dropped outside the lateral water hazard (not nearer the hole) within two club-lengths of 1) the point where the ball last crossed the margin of the hazard, or 2) at "a point on the opposite margin of the water hazard equidistant from the hole." A player, for example, would have the option of dropping on either side of a stream or drainage ditch marked as a lateral water hazard that runs parallel to the fairway. A one-stroke penalty is assessed for dropping a ball from a lateral water hazard.

3. In 1992, the Environmental Protection Agency (EPA) published *Guidelines for Water Reuse*, the USGA released *Golf Course Management and Construction: Environmental Issues*, and the American Society of Golf Course Architects published *An Environmental Approach to Golf Course Development*. In 1993, the USGA sponsored a symposium on wastewater reuse and published the symposium's proceeding in *Wastewater Reuse for Golf Course Irrigation* the following year. The year 1994 also saw the USGA publish the *Landscape Restoration Handbook* and the publication of scientific research on turfgrass in the *Journal of Environmental Quality*. The Center for Resource Management, *Golf Digest Magazine*, the National Wildlife Federation, and the Pebble Beach Resort Company held the First Conference on Golf and the Environment. The involvement of the USGA is documented at www.usga.org/green/index/html.

Hole 32: Water Quality

United States Golf Association (USGA), for example, believes that no issue is more likely to have a significant impact on the game of golf in the 21st century than how golf courses and golf maintenance affect the environment. Everything from the use of pesticides and fertilizers to proper storm-water management is on the table for discussion.

The Facts

The City of Santa Barbara supplies potable water to users within its service area. It also collects and treats municipal wastewater at a city facility, which it then sells to customers for additional beneficial uses unrelated to human consumption.

Montecito Country Club[4] is within the city's water service area and buys water from the city. It operates an 18-hole golf course consisting of about 105 irrigated acres, a clubhouse, swimming pool, restaurant, and tennis courts. The country club used potable water for golf course irrigation as well as for other uses. Faced with water shortages, the city proposed substituting reclaimed water for the potable drinking water being used by the country club for irrigation.[5] The club refused.

Santa Barbara filed a complaint with the State Water Resources Control Board, which has jurisdiction over water and wastewater issues. The city asked the board to require the country club to use its reclaimed water for irrigation purposes so that potable water could be freed up for other uses within the

---

4. In 2004, the Montecito Country Club was sold by Tsukamoto Sogyo Co., Ltd. to Ty Warner Hotels and Resorts. The new owner reached agreement with Jack Nicklaus in 2005 to redesign the course.

5. California Water Code § 13050(n) defines "recycled water," also called "reclaimed water," as "water which, as a result of treatment of waste, is suitable for a direct beneficial use or a controlled use that would not otherwise occur and is therefore considered a valuable resource." The Water Code contains numerous provisions controlling water reclamation and reuse.

city. Substitution was particularly important at the time because Southern California was in the midst of one of its recurring droughts.

To satisfy demand, Santa Barbara was augmenting its water supply through groundwater pumping. This augmentation strategy was not a permanent solution because the groundwater basins available to the city were already being used to capacity. Any long-term increase in groundwater extraction could destroy the aquifers due to seawater intrusion and land subsidence.

The country club declined to enter into a written contract with the city for the use of reclaimed water.[6] It had two principal objections. First, it was concerned that the salinity level or other pollutants in the reclaimed water might have an adverse effect on golf course plant life, especially the greens. Second, it wanted some assurances. The club wanted the city to hold it harmless for any claims or damages that might arise from use of the reclaimed water.

The Law

The California legislature has declared the public policy for water reclamation in the state. Its policy is to encourage the development of water reclamation facilities as a way of meeting the public's growing water requirements. As an adjunct to this policy, the legislature has also prohibited the use of potable

---

6. In City of Orlando v. West Orange Country Club, Inc., the plaintiff, owner of a golf course and country club, filed suit against the City of Orlando seeking to enforce an agreement by the city to provide reclaimed water at no charge for a period of 20 years. The appellate court found that the contract was not signed by either party and that its enforcement was therefore barred by the Statute of Frauds. The Fifth District further held: "With respect to the trial court's determination that the Defendants can be held liable for performance of the contract under an estoppel theory, the law is well-settled that '[t]he doctrine of promissory estoppel cannot be used to circumvent the statute of frauds.'" City of Orlando v. West Orange Country Club, Inc., 9 So. 3d 1268 (Fla. 5th Dist. Ct. App. 2009).

Hole 32: Water Quality

(drinking) water to irrigate golf courses *if* suitable reclaimed water is available as determined by the State Water Resources Control Board.[7]

The Water Board, after giving notice and a hearing to an affected party, can find that the reclaimed water supply is of adequate quality and is available at a reasonable cost. If the state Department of Health Services agrees that such use will not be detrimental to public health, the board may direct that the potable water use be stopped to allow the use of reclaimed water.

In the Santa Barbara dispute, the board made the necessary findings required by Water Code § 13550. It found that (a) reclaimed water of adequate quantity and quality is available for use at the country club; (b) the cost of the reclaimed water to the country club is comparable to or less than the cost of potable water; (c) the use of reclaimed water will not be detrimental to public health; (d) the use of reclaimed water will not adversely affect downstream water rights or degrade water quality; and (e) with the possible exception of the greens, the use of reclaimed water will not be injurious to plant life on the golf course.

There was some uncertainty as to the effect reclaimed water might have on the club's greens. Given this uncertainty, the board ordered the club to designate one green that the city could use to conduct a test to determine whether the reclaimed water would be injurious. The test was to be conducted over a 24-month period.

---

7. California Water Code § 13550 states:

   The Legislature hereby finds and declares that the use of potable domestic water for the irrigation of greenbelt areas, including, but not limited to, cemeteries, *golf courses*, parks, and highway landscaped areas, is a waste or an unreasonable use of such water within the meaning of Section 2 of Article X of the California Constitution when reclaimed water which the State Board, after notice and hearing, finds adequate to meet state guidelines [emphasis added].

The board ordered the country club to stop using potable water for irrigation purposes as soon as it was reasonably possible to begin using reclaimed water. The city also was ordered to cease supplying potable water to the country club once the system for distributing reclaimed water to the club was available.

The board rejected the country club's demand that it be held harmless in the event damage occurred, although it did observe that the city's reclaimed water service contract provided some, but not all, of the assurances sought by it. In denying the request that the city hold it harmless, the board reasoned that the law contained in the Water Code did not expressly require a supplier of reclaimed water to give indemnification assurances to users. In addition, the board found that no evidence supported the conclusion that the cost of using reclaimed water was greater than the cost of using potable water. Finally, the club presented no evidence demonstrating that the risk of litigation would be greater if reclaimed water were used instead of potable water.

Conclusion

What were the reclaimed-water test results to the green? Unfortunately, the results are nowhere to be found. Currently, the golf course uses potable water on all its greens.[8]

Today, reclaimed water is used extensively by golf courses in California, as well as in other states, for irrigation purposes and in water hazards. U.S. Open venues using recycled water on the fairways include Torrey Pines (2008), Pebble Beach (2010), and The Olympic Club (2012).

But legitimate concerns continue to exist with the salinity contained in the reclaimed water and its buildup when used

---

8. In March 2007, a golf course representative, Bill Herbert, reported during a telephone interview that the course uses potable water on all its greens. The effect since then is not known.

Hole 32: Water Quality

over an extended period.[9] For example, a typical Las Vegas golf course irrigating entirely with reclaimed water is the equivalent of applying 10 or 11 tons of salt per acre per year. The Colorado River, which provides Las Vegas with water, is high in salt content, and the recycling process approximately doubles the salt concentration.

Interest has grown in using grass strains that are less susceptible to damage from high salinity. One of the best-known strains is Seashore Paspalum, which has a high tolerance for salinity. While promising, it is not a cure-all. Other concerns have popped up. Reclaimed water contains pharmaceuticals because wastewater treatment plants are not designed to remove them.

Although extensively regulated and monitored under state regulations, the question of liability for injury arising out of the use of reclaimed water has not been litigated. One can predict with confidence, however, that it will be in the future.

---

9. Although we may be "the salt of the earth," too much salt is a bad thing. The *Old Testament* tells us that the enemy would use salt as a weapon. They would salt the land to prevent it from being used. JUDGES 9:42.

Part VI
Equal Protection

Hole 33

Gender Discrimination:
Men's only golf tournaments at a public golf course

Federal: *Joyce v. Town of Dennis*,
705 F. Supp. 2d 74 (D. Mass. 2010)[1]

G olf courses commonly include hazards, such as bunkers and water hazards. One type of hazard not commonly encountered is a federal lawsuit for gender discrimination.

The golf tournament policies and practices of the Town of Dennis (Town) have received considerable media attention.[2] Articles about its men-only tournaments being discriminatory have appeared in the *New York Times* and other prominent newspapers. Radio talking heads and Internet bloggers have contributed to the chorus of opinion.

Media coverage probably was fueled by the fact that the plaintiff, Elaine Joyce, hired a publicist. Not surprisingly, everyone seemed to have an opinion on Elaine's lawsuit and her

---

1. As indicated in the Epilogue, the Joyce case was the subject of an appeal to the First Circuit Court of Appeals and a remand to the district court on the issues of attorneys' fees and injunctive relief.

2. The case drew considerably less media attention than the public controversy championed by Martha Burk over the failure to admit women as members at the home of the Masters Tournament, Augusta National Golf Club. That controversy was different because it involved the admission practices at a private club. In 2012, Augusta admitted its first two female members, Condoleezza Rice and Darla Moore.

demand for damages for emotional injury, punitive damages, attorneys' fees, and the costs and expenses of the litigation. News of the Town's rejection of her settlement offer fanned the flames of public opinion, which some saw as support for the view that "hell has no fury like a woman scorned."[3]

The Facts

Dennis is a popular golf destination on Cape Cod in Massachusetts. The Town owns two golf courses, the Dennis Pines and the Dennis Highlands. Both courses are open to the public, and anyone can become a member for a fee. One of the advantages of being a member is the chance to play in various golf tournaments during the year.

A tournament at Dennis Pines was at the center of the controversy. The litigation about the tournament policy lasted more than five years. The Town will undoubtedly be pleased to finally say "Amen" to the dispute.[4]

In 2007, the Dennis Pines tournament schedule included mixed-gender events as well as separate men's and women's events. The men had 10 scheduled tournaments and the women had two. The fewer number of tournaments for the women was, according to the Town, based on the fact that the women members didn't want more tournaments.

Elaine Joyce, a member at Dennis Pines, is an avid and accomplished golfer. She has won numerous club championships and was ranked among the top women golfers in Massa-

---

3. WILLIAM CONGREVE, THE MOURNING BRIDE (1697).
4. The sports writer Herbert Warren Wind gave the moniker "Amen Corner" to holes 11, 12, and 13 at Augusta following the spectacular play by Arnold Palmer during the 1958 Masters. The inspiration for the moniker was the jazz recording "Shouting at Amen Corner." It is not without some irony that the 10th, 11th, and 12th holes are known as the Cape's version of "Amen Corner" at Augusta National Golf Club.

Hole 33: Gender Discrimination

chusetts. On April 20, 2007, she signed up to play golf with her dad in a men-only tournament scheduled to take place on May 5 and 6.

On May 2, three days before the scheduled event, the PGA head golf professional (Russell Champoux) called Elaine's dad (Patrick) and gave him the bad news. Elaine would not be allowed to play in the tournament because it was a men-only event. If there was any good news for Patrick, it was that he could still play in the tournament if he found a male partner. Like any good golfer, Champoux kept his head down on the follow-through. He told Elaine's dad that the decision was out of his hands and that he was simply relaying the decision made by the Golf Advisory Committee (GAC) to keep the event a men-only tournament.[5]

The next day, May 3, Elaine fired off an email to the town administrator (Robert Canevazzi) protesting the decision to exclude her from the men's tournament. She asked him to act promptly to get the current decision reversed so she could play in the weekend tournament. Elaine said she was willing to play by all the same rules as the men, and there was no acceptable reason to prevent her from playing just because she was a woman.

After receiving Elaine's email, Canevazzi consulted the director of golf and head golf course superintendent (Michael Cummings). Canevazzi then sent Elaine an email upholding the committee's decision. He said that changing the tournament rules at the last minute to allow her to play would be unfair to the membership. It would be unfair to the members who had signed up for the men-only tournament as well as to those

---

5. The Golf Advisory Committee is a volunteer group that is responsible for course policy.

other women members who didn't apply to play because they were following the announced tournament rules. Canevazzi also relied on the traditional practice of having separate men's and women's tournaments. He added that he would ask the GAC to revisit the gender-based tournament rules at its next meeting on May 14, which of course was after the tournament.

After the Canevazzi hit the email send button, he decided to talk with the town counsel. The attorney became alarmed that excluding her from the tournament might be perceived as discriminatory. The counsel's alarm bell might have gone off because he was aware that a GAC member had previously expressed the view that it was "difficult to justify" holding men-only tournaments.

During the May meeting of the GAC, the issue of gender-based tournaments was raised as promised.[6] The issue was referred to a subcommittee to formulate a recommendation. At the June meeting of the GAC, the subcommittee recommended that no changes be made to the 2007 schedule. It also recommended that, starting in 2008, all future tournaments should include a men's and a women's field.

The chairman of the GAC advised the committee that the United States Golf Association (USGA) allows women to play in all events "as long as they play exactly the same as a man." The GAC decided that women should be allowed to play in men's tournaments starting in October 2007, and thus the change in policy should not be delayed until 2008. This policy was the one Elaine initially sought.

To Elaine, the change in policy wasn't good enough. She had lost to chance to play in the May tournament with her dad. On February 15, 2008, she filed a complaint in federal district court

---

6. Elaine was expressly invited to attend the meeting by the GAC's chairman (Jim Horvath), but didn't respond to the invitation or attend.

against the Town, the golf course, the town administrator, the golf directors, and the head golf professional for gender discrimination under both federal and state law.[7]

The Law
Federal Law:
Equal Protection and Section 1983

The Fourteenth Amendment to the Constitution states:

> No State shall make or enforce any law which shall abridge the privileges or immunities of citizens of the United States; nor shall any State deprive any person of life, liberty, or property, without due process of law; nor deny to any person within its jurisdiction the equal protection of the laws.

Most federal constitutional claims against local governments are brought under Section 1983 of the Federal Civil Rights Act. It provides:

> Every person who, under color of any statute, ordinance, regulation, custom or usage, of any state or territory, subjects, or causes to be subjected, any citizen of the United States . . . to the deprivation of any rights, privileges or immunities secured by the Constitution and laws, shall be liable to the party injured in an action at law, suit in equity, or other proper proceeding for redress.

---

7. Elaine made three general claims about the policies and practices in her federal lawsuit: First, violation of the Equal Protection Clause of the Fourteenth Amendment; second, violation of the Massachusetts anti-discrimination statutes; and finally, violation of the Massachusetts Consumer Protection Act. In July 2007, Elaine filed an administrative complaint with the Massachusetts Commission against Discrimination.

Section 1983 does not create new substantive rights. Rather, it provides a remedy for the violation of a federal constitutional or statutory right. Local governments are considered "persons" within the meaning of Section 1983.[8] Liability attaches when a local government official or employee acts in a discriminatory fashion pursuant to the local government's policy or custom.

Elaine argued that the Town's official policy and practice that disqualified her from playing in the May tournament constituted unconstitutional gender discrimination. The fact that the women were afforded fewer tournaments than the men was also discriminatory. More specifically, the Town's "regulations, custom, or usage" violated the Equal Protection Clause of the Fourteenth Amendment and entitled her to relief under Section 1983.

The Equal Protection Clause has never been construed to prohibit all forms of discrimination. Rather, it has been applied to prohibit using classifications that cannot be justified on the basis of a legitimate government interest. In other words, it prevents government from drawing arbitrary distinctions.

Policies and practices that classify on the basis of gender are examined carefully by the courts. Because such classifications are considered quasi-suspect by the courts, they are subject to intermediate or mid-level scrutiny. Under this standard of review, the government must show that it has an exceedingly persuasive justification for the challenged classification to survive an equal protection challenge.

Gender discrimination is permissible only if it furthers an important government interest, which the Town was unable to identify. The only reasons offered by the Town for its policy and practices were history and tradition, and the equal opportunity for women to play in women's tournaments and mixed-gender

---

8. Monell v. Dep't of Social Servs. of City of New York, 436 U.S. 658 (1978).

Hole 33: Gender Discrimination

events. These reasons were not, in the court's view, a persuasive justification.

The officials or employees must be implementing the Town's official policy or practice for Section 1983 to apply. This requirement was satisfied. Thus, Elaine's equal protection claim was sustained, and the Town was found to be liable.[9]

Massachusetts Law: Public Accommodation

Massachusetts requires a plaintiff claiming gender discrimination to show that it occurred at a place of public accommodation. Section 92A defines a public accommodation as "any place . . . which is open to and accepts the patronage of the general public."[10] Section 98 provides: "All persons shall have the right to the full and equal accommodations, advantages, facilities and privileges of any place of accommodation. . . ." Taken together, these sections prohibit any gender discrimination in a place of public accommodation.

The district court reached three important conclusions about her state-based claim: First, a membership tournament at a public golf course is a place of public accommodation. The fact that the tournament was a non-public event only available to members was not controlling. The event was hosted at a public golf course. Thus, the decision is strong support for the proposition that the holding applies to any tournament hosted at a public golf course.

---

9. Elaine also sought to hold the defendants personally liable. The court rejected her claim that they were individually liable. The defendants were entitled to the benefit of qualified immunity. This immunity from personal liability is available unless the plaintiff can show that the infringed right was clearly established at the time of the violation. The court noted that men and women are often constitutionally separated in sports, and that the defendants reasonably believed that they were acting lawfully. Thus, the infringed right was not clearly established.

10. Mass. Gen. Laws ch. 272, § 92A.

Second, the court found that no "separate but equal" exception applies to the statute's otherwise clear prohibition of gender distinctions or discrimination. It rejected the argument that women were given "full and equal accommodations, advantages, facilities and privileges" based on the level of interest by the women membership, which was essentially a "separate but equal" argument.

The Town's "separate but equal" argument was parried against it. In the district court's view, the solution was not to schedule more tournaments for women uninterested in more tournaments, but to allow those interested women members to play in the men's events. This solution would give women an equal opportunity to play.

The district court had no difficulty in finding that excluding Elaine from the men-only tournament was a violation of federal and state law. Therefore, it granted summary judgment on the issue of liability.

Conclusion

Public golf course tournament administrators must be vigilant to avoid discriminatory practices based on gender. The federal constitution and state law are available to redress claims of gender discrimination.

Government policies that classify on the basis of gender are "quasi-suspect." This means that a court will evaluate the governmental objective underlying a gender-based policy and practice using an intermediate standard of judicial review.

A gender-based policy and practice are likely to be found discriminatory unless their defender can establish an exceedingly persuasive justification for the gender classification. In addition to having a legitimate government objective, which the Town was unable to identify, the classification must be substantially related to achieving that objective. The challenger of gender discrimination is not required to show a discriminatory intent in order to prevail.

The Town failed to meet its burden of justifying its decision to exclude Elaine from the men-only tournament. The Town's history and tradition of holding mixed-gender tournaments and separate tournaments for men and women did not suffice. Affording women fewer tournament opportunities at Dennis Pines added support to her claim, regardless of the fact that the women members were not asking for more women's events.

The district court cautioned against misreading its decision. "Finally, it bears emphasizing that the holding in this case results from the defendant's failure to advance a persuasive justification for their act, not necessarily because no justification exists."

Epilogue: The Remedies

Following the determination of liability in 2010, the Town tried to settle Elaine's claim for compensatory damages by offering her $35,001, inclusive of costs and attorneys' fees. She rejected the offer and things heated up.

Elaine moved for sanctions against the attorney representing the Town.[11] Her complaint was that the Town's attorney improperly told the media she had made a $500,000 settlement demand and that any money judgment in her favor would be paid by the Town's taxpayers. Elaine argued that these statements would materially prejudice or interfere with her right to a fair jury trial on the issue of damages.

Her motion for sanctions was denied because she had not demonstrated that the statements had a reasonable or substan-

---

11. Joyce v. Town of Dennis, 736 F. Supp. 2d 321 (2010).

tial likelihood of materially prejudicing or interfering with a fair trial. The court was sensitive to the issue of media coverage and directed both parties "henceforth to refrain from trying their cases in the media."

The wheels of justice continued to grind forward. In January 2011, the court found that Elaine could recover attorneys' fees under both federal and state law. But it delayed setting them because it reasoned that the amount of the fees would be a major factor in determining a reasonable fee.[12] The case then headed to the jury for a determination on damages.

Later in 2011, the jury awarded her $15,000 in damages and her attorneys were awarded $30,000.[13] Although the court acknowledged that the Town shared the blame for prolonging the dispute, Elaine's attorneys were lambasted by the district court. In his order, the judge found that Elaine's attorneys spent an inordinate amount of time (249 billable hours) on a "simple, uncomplicated case" where a "significant portion of the hours enumerated relate to the bickering between counsel over media coverage."

But the Town of Dennis and the district court had not seen the last of Elaine. She appealed to the First Circuit Court of Appeals.[14]

On appeal, she argued that the district court erred in failing to instruct the jury on punitive damages, denying injunctive relief, and awarding attorneys' fees in an amount substantially less than her request. The Town responded by arguing that she was not primarily the prevailing party and shouldn't get any attorneys' fees.

The First Circuit upheld the district court's denial of puni-

---

12. Joyce v. Town of Dennis, 770 F. Supp. 2d 424 (D. Mass. 2011)
13. Id.
14. Joyce v. Town of Dennis, 2013 WL 2948100 (June 17, 2013).

tive damages. Based on the record, the appellate court reasoned that a jury could not reasonably conclude that the failure to open all tournaments to women met the legal requirement of a "conscious or purposeful effort to demean or diminish the class of which plaintiff is a part" or any other factor justifying punitive damages. The GAC changed the rules to allow women to play in men's tournaments after Elaine protested. It also invited her to participate in discussions about changing the rules, but she declined. The facts simply did not support her claim of reckless or callous indifference to her federally protected rights to support an award of punitive damages.

The First Circuit remanded the issues of attorneys' fees and injunctive relief. The appellate court reasoned that reducing the requested award based on Joyce's rejection of a settlement offer and linking the fees to the amount of compensable damages was improper. Too much weight was given by the district court to the amount the plaintiff recovered in compensable damages. Citing prior case law, the First Circuit observed: "It is a mistake of law to reduce an award of attorneys' fees in a civil rights case in response to a plaintiff's rejection of a defendant's settlement offer when the judgment exceeds that offer."[15]

On remand, the refusal to settle should not be considered by the district court. In addition, the district court should clearly and fully explain the basis for its recalculation. Although the appellate court required recalculation, it also recognized that the recalibration would not necessarily produce fees at or near the amount of Elaine's request.

The district court denied Elaine's request for injunctive relief, stating only that the "defendants had 'gotten the message' and that any future conduct to the contrary would be met with

---

15. Coutin v. Young & Rubicam Puerto Rico, Inc., 124 F.3d 331 (1st Cir. 1997).

severe sanctions." The First Circuit found that the district court needed to better explain its refusal to grant injunctive relief. More specifically, it was unclear to the appellate court how the possibility of future misconduct would be dealt with absent injunctive relief. Requiring a new lawsuit to be filed by Elaine was deemed unsatisfactory to protect the right she had won.

As a result of her lawsuit, Elaine believes that she has been ostracized by the members at Dennis Pines, both men and women. It is unlikely that injunctive relief will be effective to prevent some members from avoiding or ostracizing her in the future. Unfortunately, this may be part of the price for advancing the public interest against gender discrimination at public golf courses.

Hole 34

Country Club Membership Rules:
Sexual-orientation discrimination

California: *Koebke, et al. v. Bernardo Heights Country Club*, 36 Cal. 4th 824 (2005)

Same-sex couples in America continue to challenge laws and restrictions that deny them equal rights. The *Koebke* case examines the California statutory law related to same-sex domestic partnerships. Because the final chapter on same-sex law has not been written, the case is most usefully seen as a historical guidepost on the road of social change.

Koebke is a landmark case decided by the California Supreme Court. It does not explore, however, the philosophical debate of whether same-sex "rights" are best addressed by the legislature, the judiciary, or popular vote. One thing is clear about the debate: The controversy generates strong opinions both on and off the golf course.

The Facts

Bernardo Heights County Club (BHCC) is a private golf course located just north of San Diego in Rancho Bernardo, California. It features an 18-hole, par-72 championship layout that was designed and built by renowned architect Ted Robinson.

Bernardo Heights Country Club

B. Birgit Koebke (Birgit) and Kendall E. French are avid golfers. They are also a lesbian couple who were registered as domestic partners under California's Domestic Partnership Act.[1] In 1987, Birgit purchased an $18,000 equity membership in the BHCC to take advantage of the golf and other benefits.

Birgit's membership allowed her to play golf as often as she wanted without paying any additional greens fees. The BHCC bylaws also allowed a member to play golf with a spouse without paying additional membership or usage fees. Guests could also play, but guests had to pay a greens fee each time they played. Unlike spouses, guests were limited in the number of

---

1. CAL. FAM. CODE § 297 (2005).

Hole 34: Country Club Membership Rules

times they could play, and they could not sign charge slips for food that was served on the premises.

In 1995, Birgit asked the BHCC Board of Directors to designate Kendall as a "significant other" to enable them to golf together on the same basis as a married couple. The board rejected the request. In 1998, Birgit and Kendall executed a written "Statement of Domestic Partnership," and registered as domestic partners with California and the City of San Diego. Thereafter, Birgit again asked the board to adopt a "significant other" policy, which the Board also rejected.

Birgit and Kendall tried a different strategy in 2000. The couple wrote to the board asking it to grant Kendall spousal benefits. They argued to the board that "we cannot legally marry," but "consider themselves married" because they are registered domestic partners, which the state recognizes as "legal spouses."

Although the strategy was different, the outcome was the same. The board rejected the request. The board reasoned that the BHCC bylaws contained no provision for a non-spousal partner to have the benefits of spousal membership. The board explained that it did not have the unilateral authority to simply change the bylaws, and that the proper procedure for changing the bylaws was to petition the membership and to have it vote on the submitted petition.

They saw this suggestion as a non-starter. As a result, Birgit and Kendall sued the BHCC, alleging that it unlawfully discriminated against them on the basis of sex, sexual orientation, and marital status in violation of the state Unruh Act.[2] They alleged

---

2. The Unruh Civil Rights Act, CIVIL CODE § 51, subd. (b), states:

All persons within the jurisdiction of this state are free and equal, and no matter what their sex, race, color, religion, ancestry, national origin, disability, or medical condition are entitled to the full and equal accommodations, advantages, facilities, privileges, or services in all business establishments of every kind whatsoever.

state law prohibits the BHCC from extending certain benefits to married couples that are denied to unmarried couples. In addition, Birgit cited numerous instances in which BHCC granted membership benefits to unmarried heterosexuals and other friends. They also cited instances in which Birgit encountered overt hostility as a result of attempting to get spousal benefits for her partner, Kendall. The members apparently were not playing nice.

The Law

At the time of the litigation, the California Unruh Civil Rights Act applied to discrimination based on "sex, race, color, religion, ancestry, national origin, disability, or medical condition." Neither marital status nor registered domestic partners were included on the statutory list.

The court began by finding that registered domestic partners under the Domestic Partner Act and marital spouses were substantial legal equivalents. Treating a registered domestic partner differently from a marital spouse constituted impermissible marital status discrimination. In enacting the Domestic Partnership Act, the court reasoned that the legislature made clear its intent to create substantial legal equality between domestic partners and marital spouses.[3] The intent of the legislature was that the Domestic Partnership Act "shall be construed liberally in order to secure to eligible couples who register as domestic partners the full range of legal rights, protections and benefits, as well as all of the responsibilities, obligations, and duties to

---

3. The discussion of plaintiffs' claim of damages against the BHCC under the Unruh Act prior to the 2005 effective date of the Domestic Partner Act is omitted. In the omitted part, the court found no facial violation of the act's prohibition against sexual orientation. It did find, however, that the plaintiffs should be allowed to argue on remand that the BHCC marital status rule as applied to them constituted a violation of the act.

each other, to their children, to third parties and to the state, as the laws of California extend to and impose upon spouses." According to the court, the legislature presumably determined that expanding the rights and obligations of domestic partners "would reduce discrimination on the bases of sex and sexual orientation in a manner consistent with the requirements of the California Constitution."

Having found that the Domestic Partnership Act was intended to equalize the status of registered domestic partners and married couples, the court next turned to the question of whether the Unruh Act precluded the BHCC from granting married couples benefits that it made unavailable to registered domestic partners.

The problem was that neither marital status nor registered domestic partners were expressly identified as a protected category by the Unruh Act. The court was not stymied by this seeming obstacle.[4] Based on prior case law, the court had determined that the enumerated categories were "illustrative rather than restrictive." It presumed that the legislature did not intend that the identified list be treated as comprehensive.

This form of legal jujitsu is the bane of textualists who would limit the protected classes to those actually stated by the legislature. They would object to expanding the list to categories not identified by the legislature.[5] Notwithstanding this theoretical concern, the court applied the three-part test it had previously created for determining whether a future claim of

---

4. This type of reasoning gives some jurists the yips. They maintain that the enacted test is the law, and not some implied intent about the wishes or supposed intent of the legislature. Whenever a statute is enacted, the only thing clearly agreed upon are the words in the text.

5. The constructional canon *ejusdem generis* may apply when a general phrase, such as "others," appears at the end of a list. The catchall phrase implies others of a similar kind should be included. *See* WILLIAM D. POPKIN, A DICTIONARY OF STATUTORY INTERPRETATION 74 (2007). This canon was not used by the Court in construing the statute.

discrimination, involving a category not listed by the legislature, fell within the protection of the Unruh Act.

The first step in this process examines whether new or novel claim of discrimination is based on personal characteristics, such as a person's geographical origin, physical attributes, and personal beliefs. The second step looks at whether a legitimate business interest supports the challenged discriminatory act or policy. The final step considers the potential consequence of allowing a plaintiff to proceed with the new or novel discriminatory claim that is not part of the statutory list.

Applying this framework of analysis, the court determined that plaintiffs' "marital status" claim was cognizable under the Unruh Act. Marital status decisions involve personal choices fundamental to a person's identity, beliefs, and self-definition. The court reasoned that the plaintiffs' decision to enter into a registered domestic partnership was motivated by similar considerations, including personal values and beliefs, and was more than simply asking the state to confer a legal status. These considerations, the court reasoned, lie at the essence of the statutorily identified existing categories.

Denying the plaintiffs the benefits or services that BHCC extends to married persons violates the public policy favoring registered domestic partnerships. Therefore, the court found, consistent with the first step of the analysis, discrimination against registered domestic partners in favor of married couples was the type of discrimination falling within the scope of the Unruh Act.

With respect to the second analytical step, BHCC argued that legitimate business interests were served by its policy of denying family membership benefits to any but married couples. It maintained that expanding the eligibility was a slippery slope to ruin. Granting benefits to "members' friends" might lead to overuse of its facilities, create a disincentive for such friends to apply for membership, and would discourage its "legitimate goal of creating a family-friendly environment by welcoming the immediate family of married members."

The court was not persuaded. The plaintiffs were registered domestic partners with rights and responsibilities similar to that of a spouse. Extending the spousal benefit to the plaintiffs would not create a stampede to the first tee, which was BHCC's concern. Moreover, although creating a family-friendly environment may be a legitimate business interest, that policy was not served when BHCC discriminated against the domestic partner of one of its members. Rather, by so doing, it ran contrary to the state policy favoring domestic partnerships.

The final step in the analysis examines the consequences of allowing the claim to proceed. The court found that the scope of its holding was limited to registered domestic partners and did not apply to cases involving any and all unmarried couples. It also found that the decision positively advanced the policies underlying the Domestic Partner Act.

Conclusion

The court found that the plaintiffs' claim of marital status discrimination was cognizable under the Unruh Act. It therefore reversed the grant of summary judgment in favor of the BHCC. In reasoning that would generally echo through subsequent same-sex litigation cases, the court reasoned that the social policy favoring marriage between heterosexual couples was not served by denying domestic partners protection from discrimination.

California law has been clarified by the legislature on the question presented in *Koebke*. Section 51 (b) of the Unruh Act contains now provides:

All persons within the jurisdiction of this state are free and equal, and no matter what their sex, race, color, religion, ancestry, national origin, disability, medical condition, genetic information, *marital status*, or *sexual orientation* are entitled to the full and equal accommodations, advantages, facilities, privileges, or services in all business establishments of every kind whatsoever.[6]

The addition of the category "sexual orientation" broadens the protections available under the Unruh Act beyond the marital status (registered domestic partners) issue in *Koebke*. The California legislature has endorsed the idea that the categories enumerated in the Unruh Act are illustrative rather than restrictive, and that its overarching concern is the prohibition of arbitrary discrimination.

Whether one agrees with the court's expansive construction of the Unruh Act in *Koebke* is apt to depend on one's judicial philosophy. A "textualist" would probably reject such an interpretation because the construction to include marital status as a protected category is inconsistent with the plain meaning of the enumerated categories identified by the statute. The criticism is that the court is effectively legislating rather than interpreting the language used by the legislature.

In contrast, "intentionalists" would support such an expanded judicial construction. They would be guided by discerning and carrying out the legislature's intent. To accomplish this task, all available extrinsic sources, including any legislative history, would not be out-of-bounds (OB). Similarly, "purposivists" would be guided by looking at the goals or purpose of the legislature. Not surprisingly, each of these competing judicial philosophies has its followers and critics.

---

6. CAL. CIV. CODE § 51(b).

Part VII
Sovereign Immunity

Hole 35

Federal Sovereign Immunity:
Military golf course liability

Federal: *Ventimiglia v. United States of America*, 2009 WL 2982001 (N.D. Cal.)

The *Rules of Golf* outline the various options that are available to a golfer who has hit into a water hazard, such as a lake, pond, or river.[1] Golfers expect to encounter such hazards during a round of golf. Avoiding them is part of the challenge of the game.

Water hazards are well known for appropriating golf balls and adding penalty strokes to the golfer's tally. But the water hazard in this case did much more. It resulted in the ultimate penalty: the player's life.

---

1. "Lateral water hazards" are marked with red stakes or lines around the perimeter of the hazard, whereas "water hazards" are marked with yellow stakes or lines. The Rules spell out the various options when a ball comes to rest in a water hazard. For water hazards, the player has three options: 1) play the ball without penalty; 2) play the ball anywhere on an imaginary line where the ball crossed the hazard and the hole (no closer to the hole) with a penalty of one stroke; 3) return to the place from which the shot was hit with a penalty of one stroke (called stroke-and-distance). For lateral water hazards, a player has two additional options: 4) drop within two club lengths of where the ball entered the hazard, no nearer the hole, with a penalty of one stroke; or 5) drop on the opposite side of the lateral hazard within two club lengths, no nearer the hole, with a penalty of one stroke (Rule 26).

The Facts

Each branch of the U.S. Armed Forces has a Morale, Welfare, and Recreation (MWR) program that provides discounted recreational facilities to qualifying personnel and their families. The Navy owns and operates a number of golf courses as part of its MWR program. The golf program provides recreational opportunities to promote the physical well-being of Navy personnel and their families.

One of its courses is the Monterey Pines Golf Course (MPGC), located on the grounds of the Naval Postgraduate School in Monterey, California. Known to locals as the "Navy Course," it opened as a nine-hole course 1963. In 1972, the back nine was added, making it an 18-hole course.

The course features three artificial lakes or water hazards, in Navy lingo called "Alpha Lake," "Bravo Lake," and "Charlie Lake." Alpha Lake is primarily a source of irrigation for the course and secondarily a water hazard for wayward golf balls. It is located directly to the northeast of hole 3 and to the northwest of the hole-4 tee box.

In 2001, Alpha Lake was fitted with a black plastic liner to prevent water seepage through the soil. The rim of the liner was exposed around the circumference of the lake and above its surface. This left a plastic-sheeted area, which could be slippery, between the lake and the turf.

On November 29, 2005, at about 1:00 p.m., Joseph Ventimiglia checked in at the Navy Course pro shop to play a round of golf. He was a retired Department of Defense civilian with playing privileges at the course. According to MPGC employees, Joseph often golfed by himself.

Later that same afternoon, some golfers reported to the pro shop attendant that they had seen an unattended golf bag near the southwest corner of Alpha Lake next to hole 3. As a result, the attendant retrieved the bag and had it stored.

When Joseph didn't return home that evening, his wife became worried and filed a missing person's report with the police department. The following morning, Joseph's car was found in the golf course's parking lot.

The police started an investigation. They discovered drag marks on the exposed section of the plastic liner above the lake. The police investigators requested a diver search of the lake. During the search, the diver discovered Joseph's fully clothed body approximately eight feet below the surface of the lake.

The post mortem examination determined his body contained no drugs or alcohol, and ruled his death as asphyxiation dues to accidental drowning. There were no witnesses to the drowning.

Joseph's brother, Michael, suspected that Joseph had slipped and fallen into the lake while trying to retrieve a golf ball. The discovery of Joseph's 3-iron at the bottom of the lake tended to support Michael's suspicion, especially in light of the fact that his golf bag was about 80 yards from the hole. A 3-iron would have been too much club for a shot so close to the hole. The 3-iron was the longest one in his bag, and most likely was used by Joseph in an ill-fated attempt to retrieve a ball from the lake.

At the time of his death, Alpha Lake was 12 to 14 feet deep. The slope of the underwater drop-off was steep and varied between a slope of 1:1 and 1:2. Six signs posted around the lake warned: "DANGER: PLEASE STAY OUT OF THE LAKE. NO RETRIEVAL OF GOLF BALLS."

Joseph's widow, Kathleen Ventimiglia, sued the federal government under the Federal Tort Claims Act (FTCA), as well as various private defendants, alleging safety flaws in the design and maintenance of Alpha Lake. More specifically, she claimed the Navy was negligent in failing to provide the necessary precautions, such as a guard rail or fence, to prevent golfers from accidentally falling in the lake. She also maintained that the depth, grading, and exposed plastic liner around the lake required "terraced stepping areas" to assist any golfer who might fall into the lake.

The plaintiff argued that the government was negligent and that sovereign immunity did not insulate the government from liability for the death of her husband. The federal government disagreed. It moved to dismiss her wrongful death claim on the theory of sovereign immunity.

The Law

The United States, as sovereign, is immune from being sued except to the extent that it consents to be sued.[2] In 1946, Congress enacted the Federal Tort Claims Act (FTCA) waiving sovereign immunity for torts committed by federal employees acting within the scope of their employment that cause damage or death.[3] An FTCA claim against the federal government must be brought in federal court, but state tort law governs the substantive rights and duties of the parties.

The waiver of sovereign immunity under the FTCA is subject to a number of statutory and judicially created limitations. One limitation is the discretionary function exception. A plaintiff is barred from bringing a tort claim against the federal government for actions taken in exercising or performing a discretionary function or duty.

---

2. The *Rules of Golf* do not permit the waiver of the rules. Rule 1-3 provides that players must not agree to exclude the operation of any rule or penalty incurred. This non-waiver rule, which is designed to ensure the application of a uniform code for playing the game, is often not followed during a friendly round of golf.

3. Federal Tort Claims Act, 28 U.S.C. §§ 1346 *et seq.*

Hole 35: Federal Sovereign Immunity

One might reasonably ask, why? Haven't we come a long way from the original idea underlying sovereign immunity that the king can do no wrong?

At its core, discretionary immunity is based on the doctrine of separation of powers. This doctrine forecloses the judiciary from reviewing the discretionary policy decisions by the other branches of government and that lie at the heart of our system of governance. Immunity prevents tort actions from becoming a vehicle for judicial second-guessing of policy-based decision-making. It also eliminates the actual or potential threat of liability from interfering with decisions essential to effective governance. In effect, immunity puts certain decisions beyond the legal reach of the courts.

The FTCA statutorily bars claims against the government when the government employee exercises or performs a discretionary function or duty.[4] In *Berkovitz v. United States*, the Supreme Court articulated a two-prong test for determining the existence of discretionary immunity.[5] First, did the challenged conduct involve the exercise of judgment or discretion? To the extent that a federal statute, regulation, or policy specifies or directs a course of action to be followed by the federal employee, no discretion is involved, and immunity is not available.

Second, assuming judgment or discretion is involved, the next question is whether the exercise of the discretion was based on considerations of public policy, such as those based on social, economic, and political policy considerations. This second step examines whether the alleged tortious conduct fits within the scope of decision making that discretionary immunity is designed to shield. If a decision turns on only technical,

---

4. Federal Tort Claims Act, 28 U.S.C. § 2680(a).
5. Berkovitz v. United States, 486 U.S. 531 (1988).

scientific, and engineering considerations without policy implications, then the discretionary function exception does not generally apply.

If the challenged conduct satisfies both prongs of *Berkovitz*, then discretionary immunity is available to shield the government from tort liability. In such a case, the federal court lacks jurisdiction to hear the plaintiff's tort claim.

The court reasoned that the first prong of *Berkovitz* was easily met. The Navy was not bound by any mandated course of action regarding the design of Alpha Lake, including its decision to line the lake with a plastic water-retaining membrane to conserve water. The general guidelines and policies cited by the plaintiff, without more detailed mandatory requirements, gave the Navy ample discretion to determine the appropriate way to meet any relevant guidelines.[6] No statute, regulation, or policy mandated the design features of Alpha Lake or its renovation.

But the federal government was also required to satisfy the second prong of *Berkovitz* in order to secure immunity.

The courts have generally held that decisions regarding how and whether to address potential safety hazards involve the exercise of judgment meant by Congress to be shielded from liability. Thus, had plaintiff's claim of negligence been based solely on the decision not to install warning signs, fencing, or other barriers, she would have lost. The discretionary function exception would preclude jurisdiction.

The plaintiff also argued that the government was negligent in failing to construct a proper safety shelf. The government failed to establish how the liner-construction project involved decision making susceptible to any political, social, or econom-

---

6. Bureau of Navy Personnel's (BUPERS) Instruction 1710.11C §§ 2201–2211, and Appendix K; and also MWR's Internal Golf Operating Guidelines and Financial Standards.

ic considerations. Instead, the record supported the plaintiff's view that including a safety shelf when the liner was installed was a simple, essentially no-cost safety fix that did not warrant a careful weighing of policy options or competing interests.

Thus, the government was not entitled to the benefit of sovereign immunity for the alleged safety-shelf flaws. The plaintiff's complaint for negligence in the design and maintenance of the safety shelf could proceed under the FTCA.

Conclusion

The Federal Tort Claims Act waives sovereign immunity by the federal government. But the waiver does not extend to actions fitting within the discretionary function exception.

The federal government failed to demonstrate that this exception applied to the construction project when the liner to Alpha Lake was installed. It was unable to convince the court that the design decisions were susceptible to any public policy analysis implicating political, social, or economic considerations. Absent being able to show that its employees actually engaged in a balancing of public policy issues, the government was unable to make a convincing case for the application of sovereign immunity.

Paul Harvey was a popular radio personality from the 1950s through the 1990s. He was well known for his radio broadcast segment, "The Rest of the Story." His trademark was to hold back a key point in the narrative until the end of the story, at which point he would conclude "And now you know the *rest* of the story." The rest of the story in *Ventimiglia* is the plaintiff still had to prove that the Navy was negligent under California law. In light of the signs warning golfers not to retrieve golf balls from the lake, this would be difficult.

Hole 36

Local Government Immunity:
Municipal golf course liability

Iowa: *Summy v. City of Des Moines*, 708 N.W.2d 333 (2006)

In 1995, then-president Bill Clinton and former presidents Gerald Ford and George Bush (senior) were playing golf together in a pro-am tournament at Indian Wells Golf Club in California. The score for the round says it all: Ford shot a 100 and hit one spectator; Bush shot a 92 and hit two spectators; and Clinton shot a 93 and knocked a piece of watermelon from a boy's hand with one of his more wayward shots. Golf courses can be dangerous places.

Mishit and errant shots in golf are common. Also common is the fact that a golfer who is seriously injured on a golf course by such a shot is likely to sue the owner and operator of the golf course for negligent design or maintenance.[1] Others may also be sued, including the author of the injury-causing shot. But, as the following case explores, special legal defenses may apply when

---

1. Among other duties, a golf course has the responsibility to ensure that yardage markers embedded on the fairway and indicated on the scorecard are accurate. It is reasonably foreseeable that a player may rely on such yardage in deciding whether to safely hit. Thus, a player who is injured because another player relied on inaccurate information furnished by the course is likely to sue for negligence.

the owner or operator of the golf course is a city or other local government agency.

Waveland Golf Course is owned and operated by the City of Des Moines, Iowa. Built in 1901 on wooded hillsides, it claims to be the oldest municipal golf course west of the Mississippi. The vintage 18-hole course attracts more than 40,000 rounds of golf annually. It was also at the center of a tort dispute decided by the Iowa Supreme Court involving the application of the Iowa sovereign immunity statute and the public duty doctrine.

The Facts

In 2000, Richard Thomas was playing golf at Waveland on a pass issued to his employer. His plans for a pleasant and relaxing round of golf abruptly ended on the first hole after his tee shot struck Richard Summy in the eye. Summy, who was playing golf on the adjacent 18th fairway at the time, was about 150 yards from Thomas.

A protective barrier of 60 to 80 mature trees had originally separated the first and 18th fairways, but the trees died during the 1960s. At the time of the accident, only a few small trees separated the two holes. The absence of an effective barrier between the two holes created the foreseeable risk that a golfer teeing off on the first hole might hit a golfer playing the 18th hole, which is exactly what happened.

The risk was generally apparent. Summy admitted seeing golfers warming up on the tee box to the first hole. Had Summy looked, he would have seen Thomas teeing off. But Summy didn't look. Instead, he was focused on his playing partner.

Thomas did not yell "fore" when his shot veered onto the adjacent 18th fairway. He said he didn't see anyone who might get hit. Summy thought that if the traditional warning of "fore" had been given, he might have taken action to avoid getting hit.

The deep pocket in this situation was the City of Des Moines, so Summy sued it. He alleged that the city negligently designed, operated, and maintained the course in an unreasonably dangerous condition by allowing an overlapping area of play between the first and 18th holes. Interestingly, Thomas was not a party to the lawsuit.

The City asserted several affirmative defenses. It argued that Summy was comparatively at fault, that Thomas was the sole proximate cause of the injury, and that it was immune from liability under state law. Among other rulings, the trial court found that the City was not entitled to immunity. The City asked the Iowa Supreme Court to find it immune from liability under Iowa law governing third-party tortfeasors.

The Law

The common-law doctrine of sovereign immunity is historically based on the idea that the sovereign could not be sued because the King could do no wrong. When considering the potential liability of a municipal golf course, the law of sovereign immunity under state law is in play.

The doctrine of sovereign immunity has been gradually eroded by state legislative and judicial action. With the passage of time, some states have judicially abolished the doctrine. On the other hand, legislation completely extinguishing immunity is rare.

Despite forecasts of the complete demise of municipal tort immunity, the doctrine continues to be relevant to the analysis of tort claims brought against municipal golf courses.

In pursuing a tort claim against a municipal golf course, the plaintiff has the same burden to prove the elements of negligence that would be required when suing a private party or entity. The plaintiff must prove that the municipality owes the plaintiff a duty, breached that duty, and the breach caused the plaintiff harm. But the analysis of whether a municipality owes the injured plaintiff a duty is somewhat different from a tort action between private parties.

Duty and immunity are separate legal concepts. A municipality can avoid liability to a plaintiff by claiming it owes no duty to the plaintiff or that it is immune from liability. To the extent that the plaintiff establishes a prima facie case of negligence, the municipality may still avoid liability by successfully arguing the affirmative defense of immunity. Many states employ a similar discretion-function analysis adopted by the Federal Tort Claims Act.[2]

Duty

As a general rule, a city is not liable for the actions of a third party who is not under the supervision and control of the city. This general rule does not always apply to excuse liability.

The City argued that no duty existed because of the "public duty doctrine."[3] This judicially created doctrine provides that if the duty claimed by the plaintiff is owed to the public generally, there is no liability to an individual member of the public. The doctrine typically applies in the provision of public services, such as police protection, or in the enforcement of regulatory laws. As a matter of public policy, it avoids judicial interference with the allocation and prioritization of financial resources and reduces taxpayer exposure to broad liability.

---

2. To the extent that the alleged tort is based on the enforcement of a statute or the exercise of a discretionary function, federal immunity exists. Federal Tort Claims Act, 28 U.S.C. §§ 1346 *et seq.*

3. The "public duty rule" is something of a misnomer because when the rule applies, no duty exists that gives rise to liability, even though a duty to the general public may exist. The justification for the public duty rule has been increasingly questioned.

This judicially created doctrine, which is recognized by Iowa, protects a municipality from tort liability unless the plaintiff can show that the breached duty was owed to the plaintiff individually, and was not merely a duty to the public at large.[4]

The Iowa Supreme Court rejected the application of the public duty doctrine. It held a duty is owed to invitees (golfers) on the golf course and not to the public at large. One special relationship that generates the duty to take positive acts of reasonable care is that of landowner-invitee. The court applied the principles of the *Restatement (Second) of Torts*:

> A possessor of land who holds it open to the public for entry for his business purposes is subject to liability to members of the public while they are upon the land for such a purpose, for physical harm caused by the accidental, negligent, or intentionally harmful acts of third persons or animals, and by the failure of the possessor to exercise reasonable care to (a) discover that such acts are being done or are likely to be done, or (b) give a warning adequate to enable the visitors to avoid the harm, or otherwise to protect them against it.[5]

---

4. *See* Kolbe v. State, 625 N.W.2d 721 (Iowa 2001) (holding that the duty to use care in the issuance of a driver's license is a duty owed to the public at large, and that finding liability for the negligent issuance of a driver's license to a person with Stargardt's disease who caused plaintiff's injury would "chill" the state's licensing function).

5. RESTATEMENT (SECOND) OF TORTS § 344 (1965). Comment (d) provides the following on the meaning of reasonable care:

> A public utility or other possessor of land who holds it open to the public for entry for his business purposes is not an insurer of the safety of such visitors against the acts of third persons, or the acts of animals. He is, however, under a duty to exercise reasonable care to give them protection. In many cases a warning is sufficient care if the possessor reasonably believes that it will be enough to enable the visitor to avoid the harm, or protect himself against it. There are, however, many situations in which the possessor cannot reasonably assume that a warning will be sufficient. He is then required to exercise reasonable care to use such means of protection as are available, or to provide such means in advance because of the likelihood that third persons, or animals, may conduct themselves in a manner which will endanger the safety of the visitor.

The court reasoned that the public duty doctrine does not apply "if there is a particular relationship between the governmental entity and the injured plaintiff that gives rise to a special duty." This special relationship involves the assumption of a duty based on the knowledge that the failure to act in providing a barrier between the first and 18th holes might lead to the injury of a golfer on the 18th. Thus, it rejected the City's argument that the complaint should be dismissed based on the public duty doctrine.

Immunity

The scope of municipal immunity is defined by state law. Iowa generally makes every municipality liable for the torts of its officers and employees acting within the scope of their employment or duties. But Iowa statutorily grants a limited form of municipal immunity when the injury to the plaintiff is caused by a third person who is not under its supervision or control:

> [I]n the absence of [an] express statute, the municipality shall be immune from liability [for] . . . Any claim based upon an act or omission of an officer or employee of the municipality, whether by issuance of permit, inspection, investigation, or otherwise, and whether the statute, ordinance, or regulation is valid, if the damage was caused by a third party, event, or property not under the supervision or control of the municipality, unless the act or omission of the officer or employee constitutes actual malice or a criminal offense.[6]

The Iowa Supreme Court rejected the application of this immunity provision. It reasoned that "act or omission" that

---

6. IOWA CODE ANN. § 670.4(10).

would result in immunity had to be similar to an "act or omission" involving a "permit, inspection, investigation, or otherwise."

The City argued that the golfing pass given to Thomas's employer was similar to the issuance of a permit, which was the basis for its claim for immunity. The court was not persuaded. The plaintiff's lawsuit against the City was not based on allowing Thomas to play golf on the pass. Rather, the plaintiff's legal theory was that the City failed to protect him from the foreseeable hazard of an errant golf shot, and thus was not remotely similar to the immunity provisions of the statute.

Conclusion

The only thing more certain than an errant shot on a golf course is that a person who is injured by it will sue someone. That someone is likely to include the owner and operator of the golf course.

The *Summy* case is typical of a golf course owned and operated by a municipality. Notwithstanding the fact that the ball that injured the plaintiff was hit by Thomas, who was playing a different hole, the City was sued for negligence for not minimizing an obvious risk of danger. The trial court found that Thomas was not the sole proximate cause of Summy's injury, and that the City was also negligent.

The owner and operator of a golf course have the obligation to design and maintain the facility to minimize the risk that a golf ball will hit any player. The City had a duty to use reasonable care to protect Summy from golf balls hit from the first tee.

The City's affirmative defenses were rejected. The Iowa Supreme Court found that the City's duty did not fall with the proper scope of the public duty doctrine, and its operation of the golf course was not within the scope of the Iowa immunity statute. These were important clarifications of Iowa law. They also provide useful lessons for golfers and municipal golf courses in other states.

While liability insurance may protect against injuries to persons and property, properly installing barriers or redesigning the holes to minimize the risk of injury is a practical strategy to avoiding being found liable. Golf courses also should regularly check their cart paths and other walkways for potential injury-causing irregularities or dangerous conditions.

Part VIII

Antitrust

Hole 37

The USGA and Handicap Competition:
GHIN (without the tonic)

Federal: *Handicomp v. United States Golf Association* (USGA), 2000 WL 426245 (3d Cir. 2000), cert. denied, 531 U.S. 928 (2000)

The United States Golf Association (USGA) was created in 1894 to conduct national championships, to administer and promote golf, and to oversee the codification and interpretation of the *Rules of Golf* as well as the *Rules of Amateur Status*. The USGA has a long-established regulatory relationship with regional golf associations, which receive their authority to issue USGA handicap indexes from the USGA.[1]

The USGA Handicap System establishes a set of rules and procedures for calculating a golfer's handicap index, often simply referred by golfers as their handicap. Handicap indexes are issued to a golfer by golf clubs or golf associations based on the application of a mathematical formula to the golfer's past scores. The objective is to "level the playing field" by allowing golfers of different skill levels to compete against each other on

---

1. Regional golf associations also perform other services under the auspices of the USGA. They rate golf courses, conduct USGA golf events, and locally administer the USGA's *Rules of Golf*.

an equal basis by adjusting the golfers' actual score based on his or her index.

Most golf courses are designed to allow a skilled golfer to play the 18 holes in a regulation number of strokes, usually between 70 and 72, known as "par." Golf professionals are capable of scoring below par during a round of golf, but with rare exception, amateur golfers typically shoot above par.[2] And then there is the "sandbagger." The word "sandbagger" can be traced to an earlier time when street thugs would fill a sock or small bag with sand, wrap it tightly around their wrist, and use it to beat the daylights out of someone. Golfers appropriated the term to describe a player who deliberately carries an artificially high index to improve the chances of winning tournaments or bets with fellow players. Thus, the "sandbagger's" weapon of choice is an artificially high handicap.

The USGA indexing system provides some safeguards against sandbagging. It excludes particularly bad holes and only counts the best 10 of a golfer's last 20 rounds. But the system assumes that the players are properly reporting all their scores for purposes of their index, which isn't always a sound assumption. The system isn't perfect, as many an amateur golfer has learned firsthand when they hear a sandbagger say, "It was the best round of my life." The local Handicap Committee and Tournament Committee bear the principal responsibility for monitoring compliance with the USGA handicap system. Because not all golf courses present the same degree of difficulty, the USGA course handicap system takes into account the difficulty of the golf course and set of tees from which the round is played.

The basic premise of the handicap system is that players will try to make their best score and will post each round played

---

2. A "scratch golfer" has a handicap of 0, whereas a "bogey golfer" has a handicap of 18.

Hole 37: The USGA and Handicap Competition

for peer review. The first version of the USGA handicap formula was published in the late 1890s. In 1911, it adopted a system based on a golfer's best three scores. Over the years, the formula has been modified to include a course rating system and a "net score" (a score adjusted for course difficulty) method of handicapping; a "current ability" approach, in which only a golfer's most recent scores are counted; a system of "equitable stroke control," which disallows very high scores for individual holes; an upper limit on handicaps; and a "discounting" approach, in which a handicap is calculated based on a percentage (currently 96%) of the differentials between the player's score and the course difficulty.

Handicaps are relevant when golfers compete against each other. In order for a golfer to play in most golf tournaments, from the local club level to regional events, he or she must have a USGA handicap. No handicap computation business can effectively compete in the marketplace without using the USGA handicap formula.[3] It is the gold standard for golf.

The Facts

The use of computer software systems has introduced competition into the administration of golf handicaps. Handicomp has been in the business of providing golf handicap services to regional golf associations since 1968. The USGA and Handicomp offer competing data-processing services for computing golfers' handicaps to regional golf associations, such as the Southern California Golf Association.

---

3. U.S. Golf Ass'n v. St. Andrews Systems, Data-Max, Inc., 749 F.2d 1028 (3d Cir. 1984) (holding that the computer company's use of the USGA's mathematical handicapping formula to nonmembers of the USGA was not an illegal misappropriation under New Jersey law; preventing other handicap providers from using the formula would effectively give the USGA a national monopoly on the golf-handicapping business).

In 1981, the USGA started a commercial business to sell its golf handicap computation services to regional golf associations throughout the United States. It formed the Golf Handicap and Information Network (GHIN) to sell its computational services to the same regional golf associations with which it had a regulatory relationship. As an inducement to use GHIN, the USGA allowed those participating associations to use the USGA trademarks.

The network operates through regional golf associations and does not deal directly with individual players or golf clubs. More than 70 percent of close to 100 regional golf associations are under an exclusive contract with the USGA to have affiliated player handicaps calculated using GHIN. The system allows a golfer to electronically post scores from any of the more than 19,000 golf courses within the network. It also allows a golfer to see recently posted scores as well as the golfer's current handicap.

In 1996, Handicomp sued the USGA in federal district court, alleging that a conspiracy existed between the USGA and regional golf associations to violate federal antitrust law. It alleged the USGA had created a barrier to entry in the industry.[4]

---

4. A legal barrier to entry creates an unfair interference with the operation of the marketplace. The *Rules of Golf* also deals with unfair interferences. Under Rule 23, for example, "loose impediments" may be moved without penalty as long as the ball does not move while the impediment is removed. If the ball moves, a penalty is assessed under Rule 18.

Tiger Woods famously took advantage of this rule during the 1999 Phoenix Open. On the 13th hole, Tiger's drive put him behind what may be described as a boulder, which prevented him from going for the green on his second shot. The "loose impediment" was not "solidly imbedded" as required by the definition. Thus, the PGA official overseeing the application of the loose impediment rule said that as long as the boulder could be moved without unreasonable effort, without unduly delaying play, and without causing damage, it could be moved. As a result, 12 assembled spectators assisted in pushing the boulder aside. Tiger went for the green, scored a birdie, but ultimately finished in third place.

Hole 37: The USGA and Handicap Competition

It also alleged that the USGA acquired market dominance by using television revenues from the U.S. Open Golf Championship to provide price supports to keep GHIN financially afloat. This price support arguably decimated market competition, driving many competitors from the market. In short, Handicorp claimed that the USGA illegally used its position as a neutral governing body to create a monopoly in offering handicapping services through GHIN.

The district court held that Handicomp could not prove the antitrust injury, the exercise of USGA monopoly power, or the anticompetitive conduct by the USGA. The evidence offered by Handicomp did not show that the USGA manipulated the golf rules in a way that injured Handicomp or impaired competition. Any financial losses suffered by Handicomp were caused by increased competition, not market manipulation. The theory that Handicomp could have had more sales and charged higher prices without the existence of GHIN was a nonstarter.

Handicomp appealed to the Court of Appeals for the Third Circuit. It argued that the district court ignored the evidence that the USGA abused its position as a neutral governing body in order to gain competitive advantages for GHIN.

The Law

The Sherman Antitrust Act is a federal law intended to protect consumers by preventing business arrangements "designed, or which tend, to advance the cost of goods to the consumer." It also has been used to prevent arrangements that potentially harm competition, such as monopolies.

Section 2 of the Sherman Act provides:

> Every person who shall monopolize, or attempt to monopolize, or combine or conspire with any other

person or persons, to monopolize any part of the trade or commerce among the several States, or with foreign nations, shall be deemed guilty of a felony, and, on conviction thereof, shall be punished by fine . . . or by imprisonment . . . or by both said punishments, in the discretion of the court.[5]

To establish a valid claim under Section 2 of the Sherman Act, Handicomp was required to demonstrate: (1) that the USGA possessed monopoly power in the relevant market, and (2) that the USGA willfully abused its power. The first step required showing that the USGA has "the power to control market prices or exclude competition." The second step required showing that the USGA developed or abused its monopoly power willfully. As a private party, Handicomp also was required to show an "antitrust injury," which is an injury caused by the antitrust violation and not merely a result of increased competition.

The relevant market consisted of those regional associations using the USGA Handicap Index system. Only golf associations are entitled to grant USGA indexes, and therefore they constituted the relevant market.

The existence of monopoly power within the relevant market may be inferred from dominance within that market. Handicomp argued that this principle of dominance applied because GHIN controlled 72 percent of the handicap market.

The Third Circuit was not prepared to treat this degree of market share as determinative. It reasoned that Handicomp was

---

5. 15 U.S.C. § 2 (1999). Section 4 of the Clayton Act provides the basis a private plaintiff may use to sue a private defendant under § 2 of the Sherman Act:

> [A]ny person who shall be injured in his business or property by reason of anything forbidden in the antitrust laws may sue therefor in any district court of the United States . . . shall recover threefold the damages by him sustained, and the cost of the suit, including a reasonable attorney's fee.

Hole 37: The USGA and Handicap Competition

required to prove that the GHIN system constituted a significant barrier to entry to those companies wishing to enter the relevant market. Market share alone was not enough.

In addition, the evidence did not support the existence of such a barrier. When the Southern California Golf Association, for example, solicited bids for its handicap computation service contract in 1990, it received 13 bids—including nine bids from computer service companies that had never previously provided handicap computation services to golf associations. Such facts did not support the existence of a barrier to entry.

The court also reasoned: "A skilled teenage hacker today would have no difficulty in programming a data processing system to register the rating slope of a golf course and the gross score of a golfer and produce a handicap." In fact, Handicomp's president admitted that "somebody could sit down in a matter of three weeks, develop a product and put it on the market that would compete."

Without establishing a barrier to entry, there was no violation of the Sherman Act. Therefore, the Third Circuit sustained the district court's determination that the USGA did not possess or exercise illegal monopoly power. There was no evidence that the USGA was controlling prices or harming competition within the relevant market.

Conclusion

Handicomp failed in its appeal to the Third Circuit. The Supreme Court of the United States refused to hear Handicomp's claim that accused the USGA of unlawfully trying to dominate the business of calculating golfer handicaps when it created the Golf Handicap and Information Network (GHIN) system.

Handicomp's alleged financial injury didn't square with the

purpose of antitrust law. The Sherman Act is aimed at protecting consumers from manipulated high prices. Plaintiffs who want to charge higher prices for their services essentially plead themselves out of a successful antitrust claim.

Life goes on after losing a round of golf as well as losing a lawsuit. Handicomp is still in business today. It provides an Internet-based USGA Handicap Index computation service for certified golf clubs and amateur associations. It also has a Golf Tournament Network, which provides an Internet-based tournament management software system designed for clubs, associations, and individuals, as well as a Golf League Network.

Part IX

Tax

Hole 38

Internal Revenue Service:
Wannabe tour player teed off at IRS

Federal: *Courville v. Comm'r,*
71 T.C.M. (CCH) 2496 (U.S. Tax Court) (1996)

Some golf professionals have tangled with the IRS. For example, Jim Thorpe (Jimmy Lee Thorpe), a well-known American professional golfer, recently rejoined the Champions Tour after being released from prison for tax evasion. He was charged with failing to pay $1.6 million in taxes, and pled guilty in 2009.

Sergio Garcia ("El Nino")[1] and Retief Goosen[2] also have tussled with the IRS over how their endorsement income from sponsors should be treated. Neither player is a citizen of the United States, but that isn't the controlling consideration. Personal services income is subject to ordinary United States federal income tax, whereas royalty income is not. The question before the Tax Court was the proper allocation of the endorsement payments between personal services and royalty income. Garcia wound up paying more in federal taxes because the Tax

---

1. Garcia v. Comm'r, 2013 WL 999377 (2013).
2. Goosen v. Comm'r, 136 T.C. 547 (2011).

Court allocated more of the payments to the personal services category. But, unlike Jim Thorpe, Garcia simply wound up paying more in federal taxes. In contrast, the Tax Court found that Goosen's tax allocation was correct.

Will Rogers once remarked that the income tax has made more liars out of the American people than golf. I suspect if he were alive today, he wouldn't revise his viewpoint.

The Facts

William Courville was an optical engineer for many years. As a result of corporate downsizing at Lockheed Missile & Space, he was laid off from his engineering job. Following the loss of his job, he was faced with the decision of what to do with the rest of his life. For William, the answer was obvious: golf.

Now that he was unencumbered with the workaday demands of his former engineering job, William decided to pursue his lifelong goal of becoming a professional golfer. He had played golf since he was a kid and had developed some talent for the game. As an amateur golfer, he carried a handicap of 5 and was confident that he could improve his game. William had distinguished himself by winning several local club championships. But none of them carried any prize money.

William set his sights on playing on the Professional Golf Association (PGA) Senior Tour (now called the Champions Tour), which is open to qualifying golfers who are 50 and older. TV commentator Bobby Clampett has called the process for qualifying "the most complicated system known to man," and added that "not a single player understands it fully." The likelihood of success in being admitted is slightly better than winning the lottery. Each year, only a handful of golfers out of more than 300 qualify from Q-school.

Undaunted by these statistics, William tried to qualify

Hole 38: Internal Revenue Service

through the Q-school. He failed. He then tried to qualify through individual tournaments. The best he did was to make it as an alternate. William did not give up his dream. He continued to practice and take golf lessons from various players he met at the qualifying tournaments. He also sought counseling from a psychiatrist. The problem, in his view, was not his golfing ability, but his "thought process."

In 1995 William became a golf instructor to finance his continued effort to qualify for, and join, the PGA Senior Tour. Golf became his life. When he was not teaching, he was either practicing or playing golf. Some might say he was "living the good life."

William's problem with the IRS started when he filed his 1991 federal income tax return. On his tax Schedule C (Profit and Loss from Business), he reported zero income and more than $16,000 in expenses. After 1991, he did not file a Schedule C for his golfing expenses. The tax law is a nightmare to understand, but his explanation was straightforward enough for the average taxpayer to understand: "I had no [wage or Schedule C] income, so how could I write off my expenses against no income?"

Along with many taxpayers, William detested record keeping. He kept no formal books or records, although he did keep an informal sheet of paper he labeled "Tax Info." It listed his golfing expenses for 1991, but, unfortunately for William, the amounts he claimed on Schedule C did not match with the amounts listed on his informal tally sheet. On the plus side, he did have some receipts for various expenses related to his golfing activities.

The Internal Revenue Service took an interest in William's tax returns. The IRS took so much interest in his tax situation that it honored him by naming a case after him: *William James*

Courville v. Comm'r.[3] The honor of seeing his name in print was short-lived, however.

The Law

The Tax Court denied William certain deductions that he claimed for his golfing activities and socked him with accuracy-related penalties equal to 20 percent of his tax underpayment.

The Internal Revenue Code contains rules for deducting business expenses.[4] The Code provides that if an activity is not engaged in for profit, no deduction attributable to such activity is allowed.[5] The critical question before the Tax Court was whether William was engaged in the activity with the actual, honest objective of making a profit.

William had the burden of proving the necessary intent, which he failed to do. Why was William unable to convince the Tax Court?

To qualify an activity as a business and be entitled to business deductions, it is not necessary to actually show a profit. The taxpayer, however, must intend to make a profit. A proper business activity is one in which the taxpayer has the objective

---

3. Courville v. Comm'r, 71 T.C.M (CCH) 2496 (1996). The Tax Court's opinion was affirmed by the U.S. Court of Appeals, 9th Circuit, in an unpublished opinion on March 13, 1997. Courville v. Comm'r, No. 96-70475 (9th Cir. Mar. 13, 1997).

4. Section 274 contains several exceptions to the deductibility of ordinary and necessary expenses incurred in carrying on a trade or business. Expenses paid or incurred for membership in any club organized for business, pleasure, recreation, or other social purpose are not deductible. I.R.C. § 274(a)(3). More specifically, expenses paid for golf and country club dues are not deductible. Income Tax Regs. § 1.274–2(a)(2)(iii)(a). In addition, the legislative history emphasizes that it is a strict nondeductibility rule. No one, including golf professionals or instructors, may deduct club dues. Congress explained that the nondeductibility rule eased compliance with former law that required determining whether the primary purpose of belonging to the country club was personal.

5. I.R.C. § 183(a) and (b).

Hole 38: Internal Revenue Service

of making a profit, as opposed to the activity simply being a hobby or pastime.

The taxpayer's intent to make a profit is determined by reference to a variety of criteria contained in the Income Tax Regulations. They include, for example, the success of the taxpayer in carrying out the activity, the history of income and losses, and the elements of personal pleasure or recreation from the activity. From a professional and financial standpoint, the court found that William's time and effort had been without much success. He failed to qualify for any PGA-sponsored tournament and had not earned any income as a professional golfer.

William clearly gained personal pleasure from playing golf. While there is no requirement that a taxpayer not derive pleasure from the activity, the elements of recreation and pleasure, when considered with other factors, are relevant to determining whether golf will be considered a legitimate business activity. In the Tax Court's opinion, William failed to establish that his golfing activity was carried on with the actual and honest objective of making a profit.

Under the Internal Revenue Code, accuracy-related penalties can be imposed for the underpayment of tax attributable to the taxpayer's negligence or disregard for rules or regulations. The court observed that "petitioner's activity was far from being a for-profit activity." In addition to failing to keep regular books and records of his golfing activity, William failed to present any evidence to show reasonable cause as to why he should not be held liable for this type of penalty.

Conclusion

William failed to convince the Tax Court that his deductions were legitimate business expenses. The information furnished to support his claim was also suspect, and might be treated as a reminder of golf's "wrong information" rule.[6]

The term "rub of the green" is used by golfers to describe the situation when a ball in motion is accidentally deflected or stopped by an outside agency. William unhappily found out that the IRS is a formidable outside agency with the dexterous ability to rub the green out of a taxpayer's pocket.

---

6. The rules are different for match play (Rule 9-2) and stroke play (Rule 9-3). The difference is based on the distinction that in match play only the player and his or her opponent are involved in the outcome of the competition, whereas in stroke play every competitor in the field has a direct interest in the outcome.

In match play, a player who gives the wrong information, such as the incorrect number of strokes taken (including any penalty strokes), to an opponent is penalized loss of the hole, unless the information is corrected before the opponent plays his or her next stroke. The penalty does not depend on whether the player is acting in good faith. Nor does the penalty depend on whether the player is responding to a question asked by an opponent or simply volunteering the information to be nice. Wrong information is wrong information, and it may affect what the opponent does next. And silence is not golden. In the unlikely situation that a player refuses to tell an opponent the number of strokes played, the player who remains mum is also penalized loss of the hole.

In stroke play, the rules are different. A player should inform the opponent of any incurred penalty as soon as practicable. But no penalty is imposed for giving the wrong information to a competitor as to the number of strokes. Other rules may apply, however. For example, submitting the wrong score, which is lower than actually taken, results in disqualification under Rule 6-6.d.

If the recorded score is higher than the score actually taken, the higher score stands under Rule 6-6.d. This type of overreporting problem in stroke play happened to Roberto De Vincenzo at the 1968 Masters. Roberto and Bob Goalby were tied when the final putt found the bottom of the cup on the last day. Unfortunately, Roberto signed for a score that was one more stroke than he actually scored during the round. The additional stroke stood under the rules, and Roberto lost the chance of playoff with Bob Goalby, who won the Masters by one stroke because of the error.

Part X
Americans with Disabilities Act

Hole 39

Americans with Disabilities Act of 1990 (ADA):
The nature of the game of golf

Federal: *PGA Tour, Inc. v. Martin*, 532 U.S. 661 (2001)

The Supreme Court of the United States is the highest court in the land. It deals with weighty issues involving the interpretation and application of federal law. The Court rarely considers cases involving golf. Thus, the *Martin* case is an important exception to the general rule.

The Facts

To some golfers, their greatest disability is correctly tallying up their score at the end of each hole. Other golfers face more serious challenges. Casey Martin fits in the latter category.

Casey has a physical disability. He was born with a rare muscular and circulatory disorder in his right leg, known as Klippel-Trenaunay-Weber syndrome. The primary vein in this leg is missing, and the smaller veins are malformed. Thus, the leg is malnourished and half the size of his left leg. Because the

Casey Martin

veins do not return blood from the leg, the blood pools there. The disorder causes Casey to limp with severe pain when he walks. Neither the existence nor the severity of his congenital disorder is in doubt. In fact, the problem is sufficiently severe that the progression of the disease may ultimately require the amputation of his leg below the knee.

The PGA Tour, a nonprofit association consisting of the best professional golfers in the world, has a "walking-only" rule for most competitions unless the PGA Tour Rules Committee grants permission to ride, which it rarely does. Whether this rule conflicts with the protections of the Americans with Disabilities Act of 1990 (ADA) was at the center of the litigation.

Casey would prefer to walk during tour competition, but it is too painful due to his disability. He needs to use a motorized cart to get from shot to shot. The walking-only rule forced him to sue the PGA Tour in Oregon federal court. His theory was that by not allowing him to use a motorized golf cart, the PGA Tour failed to make its golf tournaments accessible to disabled individuals in violation of the ADA.

Casey won the first round. The federal district court found that the ADA applied. It also held that allowing him to use a motorized golf cart would be a reasonable accommodation and would not frustrate the purpose of the Tour's walking rule or alter the fundamental nature of professional golf tournament competition. Therefore, the Tour was directed to allow him to use a golf cart during Nike and PGA Tour events.

A three-judge panel for the Ninth Circuit Court of Appeals also ruled in favor of Martin. But events in the world of golf were happening elsewhere that confused the matter. Almost on the same day that the Ninth Circuit ruled, the Seventh Circuit held, in a remarkably similar ADA case, that the nature of the competition would be fundamentally altered if the walking rule were eliminated.[1] The Ninth and Seventh Circuits had different views on the nature of the game, the walking-only rule, and the application of the ADA.

The Supreme Court of the United States resolved the split between the Ninth and Seventh Circuits.

The Law
The Americans with Disabilities Act of 1990 (ADA)

In 1990, Congress enacted the ADA to protect the disabled from discrimination. It was designed to require the removal of barriers that prevent persons with disabilities from sharing in and contributing to the vitality of American life. The thrust of the law is to require businesses and public entities to provide reasonable accommodation for disabled persons unless the businesses or public entities can show that the accommodation would fundamentally alter the activity in question.

Martin argued in the district court that the Tour's "no-cart" rule violated Titles I and III of the ADA. Title I prohibits entities covered by its provisions from discriminating against qualified persons with disabilities in all employment situations. But an employer does not have to provide an accommodation if doing so will result in an "undue hardship."

Title III prohibits discrimination in places of public accom-

---

1. Olinger v. U.S. Golf Ass'n., 205 F.3d 1001 (7th Cir. 2000).

modation. It provides that "no individual shall be discriminated against on the basis of disability in the full and equal enjoyment of the goods, services, facilities, privileges, advantages, or accommodations of any place of public accommodation by any person who owns, leases, or operates a place of public accommodation." Title III does not apply if the entity can show that the modification would fundamentally alter the nature of the goods, services, or facilities or constitute an undue burden.

The Supreme Court considered two questions concerning the application of the ADA. The first was whether the Tour tournaments are subject to the ADA as places of public accommodation. The answer to this question depends on what Congress intended when it wrote the law. If the ADA applies, the second question was whether allowing a disabled contestant to use a motorized cart would fundamentally alter the nature of the competition by giving Martin a special advantage over other competitors who must walk. If walking is considered an essential part of the Tour competition, the Tour would be able to refuse Martin's request to use a cart.

Places of "Public Accommodation" and "Clients and Customers"

The Tour argued that it was exempt from the ADA because it was a private club or establishment, not a place of public accommodation. It claimed that Congress never intended that a private organization, such as the PGA Tour, be required to change its tournament rules to accommodate a would-be participant such as Martin.

The Tour conceded that the ADA expressly listed golf courses as places of public accommodation. But it argued that a golf course is only a place of public accommodation when it is engaged in the ordinary and usual operation of selling tee

Hole 39: Americans with Disabilities Act of 1990 (ADA)

times to the general public or providing spectator areas for tour events. In other words, the Tour maintained that the parts of the golf course on which its tournaments are played—"inside the ropes"—were not places of public accommodation because the public was not allowed there.

The Tour also maintained that Title III applies to clients and customers seeking goods and services at places of public accommodation. Martin should lose, it argued, because he was not within the protected class of clients or customers. As a playing competitor, Martin should be considered an entertainer or provider of entertainment and outside the protection of Title III.

Rather than driving into the rough of semantic gymnastics, the Supreme Court found Martin was in fact a "client or customer." Why? He paid the Tour money for the opportunity to compete. The Court reasoned that "it would be entirely appropriate to classify the golfers who pay petitioner $3,000 for the chance to compete in the Q-school and, if successful, in the subsequent Tour events as petitioner's clients and customers."

What is fundamental to the game of golf?

But finding that the ADA applies to Tour competitions was half the legal battle for Martin. Title III requires accommodation "unless the entity can demonstrate that making such modification would fundamentally alter the nature of such goods, services, facilities, privileges, advantages, or accommodations." The Tour claimed that allowing Martin to ride in a cart would fundamentally change the nature of the professional competition, and therefore no accommodation was required.

The record included testimony on the nature of the game from some of golf's greatest players. Arnold Palmer, Jack Nicklaus, and Ken Venturi each testified that fatigue can be a critical factor in a tournament, particularly on the last day, when psychological pressure is at a maximum. Moreover, their testimony was that using a cart might give some players a competitive advantage over those players required to walk. Giving a player a special advantage is inconsistent with the Rules of Golf. Not surprisingly, these golfing legends did not express an opinion on whether allowing Martin to use a cart actually would give him a competitive advantage.

The Supreme Court determined that allowing Casey to use a cart would not fundamentally change the nature of the competition or give him an unfair advantage. It reasoned that the essence of the game of golf is the ability to make a good shot, not how one gets to the ball to make the shot. In the Court's view, how a golfer gets to the ball in order to make the shot arguably is irrelevant. The idea is to find out who is the best at getting the ball in the hole with the fewest number of strokes. This view applies with equal force to the professional golfer on the PGA Tour as well as to the amateur.

The Court looked to the history of the game. It found that the tradition of walking existed until a sensible alternative was introduced shortly after World War II, when motorized carts were first marketed. Thus, "tradition" seemed a weak rationale for saying that walking is inextricably bound up in the essence of the game. In addition, the Court recognized that the sport of golf has regularly embraced advances in technology over the years. In a relatively short period of time, professional golfers have moved from wood clubs to steel clubs to titanium clubs to tri-metal clubs. The technological development of the golf ball used by professionals also suggests a willingness to embrace change.

What guidance did the *Rules of Golf* provide? The Rules do

not state that walking is fundamental to the game.[2] There is an important exception, however. When a cart is being moved by one of the players sharing it, the cart and everything in it are considered to be that player's equipment as long as the operator is not a team partner. Therefore, no penalty would be assessed when the player's ball is accidentally deflected or stopped while the cart is being driven or moved by a fellow competitor (Decision 19/1).

Moreover, when administratively convenient, the Tour has made exceptions to the no-cart rule. The power to do this is found in the Tour's Conditions of Competition and Local Rules, which provide that players shall walk at all times during the stipulated round *unless* permitted to ride by the PGA Tour's Rules Committee. In other words, when it is convenient to the Tour's Rules Committee, carts may be allowed. This often occurs, for example, in open and sectional qualifying tournaments. Carts are also frequently used to shuttle players between the ninth green and tenth teeing ground, and back to the teeing ground after discovering that a player's ball is lost or out-of-bounds. Professionals who play on the Senior Golf Tour also are given the option of using motorized carts.

Conclusion

The *Martin* case illustrates that the rules of sport competition are not beyond the scope of judicial inquiry. In delivering the 7-2 majority opinion, Justice Stevens held that the ADA applied and that the Tour's walking-only rule was at best peripheral and not

---

2. Under the rules, a golf cart, whether or not it is motorized, is treated as "equipment." When a motorized cart is shared by two players, the cart and everything in it are considered the equipment of the player whose ball is involved. Should a player's ball accidentally be deflected or stopped by his or her equipment, a penalty is assessed under Rule 19-2. In match play the penalty is loss of hole; in stroke play it is two strokes.

an indispensable feature of golf at any level. A wholesale change in the Tour's rules was not required, but the impact of its rules on individuals must be taken into account. Accommodation required his being allowed to use a cart.

Justice Stevens cited the Tour's failure to consider evidence of Martin's disability. Martin had given the Tour a videotape corroborating his disability, which was evidence that allowing him to use a cart would not give him any special advantage. The Tour returned the videotape with the explanation that the ADA, in its view, was inapplicable, and it wouldn't consider the specifics of his condition. It turned out their reasoning and analysis was wrong.

Tim Finchem, a lawyer by training, was in his fourth year as PGA Tour Commissioner when Martin sued the Tour. In an interesting twist of fate, Finchem was the unexpected source of the news to Martin that he had won the Supreme Court case in 2001. Finchem telephoned Martin with the news in the early morning on the day the Court announced the decision.

Martin enthusiastically responded to his victory in the Supreme Court by saying, "Now, I'm prepared to play golf, just like everyone else." But the decision has produced mixed reviews from professional golfers and the media. In his dissenting opinion, Justice Scalia called the result a distortion of the text of Title III, the structure of the ADA, and common sense. He lamented the Court's willingness to determine whether walking is "fundamental" to the game and nonessential when the Tour deems otherwise.

Justice Scalia predicted that the case will be a "rich source of lucrative litigation." It is not clear this has happened. The *Martin* case has however, helped other golfers seeking accommodations for disabilities, such as MacKinzie Kline of the Ladies Professional Golf Association. Regardless of his future success as a professional golfer, Casey Martin has left his mark on American jurisprudence.

Epilogue

In May 2006, Martin was named head coach of the men's golf team at the University of Oregon. He played in the 2012 U.S. Open but narrowly missed the cut. Thanks to his perseverance in litigating his ADA claim, he was able to compete and use a one-man cart between holes during the event.

In 2013, Martin was back in the news. This time the USGA denied him the use of a cart while he was recruiting for the Oregon golf team at the U.S. Junior Amateur qualifier at Oceanside, California. The USGA has a rule that prohibits spectators from using carts. The USGA responded by saying that it extended Martin the same accommodations it offers all disabled spectators. We may hear more about this in the future.

Index

A

Abandonment (legal), 193

Abandonment of provisional ball (rule), 49, 193, 194

Acushnet, 213–225, 265–272

Amateurs, 99, 110, 113

Americans with Disabilities Act of 1990 (ADA), 375–384

Anand v. Kapoor, 41–49

Assault, 128, 187–191, 294

Assumption of the risk, 6–9, 16–21, 37, 39, 45–47, 184, 346

B

Ball, identifying (rule), 3, 4, 118–119

Ball technology, 217–218

Ball use (rule), 29, 49, 179, 188, 193–194, 214, 227, 230

Bernardo Heights Country Club v. Community Association of Bernardo Heights, 193–199

Berryhill, Jimmy, Jr., 135

C

California Supreme Court, 65–66, 321

Callaway Golf, 291

Callaway Golf Co. v. Acushnet Co., 213–225

City of Santa Barbara Against the Use of Potable Water by the Tsukamoto Sogyo Company, Department of Water Resources Control Board, 297–303

Cobaugh, Amos, 100, 104

Cobaugh v. Klick-Lewis, Inc., 99–104

Coffey v. State Farm Mut. Auto. Ins. Co., 118

Colorado Supreme Court, 75

Consortium, 79–85

Contracts, xiii, 16, 67, 69, 89, 90, 94, 97, 101–104, 110, 113, 130, 136, 142–143, 189, 196–197, 241–242, 243, 245–246, 300, 302, 356, 359

Copyright, 153, 190, 244, 255–257

Course design, xiii, 10, 15, 19, 21, 52, 249–262, 269, 277, 321, 336, 338–339, 341, 343, 347–348, 354

Courville, William, 366–370

Courville v. Comm'r, 365–370

D

Dallas Athletic Country Club, 173–177

Daly, John, 229, 239, 241–246

Data-Max, Inc., 152, 355

DeSarno, James and Susan, 180–184

DeSarno v. Jam Golf Management, LLC, 179–184

Discrimination, xiii, 307–318, 321–328

Dolan, Edward, 127–131

Dolan v. State Farm Fire & Casualty, 127–131

Domestic Partnership Act, 322, 324–325, 327

Dowdle, Archie, 135, 137

Dowdle v. Mississippi Farm Bureau Mutual Insurance Co., 133–138

Dunlop, 203–206, 208–210, 241–243

Duty to disclose, 92–93, 95–96

Duty to warn, 18, 28, 42–47

E

Easements, 180, 182–184, 193–199

Endangered Species Act, 277–286

Equipment, xiii, 28, 133, 136, 240–242, 245, 381

Equipment (rule), 227–237

Equivalents, doctrine of, 203–211

Etiquette (rule), 10–11, 38, 293

ETW Corporation v. Jireh Publishing, Inc., 167–171

F

"Fair Use" principles, 169–170, 245–246

Fairview Golf Course, 100

Federal Circuit Courts of Appeals

  First Circuit, 316–318

  Third Circuit, 152, 357–359

  Fifth Circuit, 255

  Sixth Circuit, 169–171

  Seventh Circuit, 377

  Ninth Circuit, 235–236, 377

  Federal Circuit, 206–210, 219–220, 222–225, 269–271

First Amendment, 162–164, 169–171

Fish and Wildlife Service, 280–286

"Fore," yelling, 6, 15, 35, 38–39, 45, 47–49, 191, 342

forfeiture, law of, 289–295

Foursome, 14, 53, 58, 99, 118, 167, 174

Fraud, 117–124,

  Hole in one contest, 117–124

  Purchase of real property, 92, 94–95, 97

Frog, California Red-Legged, 278–281, 283–285

G

Genstar Development, Inc., 194–196

Gilder, et al. v. PGA Tour, Inc., 227–237

God, acts of, 23, 29, 31, 82

Golf ball design, 203–206, 208–210, 214, 217–218

Golf carts, 14–15, 34, 51–59, 133–134, 136–138, 289, 380–381, 383. *See also PGA Tour, Inc. v. Martin.*

Golf clubs, 63, 73–77, 127–128, 225, 228, 230–237, 292–293, 380

Golf clubs (rule), 228, 230–237

Golf Handicap and Information Network (GHIN), 356–359

Index

Golfing Gizmo, 61–64, 66–70

Governmental immunity, 333–339, 341–348

H

Handicap index, 149–154, 353–356, 358–359

Handicomp v. United States Golf Association, 353–360

Harbour Town, 251, 253–255, 258–259, 261–262

Harms, Jennifer, 109–114

Harms v. Northland Ford Dealers, et al., 107–114

Hauter v. Zogarts, 61–71

Hawaii, 13, 21, 289–291, 293

Hawaii Supreme Court, 16–18

Hennessey, Eileen, 187–191

Hennessey v. Pyne, 187–191

Hippo Golf, 241–242, 244–246

Hole-in-one, xiii, 211
  Contest, 99–104
  Fraud, 117–124
  Insurance, 141–144
  Right of publicity, 157–164
  Rules, 107–114

I

Indiana Supreme Court, 34, 36

Insurance policies, 109, 111, 113, 120, 128–130, 133–138, 141, 143–144, 348

Internal Revenue Service, 365–370

Intoxication, 127–131

Iowa Supreme Court, 343–347

J

John Daly Enterprises, LLC v. Hippo Golf Co., 239–246

Jones, Bobby, 25, 117–118, 124, 168

Joyce, Elaine, 307–310, 312–318

Joyce v. Town of Dennis, 307–318

K

Kansas Supreme Court, 28, 31

Karsten Manufacturing, 230–237

Koebke, Birgit, 322–323

Koebke, et al. v. Bernardo Heights Country Club, 321–328

Kolenda, Kevin, 141–144

Krilich, Robert, 118–124

Kurash, Naomi, 82–83, 85

Kurash, Stanley, 79–85

Kurash v. J.C. Resorts, Inc., 79–85

L

Lanham Act, 255, 257, 262, 269–270

Liability
  Golf course, 13–21, 23–31
  Golfer, 3–11, 33–39, 41–49
  Intellectual property, 242, 256, 269
  Manufacturer, 51–59, 61–71, 73–77
  Spectators, 33–39

387

Lie of ball (rule), 29
Lightning, 23–31
"Lost" ball" (rule), 49, 193–194, 381

M
Malouf, Edward, 173–174
Malouf v. Dallas Athletic Country Club, 173–177
Married Women's Property Acts, 84
Martin, Casey, 375–380, 382–383
Masters Tournament, 167–168, 252
Masters, et al. v. Burton, et al., 89–97
Maui Bird Conservation Center, 292
Mendoza, et al. v. Club Car, Inc., 51–59
Misrepresentation, 61, 69–70, 97
Mississippi Supreme Court, 135–137
Montecito Country Club, 299
Monterey Pines Golf Course, 334–339

N
National Hole-in-One Association, 120, 123, 157–164
Nature of golf, 8, 11, 231–232, 375–382
Negligence, 4, 6, 7, 9, 17, 21, 27–28, 31, 35–36, 38–39, 44–46, 48, 52, 55–56, 58, 66, 83, 85, 103, 128, 134, 175, 184, 191, 339, 343–344, 347

Nene, 290–293
New York Court of Appeals, 47
Newport Golf Club, 149
Nicklaus, Jack, 67, 168, 379
Nike, 169, 376
Nitro Leisure Products, LLC v. Acushnet, 265–272

O
Oaks North Country Club, 79–80
Obstructions (rule), 154–155
Ohio Supreme Court, 170
Olson, Walter, 127–131
"Out of bounds" (rule), 45, 49, 154, 173, 188, 193
"Outside agency" (rule), 230, 370

P
Palmer, Arnold, 157–158, 261, 379
Patent law, xiii, 203–211, 213–225, 256–258
Pebble Beach, 278, 302
Pebble Beach Co. v. Tour 18 I Ltd., 249–262
Pfenning v. Lineman, 33–39
PGA Tour, Inc. v. Martin, 375–382
Pinehurst, 251, 253–255, 258–261
Pooley, Don, 157–159
Pooley v. National Hole-in-One Association, 157–164
Price, David, 73–77
Price v. Wilson Sporting Goods Co., 73–77

Index

Professional Golf Association (PGA) Senior Tour, 367, 381

Professional Golf Association (PGA) Tour, 99, 117, 157, 167, 227–228, 230–237, 241, 293, 375–376, 378, 380–382

Publicity, right of, 157–164, 167–171, 239–246

Pupus, Terry, 291–293

Pyne, Michael, 187–191

R

Rhode Island Louisquisset Golf Club, 187

Rhode Island Supreme Court, 191

Risk, assumption of, 7–9, 16–18, 20–21, 37, 39, 45–47, 184

"Rub of the green" (rule), 370

Rules of Golf
Abandonment of provisional ball, 193
Clubs, xiii, 228–237
Equipment, 227–237
Etiquette, 10–11, 38, 293
Game, nature of, 375–382
Lie of ball, 29
"Lost" ball, 49, 193–194, 381
Obstructions, 154–155
"Out of bounds," 45, 49, 154, 173, 188, 193
"Outside agency," 230, 370
Provisional ball, 49, 193
"Rub of the green," 370
Unplayable ball, 81
Water hazards, 49, 193, 333

Wrong ball, 193

"Wrong information," 370

Rush, Rick, 168–171

S

St. Andrew's Shinnecock Hills Golf Club, 149

Sandalwood Golf Course, 290–292

Sall v. TS, Inc., d/b/a Smiley's Golf Complex, 23–31

Sea Pines, 258–261

Service mark, 150–154, 252, 254–262

Sharp Park Golf Course, 277, 279, 281–284, 286

Sherman Antitrust Act, 357–360

Shin v. Ahn, 3–11

Snake, San Francisco Garter, 278–281, 283–285

South Dakota Supreme Court, 110, 113

Stackhouse v. Royce Realty and Management, 85

State v. Terry Pupus, 289–295

State of Washington v. Kevin Kolenda d/b/a Hole-in-Won, 141–144

Strict liability, 18, 59, 61, 65–66, 71, 75, 77

Sullivan patents, 214, 218, 222

Summy v. City of Des Moines, 341–348

Supreme Court. *See* United States Supreme Court

389

T

Taxes, 365–366

Trade dress, 255–256, 260–262

Trademark, 150–151, 168–169, 204, 215, 225, 240, 242–243, 245–246, 255–258, 260, 265, 267–272, 356

Trespass, tort of, 173–177, 179–184, 187–191

Trial court, 7–8, 16, 28, 31, 35, 46, 57–59, 65–66, 94–96, 101, 110, 129, 135, 150–151, 153, 176, 191, 197, 343, 347

U

Unfair competition, 150, 152, 159–160, 169–170, 243, 255, 257, 268

Uniform Commercial Code (UCC), 67–68, 71

United States v. Krilich, 117–124

United States Golf Association (USGA), xiii, 10, 29, 149–154, 228–233, 236–237, 299, 310, 353–360, 383

United States Supreme Court, 162, 189, 206, 225, 271, 337, 359, 375, 377–382

Unplayable ball (rule), 81

Unruh Civil Rights Act, 323–328

U.S. Golf Association v. Arroyo Software Corp., 149–155

U.S. Golf Association v. St. Andrews System, Data-Max, Inc., 152

V

Ventimiglia v. United States of America, 333–339

Venturi, Ken, 380

W

Warner-Jenkins Co. v. Hilton David Chemical Co., 210

Warranty, 18, 52, 55, 58, 61, 67–69, 71, 268

Water hazards (rule), 49, 193, 333

Water supplies, 297–298

Waveland Golf Course, 342

Wild Equity Institute, et al. v. City and County of San Francisco, 277–286

Willful and wanton conduct, 37, 44, 190

Wilson v. Dunlop. See Wilson Sporting Goods v. David Geoffrey & Associates, 203–211

Wilson Sporting Goods v. David Geoffrey & Associates, 203–211

Woods, Eldrick "Tiger," 33, 41, 155, 167–171, 229

Wrong ball (rule), 193

"Wrong information" (rule), 370

Y

Yoneda v. Tom and Sports Shinko (Mililani) Co., Ltd., 13–21

About the Author

John "Jack" H. Minan is a Professor of Law at the University of San Diego and an avid golfer. During his more than forty-year teaching career, he has held a numerous administrative appointments, including Associate Dean for Academic Affairs, Acting Dean of Summer Programs, Director of Internship Programs in Washington, D.C., and Director of USD's International and Comparative Law Programs at Trinity College, Dublin, at Magdalen College, Oxford, and in Florence, Italy. Jack has authored or coauthored numerous books, including the ABA's best-selling *The Little Green Book of Golf Law* and *The Little White Book of Baseball Law*, and more than forty scholarly articles on a wide variety of topics. He has been interviewed about golf law on the radio, by the national print media, and has been the guest speaker at professional and nonprofessional educational programs.

Professor Minan has a B.S. from the University of Louisville, an M.B.A. from the University of Kentucky, and a J.D. from the University of Oregon. He has completed postgraduate course work in Operations Analysis at American University. Following law school, Jack practiced law as a trial attorney with the Civil Division, U.S. Department of Justice. He has qualified as an expert witness on matters involving Land Use Planning and Real Property.

Jack has an extensive record of public service. He has served as a gubernatorial appointee to the California Regional Water Quality Control Board, including six consecutive one-year terms as its chairman. Professor Minan has served on the Board of Governors of the Southern California Wetlands Recovery Project, an organization consisting of seventeen state and federal agencies. He has been on the Board of the San Diego River Conservancy, and served as its vice-chairman. Jack is active with the ABA. He has served several terms on the Governing Council, Section of State and Local Government, has been the chairman of the Environmental Law Subcommittee, and on the Section's Publication Oversight Board. He also has been active with the ABA Section of Environment, Energy, and Resources.